As the Crow Flies

A Walk from Edinburgh to London in a Straight Line

JANET STREET-PORTER

First published in Great Britain in 1999
by Metro Books (an imprint of Metro Publishing
Limited), 19 Gerrard Street, London W1V 7LA

Cover photograph: © Country Living/Gary Swann
Photographs of Janet Street-Porter with David Steel and
with Sting supplied courtesy of Screaming Productions.
All other photographs supplied by the author.

British Library Cataloguing in Publication Data. A CIP
record of this book is available on request from the British
Library.

ISBN 1 900512 71 8

10 9 8 7 6 5 4 3 2 1

Typeset by Wakewing, High Wycombe, Buckinghamshire
Printed in Great Britain by Caledonian, Glasgow

ACKNOWLEDGEMENTS

Thanks to:

Darryl Burton, Janet Cristea, Virginia Allport,
Susan Proctor, Charlie Courtauld, Vic Reeves.

TV production team

Director: John Bush
Producers: Elizabeth MacIntyre, Judith Mackay
Research: Louise Randall, Sarah Spencer,
Ginnie Herrington, Will Stern, Cathrin Starkmann

A BBC production in association with
Screaming Productions;
As the Crow Flies.
Transmitted on BBC2, 1999

CONTENTS

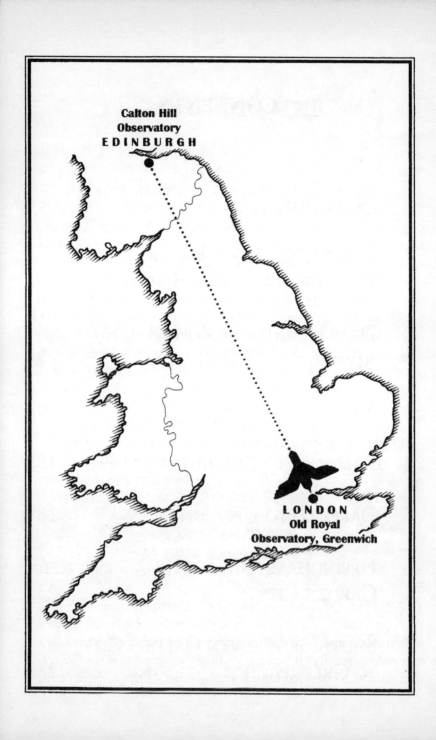

INTRODUCTION

This is the story of a straight-line walk from Calton Hill Observatory in Edinburgh to the Old Royal Observatory in Greenwich, London. Like any potty project, it had its high and low moments. The original concept emerged one sunny afternoon sitting by Vic Reeves' swimming pool in Kent, drinking.

Vic is a keen walker who had accompanied me on part of my previous marathon ramble, coast-to-coast, which started at Dungeness in Kent and ended months later in Conway Castle, North Wales. He was desperate to walk in a completely straight line, through rivers, over walls, the lot. I went away and came up with this route – before Greenwich was declared the home of time, Edinburgh had its own time, which was 12 minutes different!

The Ordnance Survey drew the line connecting the two observatories on dozens of maps for me. I soon saw that to stick to it 100 per cent would be extremely hard, but I would do the very best I could. I'd cajole landowners into letting me cross their moors and their fields. I'd walk through factories and people's homes. In the end it took over 450 miles and 41 days of walking, mostly in atrocious weather. I arranged to meet some famous people – from Sting to Elton John to Kathy Burke en route – for entertaining chat, I hoped. I walked with Vic Reeves into Leeds, his birthplace.

My lowest ebb was in the North Pennines, and I wept in Welwyn Garden City. I hurt my knees plodding through endless potato fields, and I fell down in the bogs of County Durham over and over again. But it was the ordinary people I met on the way who constantly cheered me up, brought me drinks and made me tea. Thanks a lot. By meeting a huge cross-section of Britain from redundant miners to grouse-moor owners, from hill farmers to steel workers, I came home with a portrait of Tony Blair's Britain unlike any other. Perhaps it's about time the politicians put on their own walking boots and really met the electorate.

PART ONE

Calton Hill
Observatory, Edinburgh

to Deaf Heights

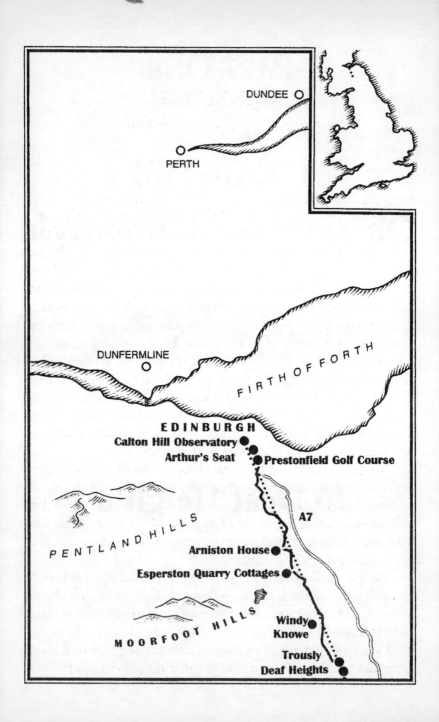

EDINBURGH

I plot my course and have a dental disaster

Now that Scotland is to have its first elected Assembly since 1707, what better place to start my walk? My destination is Greenwich – not the Millennium Dome, but the Royal Observatory, since 1884 the home of time. I'd decided to emphasize the new relationship between Scotland and England by starting my walk at the Calton Hill Observatory, home of Edinburgh time. Up until Greenwich won the battle as official time-keeper, local time prevailed in Scotland. And Edinburgh was 12 minutes different to London. How exciting a concept!

I had asked the Ordnance Survey to plot me a straight-line route from Edinburgh to Greenwich, and now rolled up in a giant cardboard tube in my hotel room was a set of large-scale maps of England and Scotland, with a black line drawn right across them. Interpreting this line and deciding how closely to stick to it was going to be one of the challenges of this walk.

For the purposes of the television series, I walked out of Waverley Station and up the steps into Waterloo Place. Like all filming, the first day is a bit like re-inventing the wheel. I seemed to have to go up the same set of steps about six times, while they shot enough footage to recreate the 39 steps. At this rate, I'd never get to Greenwich by Christmas.

'I'm not walking anything else twice,' I bawled, oblivious to the stares of commuters arriving for work. We'd only been filming an hour, and I'd covered only 300 yards and already lost my rag. It didn't bode well.

I walked east up Waterloo Place and then took a steep tarmacked path up Calton Hill towards the Observatory. These gardens with their fine wrought-iron railings and neo-classical stone buildings, were unlocked at night, and so were a dossing-down spot for dozens of hippies, junkies and festival hangers-on without a room. Rubbish was everywhere you looked: bins overflowing and grass littered with beer cans, plastic supermarket bags and polystyrene food containers. It was a rather inauspicious beginning to my walk.

I went through a gateway and met Graham Rule, the secretary of the Astronomical Society which runs the Observatory entirely on donations. Graham was in a lather about his unwanted overnight guests, and he and some fellow astronomers had already done a tour round the outside of their building picking up the droppings of festival folk. He had ginger hair and specs, and a suitably oblique way of explaining time and longitude. Star-gazing is very popular here, and his society has over 100 members, one of the largest of its kind in Britain. In the main room, there was an interesting display of photographs of the Northern Lights, and a pathetically subtle sign asking for donations. There was no admission fee, a condition of the city council giving them the building.

As we climbed the narrow wooden steps up to the dome and the big telescope, Graham explained how before accurate clocks were invented, every important town needed an observatory because star-gazing was the only accurate way of measuring longitude, and therefore time. Longitude, said Graham, was an unnatural non-parallel line (unlike latitude) going through both poles, North and South. The distance between latitude is constant, but longitude depends on where you are. The difference of your angle to the sun sets your time, so Edinburgh and London were 3 degrees different, which worked out at 12 minutes.

I was totally confused. But Graham had become addicted to all this stuff as a small boy watching the Apollo landings, and explained that the 12-minute difference disappeared when a 'mean' (or average) time was introduced. I asked him how hard it would be to set my course to Greenwich. 'Greenwich is roughly 25 degrees to the east, or left, of the due south line,' he replied. 'Unfortunately the compass is five degrees out because the magnetic North Pole isn't exactly where the North Pole is.' Never ask a boffin a simple question!

At least I could look through the telescope. But when I did everything was upside down. All I could see was the rocky outline of Arthur's Seat, and in front of it, Salisbury Crags. These tremendous protuberances were sitting in Holyrood Park, bang slap on my route. The trouble was that there were several high-rise council blocks between Calton Hill and Salisbury Crags. The dynamics of Edinburgh are unique in Europe with the castle atop one crag, with sheer drops and steep hills all around, and Arthur's Seat forming a green mass on the skyline, a counterpoint to the castle, right in the heart of the city. 'I'd suggest walking round it rather than over it,' was Graham's last advice.

I said goodbye, and stepping around the hordes of tourists, I dropped down the hill and took Jacob's Ladder, a set of steps down the side of St Andrew's House. Inside the forecourt I could see the flattened grey outline of a man lying on the ground. Was it an artwork or the body of a rambler attempting the same route? I would never know. I crossed under the railway line leading into Waverley Station (where I'd started) and up Old Tolbooth Road to Canongate, on the Royal Mile. In 1724, Daniel Defoe thought this 'the largest, longest and the finest street for buildings and number of inhabitants not in Britain only but in the world'.

He obviously hadn't visited it at the height of festival madness. The pavements were chock-full of tourists, backpackers, rucksack wearers, performance artists and, worst of all, clowns, not to mention the people thrusting flyers into your hands every ten feet, begging you to attend their shows. A zoo would seem calm compared to this. It was 10.30 am and Edinburgh was officially full.

The largest arts festival in the world was out of control in my book. How many drag acts can one city take? Please don't write in and tell me. A million visitors would pass through over a three-week period and performances were happening 24 hours a day.

But how much of it was any good? After a few beers, can anyone tell? Don't worry, I'll still be back next year, it's addictive.

I'd arranged to meet comic and actor Alan Davies outside a pub on Canongate. People were astonished when I ordered a mineral water. But I did have to climb all those crags... Alan sloped down the street, immediately recognizable, his tall frame topped with that trademark mop of twirly curls and a large smile. He handed me the leaflet for his show *Urban Trauma*, which I'd seen the night before. Two things confused me – why did the photo of him on it show a truly bizarre pose – he seemed to be about to pull a piece of chewing gum off his right foot. Or had he just stepped in a large piece of dog poo? And why was his face bright red? Alan was unforthcoming about the 'comedy' pose, but did allow, 'I've got a bit of a sun tan.' I thought he looked as if he had scarlet fever. As his show ran for only 14 nights, and had sold out in advance, the leaflet was redundant anyway.

As we walked along the street up the Royal Mile, Alan was spotted by locals at every step. According to him, though, everyone else was a tourist and the locals were well outnumbered. It was boiling hot, and I was already regretting the 8 am start. But what time did he have to get up when he was filming *Jonathan Creek* for BBC1? 'I get picked up about six usually and leave my house which is in Islington, then I'll be filming somewhere in Wiltshire.' Quickly I stopped moaning.

I told Alan I was glad I'd decided to start my walk during the Festival, as I'd be able to combine it with seeing a few shows. I'd gone along to his the night before and been surprised to see children in the audience. After all, it didn't start till 9.15, and included plenty of references to Monica Lewinsky, oral sex and wanking. I suppose they know all about it anyway.

Alan decided to be my tour guide to the Royal Mile, a part of Edinburgh I've always tried to avoid. 'The first Edinburgh show I did was at a venue up here. I was a student. Now the Royal Mile is a tourist haven just here, hence the Mexican restaurants. But just on the right up here, we can go down some steps and see the first venue performed at when I was a student. It was a musical version of *Lysistra* and I had a big false cock stuck on me.'

Was it a sell out? I asked. 'Yeah, not as much a sell out as being a bank commercial,' Alan replied, having just done a very lucrative TV commercial for Abbey National. How long ago was Alan's debut? 'It was 1986, I was 20 and I had to do singing and dancing. It was a bloody good way to get my life in showbiz started. *Lysistra* is a comedy about women depriving the men of sex so they'd stop having wars. So we have to run round halfway through the show, going, "Please have sex with us, we won't fight any more." But we did it in the style of *Oklahoma!* I was incredulous. 'We were called a bawdy romp in my first-ever review, and that gave me the hump even then.'

Undeterred, Alan kept returning to Edinburgh, but without a strap-on papier-mâché cock! How many years had he played here? 'I've been in about six or seven shows and come up about eight or nine times to visit.'

Since Alan started coming here the Festival has exploded and now it's got almost 10,000 people performing, particularly comedy and stand-up. So why, as Alan is a big success, with a British Academy Award, a hit TV commercial and a successful comedy series, does he keep coming back to Edinburgh? Wasn't he denying less successful, less well-known comedians a place to perform? Wasn't the Fringe now just mainstream?

'I know what you mean, and it's true. One of my first-ever stand-up spots was in the Fringe Club in Edinburgh down around the corner, and I was greeted with total indifference. That was ten years ago. But I didn't care because I really like doing it. And I still like doing stand-up comedy, so what am I supposed to do now, go to some sort of posh place where only famous people perform, like Glyndebourne?'

We turned off the Royal Mile down a dank alleyway and went down some steps to see the birthplace of Alan's career. It was a church hall, and the audience had only had to pay two quid to get in, Alan assured me. It held about 60 people but their

Oklahoma!-style *Lysistra* only attracted 15 or 20 people a performance. 'There were about eight of us in the show and I think six of us stayed in one flat with two bedrooms. There were four boys in one room and two of them were going out with each other. But there was only one bed and we were there for a fortnight and they obviously wanted the bed, but me and my mate said, "Look, we've got to have a bed for one week at least." So we had it for the first week.' Did he get lucky? 'No, I didn't. Every time I met a girl, I would say I'm sorry but I've got two gay boys in my bed and they bicker over the duvet all night long.'

I went inside to investigate, while Alan loitered outside. At this precise moment a ghastly cacophony of drumming was underway, but we were handed a leaflet announcing that Arthur Smith's live bed show would be on that evening. It had been performed with Paul Merton and Caroline Quentin in the West End, and now it was back on the Fringe again where it started. Alan had premièred his show in London too, so it was hardly Fringe material, was it? 'I've done it in New Zealand as well,' he said triumphantly. I think we can call that the Fringe, I allowed. 'Anyway,' he said, changing the subject, 'this is where I was in 1986. I was rubbish.'

I asked Alan if he was a keen rambler. 'Very verbally,' he said. 'I like walking my dad's dog in Epping Forest. That's where I grew up.' We retraced our steps, passing an Amnesty shop window where a large poster announced the charity show Alan was doing that very night. We both agreed the window display was rather ruined by a tasteless picture of David Bowie.

Back on the Royal Mile I headed for Holyrood Road and Salisbury Crags, while Alan went off to rehearse his show.

I left the swirling mass of Canongate behind me, walked down an alleyway, and emerged on to a giant building site – Holyrood Road. Not only is the new parliament building under construction on the site of a former brewery, but new newspaper offices for the *Scotsman* and *Scotland on Sunday* are going up too, as well as Edinburgh's answer to the Millennium Dome, the Dynamic Earth project. I crossed the road and surveyed the large sign announcing the scheme, with an award of £15 million from the Millennium Commission (the Lottery), and an equal amount from a brewery, the City Council, Lothian and Edinburgh Enterprise Ltd, and a property company. Designed by Sir Michael Hopkins, the blurb claimed, 'Visitors will experience the thrill of travelling back in time … '

Educational it might be, but a dome plus that 'experience' word sounds worrying to me. You might discover how the earth was formed, but at a cost of £30 million. A few hours earlier I'd seen the volunteers at the Calton Hill Observatory struggling along just on donations. Just as educational. Stars not volcanoes. They even had their own dome housing the telescope. And you can't tell me Dynamic Earth was going to be free to visit. We have a weird sense of priorities for the Millennium.

On the opposite side of the road was a tea stall where I stopped for a cuppa. Even though its owner was bound to profit from all the new buildings, she was scathing about the lot, and particularly rude about the design for the new parliament by Spanish architects Enric Miralles y Moya in conjunction with a local firm. 'It's supposed to be in the shape of an upturned fishing boat, but who wanted it?' she moaned. 'Apparently the architect used to spend his holidays in the west of Scotland when he was a wee boy. So this is what Scotland means to him, an upturned fishing boat – there's a lot more to us than that!'

I sat on the grass by the car park south of Holyrood House and ate my sandwiches in the sunshine. As I ate a peach, a huge lump of my front tooth fell out! I couldn't believe it. Day One and I was on the mobile phone searching for a dentist. Luckily I'd found the bit of tooth. Now I needed someone to glue it back on.

I followed the path around under Salisbury Crags, and climbed up a steep slope, finding footholds in the rocks, to skirt round for the final ascent of Arthur's Seat. I wasn't in the prime condition I'd hoped, and before long I was sweating profusely. The summit was slightly off my line, but it seemed churlish not to climb up and admire the finest views in the city.

I'd arranged to meet actress Elaine C. Smith at the top, to grill her about her career. Was she going to swap her success as Rab C. Nesbit's long-suffering wife Mary Doll for a future in politics as an SNP candidate for the new parliament? Elaine is far and away the most famous female comic actress in Scotland, with millions of fans. She's a very patriotic Scot who campaigned for the SNP in the referendum in 1997 on whether Scotland should have its own parliament. Her ready wit, fame, and obvious compassion would make her a powerful political opponent.

I reached the top of Arthur's Seat first and was plagued with fat, large black flies and a lot of American youths strumming acoustic guitars and re-enacting some version of Woodstock. Elaine appeared in jeans and a once-crisp white shirt, staggering up the rocky path from the other side of the crags, clutching a bottle of mineral water, sweating almost as much as me. 'Whose idea was this?' she said. 'Can I turn away from the camera while I sort myself out.'

While Elaine was composing herself I mentioned that some local kids had thrown rocks at the heads of walkers struggling up behind me. She laughed, 'It's just the natives from Midrie who come up here and do that just to say welcome to mime artists.'

We sat down and looked at the view – a perfect panorama from the Clyde to the Highlands, the city and my route so far, and away to the south, the Moorfoots, my next set of hills. What was it about Edinburgh at this time of year that flushes out a lot of very unfortunate people like the guitarists we were enduring behind us? 'It brings out an incredible anger and rage in me,' sighed Elaine. 'Years ago I used to want to run up and just take a punch at guys who painted their faces white and now I feel the same about stand-up comics. I wanna go up and go, "Oh shut up, I'm sick of you!"'

I immediately warmed to this woman of strong opinions, rather like myself. What did Elaine think about her fictional alter-ego? What would Mrs Nesbit make of all the talk of devolution? 'I don't think she'd give a toss,' said Elaine, 'but personally, I think that there is a great malaise amongst the ordinary working punters in Scotland. They don't trust anything to do with politics and they feel they are at the bottom of the pile. They are the people dealing with drugs and dealing with poverty and dealing with unemployment and dealing with the sharp end of it. Therefore cigarettes and the occasional Carlsberg lager is all that really matters and if can you pay your bills at the end of the week.'

To Elaine, devolution was just a step along the way. But if we split Britain into the Welsh Assembly and the Scottish Assembly, won't we have to have an English Assembly eventually? 'You've got one,' said Elaine. 'It's Westminster. On certain issues, of course, all the countries of Great Britain would join together if they are in agreement on something – on defence or on fishery policy or agriculture. But on other issues I think it's really important that Scotland and Wales and Ireland and England have a voice. I know that there are a lot of people in England who feel completely ignored and don't feel that they are being listened to. It's better for an individual country to have its own individual voice there, as opposed to one that they don't necessarily agree with. One of the problems over the last 20 years was that we had Thatcher's government, which the vast majority of Scots didn't agree with.'

I could see why it was important for a prominent woman like Elaine to come forward and encourage other women to vote in the referendum, but now there was to be a Scottish Assembly was it something she would like to continue to be involved in? The *Daily Mail* had already run a bitchy piece saying, 'How could we have Mary Doll on the front benches?' 'My mother was outraged – she was going to write to the *Daily Mail*, but there's no point and I said it's just part of being in public life that you get that sort of stuff. I think I certainly would stand in elections in the future for the SNP, but I would want to be driven by women's issues probably and the arts.'

Finally I asked Elaine what the difference was between racism and ardent nationalism? Was there any? 'It's a really difficult question and I think it is a right question to ask. It did seem to me that rampant nationalism brings out the worst in people. Any country in the world deserves to have its own heritage and preserve all that, but it has to be also in cooperation with other countries. When I hear ours blame the English for everything it's just adolescent, like blaming your parents for the fact you can't get out after 11 o'clock. Just grow up.' Did Elaine have any advice for me as I headed south towards Selkirk? 'Yes, drink a lot of water and alcohol to see you through. It will help your feet and it will keep you hydrated. And take a potty or something with you as well – you know, a po.' I told Elaine I could just go behind a bush! 'If you're that perfect,' she said, 'get a few leaves to wipe your arse and you will be fine.'

I drew the line at that. There would be no bottom-wiping with leaves on this walk. When I was little we used to go to Cornwall for our holidays and have a potty in the car. We had to pee in it and my dad would throw it out of the window. The car was an old hearse. I'd never been so embarrassed in my entire life going down to Mevagissey in a funeral car. It definitely affected me.

We said goodbye. 'Don't jump down, Janet,' said Elaine, as we set off in our separate directions. I had a date with a dentist and a tube of superglue.

DAY 2

SAMSON'S RIBS TO ARNISTON HOUSE
Golf, ostriches and open country

Last night a friend took me to a wonderful old pub he visits at the same time every evening. Beautiful sand-blasted glass, one long bar and the same regulars sitting about as usual, discussing the racing results. After a couple of large gin and tonics he had trouble dragging me on to eat. This was the other Edinburgh, the part the festival doesn't touch, thankfully. The streets were awash with revellers, but as it was only the first week of the cultural and comedy maelstrom that engulfs the city each year, the mood was not yet at the fever pitch reached by the last weekend in August. I've never understood why the Book Festival, the Television Festival, the Fringe Festival, the Film Festival and the International Festival all have to be crammed into the same four weeks, as well as the Tattoo, that orgy of bagpipes and fireworks. Every restaurateur must be praying that someone sees sense and spreads it all out over July and September. But it seems that none of the Festivals involved want to back down. So August means Edinburgh is probably the most culturally overworked city in Europe. I've been coming here for 15 years, and it never disappoints.

This morning I was rather regretting my festive mood of the previous night, as I had to get up early and do an interview at 8.45 am on Radio Scotland's *Fred Macauley Show*. He turned out to be in Glasgow, with a crowd of people in the studio, so it was a bit surreal to be sitting in a booth alone in the BBC studios at Queen Street trying to be in the party mood with a splitting headache! I talked about my last long walk coast-to-coast across England and Wales, and the book I'd written about it. I was going to be doing a talk at the Book Festival the coming Sunday and the point of this early-morning chat was to flog tickets. (Luckily for me it turned out to be a sell-out – phew!) I don't know how many people listen to Fred Macauley, but I mentioned in passing that I was at the start of my walk from Edinburgh to London, and all day people waved and said hello to me. Lorry drivers tooted as I walked along main roads and mothers left their children in the car to come and shake my hand. Good old Fred – he certainly made my walk out of the city and through suburbia a lot more enjoyable.

I started my walk at the foot of Arthur's Seat, by some rocks known excitingly as Samson's Ribs. So far so good. It was a fine sunny day and I was sporting my baggy shorts (when I looked at the subsequent film I realized I looked less like a groovy skateboarder and more like a demented scout mistress than I had hoped) and confidently strolled across the mown grass and on to the Innocent Railway, a disused line used as a cycle track. Now I had to follow my line over Prestonfield golf course. I could see a door in its high perimeter stone wall, but how did I get to it? There was a six-foot drop into nettles from the cycle track, and between me and the door was an overgrown area and a pond. A sign declared it was a nature reserve. I wasted ten minutes walking up and down and pondering (excuse the pun) what to do.

In the end I accepted that the price I would have to pay to keep my line meant a dash through the nettles. The door was unlocked. I went through from the plant frenzy of the nature reserve to a world totally unlike any other – golfworld – a place where the landscape had been ruthlessly controlled, no weeds were tolerated, every blade of grass knew its place and where all was a perfect, unreal shade of chemically enhanced green.

As I took my first steps on to the lush carpet in front of me a distant braying started up. 'You – off our course! Get off! Get back!' I leapt back and hugged the stone wall. Advancing towards me down the fairway were four very irate lady golfers, clad in eyeshades, sweaters with V-necks, golfing trousers and divided skirts. They were deadly serious. Behind them I could see another four. As I stepped forward again the second four started whacking balls feet from my nose. Wow! This was more frightening than last year's feat of climbing the Rhinog mountains in a gale and torrential rain. The first four strode up and demanded to know what I was doing. Saying I had permission cut no ice at all. They were in the middle of a one-day ladies' tournament. After a chat, they softened up a bit and we chatted about my walk. About half had seen the last one on television.

Ducking a hailstorm of balls, I made my way to the 16th hole, where I met the only man on the course that day, Ronnie Corbett. A local, Ronnie had his first taste of stardom, playing the Wicked Aunt in a panto at his youth club down the road. Things had gone on from there, and we met in my previous life as a BBC executive, when I had asked him to host a game show called *Small Talk*. He was delightful company, and so I'd asked him to meet me and explain why golf is so important to showbiz types like him. In fact, why has golf taken over the British landscape? On this walk I was to walk over more golf courses than I want to remember. Is golf Scotland's great gift to the world?

He looked, as ever, immaculate. The little checks on his trousers matched those on his sweater and he was wearing a brand new pair of golf gloves he'd bought in the shop at the clubhouse. He gave me a kiss on each cheek (on film it looks a bit like a giraffe meeting a Jack Russell), and said he hoped he wasn't too garlicky as he'd had an Indian dinner the night before! I assured Ronnie that he was both odour-free and immaculately turned out, which pleased him enormously. Had Ronnie any connections with this course? His answer totally surprised me: 'My dad played on this course, and in fact my dad died on this golf course as well. Years and years ago, on the 15th hole, playing his third round of the week at the age of 76.' 'What a fantastic way to go,' I said rather tastelessly, adding, 'especially if you're a keen golfer...' 'The way to go,' said Ronnie, 'but not for my mum, of course, who was waiting looking out of the window with the tea all ready and everything. In fact, they have a trophy here that I gave to the club in his name so it's lovely to be here, and I used to play here a lot with my dad as a boy.'

I asked Ronnie where he'd gone to school. 'Here at the Royal High in Edinburgh. I was no good at school, really. Medium rubbish, and I went through there unnoted, was reserve for the sixth rugby team and the scorer for the cricket team and all that real ordinary stuff. And then I did this show at St Katherine's the Grange Youth Club at the age of 15½, 16, and suddenly saw this little light at the end of this tunnel, you know ... as the wicked aunt. I was in drag straight away.' I cracked up laughing as Ronnie added, 'And I haven't been able to keep out of it ever since, as you know.'

I told Ronnie I started off my career in showbiz in a school play playing Joseph and I had a blanket over my head and they took the glasses off me, so I couldn't see my cues, and my acting career nose-dived after that. But what about golf – was it possible to be successful in show business and not play golf? Look at Bruce Forsyth, Bob Hope, Bing Crosby, Danny Kaye and Max Miller. They all played golf. Ronnie thought and then said, 'I think that it's possible. Ben Elton's an example of that. Mind you, I think he does want to start.' Even Chris Evans has taken up golf.

Ronnie added, 'But seriously, it's a terrific game for us, you see, because we could come out here on the golf course in the old theatrical touring days. You'd arrive in the town, Sheffield or wherever, and you did your band call, you did your first show on the Monday, on the Tuesday you're at your variety club or your stage golfing society, you saw the little golf course and you rang up the secretary, do you mind if I come and play, and that was you sorted for the week. You'd play a few holes at 11 o'clock in the morning, have lunch in the club, go home and have a wee rest and do your show at night. So it was like making a, you know, home from home. You weren't just stuck in the digs, so it's a wonderful game for us. And for people who are in the public eye, who are always being looked at wherever they go, you come out here, it's nice and peaceful and that's the great thing about it.'

Of course Ronnie Corbett would be recognized anywhere, on or off a golf course. It's not just the lack of height, but that distinctive booming voice! A bit like me, but in reverse really.

Finally, surely Britain was being over-run with golf courses. How many were there around Edinburgh? Not too many for Ronnie, as it turned out. 'I once played one hole in each of 14 golf courses within the Edinburgh city limits. That includes, you know, the Braid Hills where I grew up, or didn't grow up...' As I cracked up, he said, 'Sorry, I've tried to ignore small jokes.' Emboldened, he added, 'I've heard that I'm the only citizen in the United Kingdom with a full-length picture in my passport... I was brought up on the Braid Hill just over the road here and every Sunday afternoon after church we'd walk from one side of the Braid Hills to the other. Every Sunday afternoon without fail, because of course the public courses in those days in Edinburgh weren't open on a Sunday but they are now. So there are masses of golf clubs and little boys can start and it's not an expensive game, you can have a really cheap game of golf. My dad was a baker and there's a great history of artisan golf in Scotland. It doesn't have the same kind of snooty thing that it does down south, you see.'

But in my nightmare golf scenario, if everybody who wanted to play golf could get on a course at the time they wanted each day, I believe that soon the whole of Britain would just be a golf course. Even Ronnie thought that might be a bad thing. 'I like to play a lot of solitary golf like this, in the evenings just with the dog, seven or eight holes. It's been a terrific tranquillizer.'

Looking at the women playing in the tournament, they didn't seem very tranquil. Ronnie said enigmatically, 'Oh, they won't be tranquil. They are the least tranquil.' I laughed as we said goodbye and I left Ronnie to his solitary but tranquil game among the ferocious females.

I walked out of the golf course and past the posh Prestonfield House Hotel, a fine detached mansion that I'd visited for dinner many times when I was in telly exec world. I'd had dinner with them all there, from Rupert Murdoch to John Birt, from Verity Lambert to

William G. Stewart. But what did they say? And what jolly games did we play? I'm saving that for my autobiography. Let's just say that as I'm a rather outspoken person, networking isn't my forte.

I walked down the driveway and out through the gates. Now I was in suburbia, and getting closer to the city centre. Serried ranks of immaculate detached bungalows lined the streets, each with individual gardens expressing the owner's flights of fantasy (or lack of).

Before I could turn on to Priestfield Road, a large Jaguar pulled up. Out stepped the owner of the hotel, who had heard me on the radio. Was I related to Cecil Street-Porter (my first father-in-law)? Please pass on his regards; they knew each other at Lloyds. Then he whooshed off with no mention of a bargain break. I turned right along Peppermill Road, a dreary sprawl of shops and houses, to a large roundabout where I took the busy Old Dalkeith Road out of the city. It was hot and boring, so I turned up Kingston Avenue and skirted round my second set of greens of the day, the Liberton Golf Club. Then back to traffic hell and a long stretch down Gilmerton Road. Once a village, it has now been swallowed up by Edinburgh's sprawl.

I climbed up a hill and turned right on Ravenscroft Street past some cottages, then left on a track behind some farm buildings. The track finally went between two fields and I looked ahead to the bypass at the bottom of the hill and saw a broad swathe of countryside. In my excitement I walked through my first cow pat – now I was well and truly on my way! I sat on the scrubby grass by the side of the track and ate my sandwiches. It was boiling hot (not a weather option I was to encounter again on the entire walk!) and I drank a lot of water. I had decided to eat only brown bread smoked-salmon sandwiches en route, as this gave little opportunity for the sundry hotels and grocers who would be providing them to fuck up. Last year I had crossed England and Wales on prawn mayonnaise and with one or two ghastly exceptions (like the white bread coleslaw monstrosity I encountered in Brecon) I was quite pleased with the result. Please don't write in and tell me I'm an obsessive. Every serious walker is like this about what they eat, aren't they?

I went under the bypass on Lasswade Road, which crossed the North Esk River. Bonnyrigg was up the hill, and I took the opportunity to stop in the High Street at the chemists and purchase a selection of factor-8 sun creams (never to be used again), headache pills (a jumbo supply that quickly ran out), throat lozenges (I was hoarse from shouting at the director) and an impulse purchase of a couple of plastic rainhats, one spotted and one plain from the bargain box – a snip at 50p each. I planned to give one to Vic Reeves for his journey into Leeds, and use the other myself. I felt the plain one complemented my scout mistress shorts.

I continued out of Bonnyrigg, past a new housing development, and then took a right turn at a bridge down a small road to the sawmill at Dalhousie. The mill itself was closed and up for sale, but in a driveway next to the caretaker's house, a man was using the balmy late-afternoon sun as an opportunity to polish an immaculate old Vauxhall 10. We said hello. David Brumpton had lived here for 40 years, and had owned the car for 28 of them. He'd had to wait till his retirement four years ago for the time to restore it properly. Another more modern vehicle sat hidden next to the house. He referred to it as his 'shopping' car and the Vauxhall as his 'weekend' car. When the sawmill had closed, the price of imported timber it used making it uneconomic, 25 people lost their jobs. Once the pits had been another major employer in the area, but they'd closed too.

I walked on through farmland and sporadic houses, turning left to Aikerdean Farm, and then followed a track to Carrington Barns Farm. By now I was pretty tired as although my route might have been 7½ miles as the crow flies, I'd walked nearer 15, and it was now 4.30. I stopped for tea in the farm kitchen with Hugh Mann and his daughter-in-law Lyn. Lyn revealed that she used to work for the local television company, and had fallen in love with Hugh's son Christopher when sent to film a story on the farm. She'd relentlessly pursued him and was now happily married, a farmer's wife. The farm had been rented by the family for over 100 years and Hugh told me that until five years ago they reared cattle and farmed arable land like everyone else in the area. Then Christopher persuaded them to diversify into something more unusual.

Hugh was tall, straight-backed and a keen walker. He seemed to have a dry sense of humour, but even I wasn't prepared for the surprise he unleashed on me at the end of the track. Behind high wire fences 30 ostriches were running up and down in pens, having a whale of a time. The sight of my lime-green fleece sent them into a frenzy and they belted off at about 25 miles an hour. They eyed me in a blatantly hostile fashion, beaks at the ready for a quick nip. This was one crop I'd never seen before. Hugh explained that the meat was mainly exported to the Continent, and the skin was turned into leather handbags and purses. The eggs were blown and sold to decorators. Five years ago Hugh had been a pioneer, teased by his neighbours. Now there were about 30 other ostrich farms in Scotland and about 200 in the whole of Britain.

I asked Lyn if she gave them all names. 'No, there's too many, the very first chick we ever got we called her Henry, and then we realized she was female so we changed it to Henrietta. Normally they're curious and they would come round and stand about here and be going for a peck if they see anything unusual, but they are a bit shy today.'

I asked Hugh if he'd recommend the meat. 'Its meat's got no cholesterol and it's fat free. I have eaten some of the meat, yes. But I don't eat the meat now because I've reared them from chicks and from the shell, and they are a lot like friends in a way, and that's the only reason I don't like eating them.'

I asked Lyn if she'd ever been pecked by one of them – they had a spiteful look in their eye to me. 'If they see a button or an earring or anything shiny or colourful, they will usually come for a peck. Then they can peck a bit harder and try and get it off you, but it's just curiosity, they don't do it out of viciousness at all. The only way that they attack would be with a kick, and they pull their chests back and it's quite a powerful kick, given the size of their thigh and the size of their feet. But we've had them for five years and no one's ever been attacked.'

Knowing that Hugh was a fanatical walker, I asked him if he had any advice for me on my long walk south: 'My advice is at the end of the day when you are absolutely dog tired, don't drink any alcohol, have six cups of jolly good strong sweet hot tea. That's what I found was the best survival tip of the lot.' I said it sounded dreary. 'It's not dreary when you're tired, I can tell you,' Hugh laughed.

I asked him for help with my route, and he offered to show me a short cut to Esperston via Arniston House. He'd damaged his knee cartilage but that didn't seem to deter him, as he hobbled along at a cracking pace with a stick.

Our track fizzled out, and Hugh led me over a fence and through three-foot-high nettles to drop down a field to a beautiful stone bridge over a river, the back way to Arniston House, when the Dundas family would have gone on carriage rides. This Palladian mansion with its exquisite proportions and elegant tier upon tier of graceful windows, was remodelled by William Adam in 1725. It's surely one of the finest houses in Scotland, tucked away down a long driveway.

As I walked around the back and then the side of it, I expected to be stopped and challenged any minute. But there wasn't a sound. The windows glistened in the late afternoon sun and the owner apparently knew I was walking through. I couldn't imagine living alone in such a huge temple of perfection. Not even a dog barked and it seemed like the dream house from Jean Cocteau's *Beauty and the Beast*, sleeping and silent. I knew it was open to the public three afternoons a week during the summer. But today it was empty, its secrets firmly locked up. I would have to return to uncover them.

I walked down the long driveway to the main road, happy at the end of a perfect day.

DAY 3

ARNISTON TO TROUSLY –
THROUGH THE MOORFOOTS
I don't meet a hedgehog

To say I started the day with a hangover would be an understatement. I'd had a riotous evening in Edinburgh with two architects, Andy Doolan and Piers Gough. Andy is a hilarious Scot, a developer who did up a former Co-op building in Edinburgh and turned it into the Point Hotel. Piers was at the Architectural Association with me back in the 1960s, before I dropped out to become a writer, and he had designed my house in London. Piers and Andy are always cooking up schemes and dreams, both men with excessive temperaments that match mine only too well. We all eat and drink and talk a lot. We'd started in the bar at the Point, then had dinner and finally I seemed to have turned my room into a disco at 2 am – at 8 am I crawled out of bed, put cold water on my face, and tried to ram my belongings back into the two giant blue suitcases. It was only day three and already I was lapsing on the fitness regime! The drive out of Edinburgh passed in a blur as I clutched a large mug of black coffee and concentrated on not throwing up.

At the end of the driveway to Arniston House was an impressive stone gateway. I followed the road down to Castleton, just a collection of worker's cottages. Already I felt I'd left the city far behind and was walking along deserted country lanes. I don't know if it was my condition, but I felt freezing. A grey sky looked ominous and a strong breeze was whipping up. I put on my fleece and decided to wear my mapholder in order to placate the person who'd given it to me. Ordinarily I never use these clear plastic folders on a naff white plastic cord. To me it always looks as if you're a wally wearing a large label announcing who you are and where you are. But as it had started to rain, and I was shortly to strike off across the hills and off paths for the first time on the walk, I thought it best to be prepared. No one (except TV viewers) would see me anyway.

The houses I passed were solid, well-built single-storey estate-worker's cottages, with well-tended gardens and immaculate dark-red or white paintwork. The Scottish system of large sporting estates produces this respectable everything-in-its-place building, which gives the Borders a very definite character.

At a junction of ways, I turned left to Esperston quarry Cottages, where two little houses had been knocked into one and had been the home of Roland and Mae Carter for 30 years. Mae, with her fluffy white hair, glasses and dry wit, was very funny, and I kept thinking she was Stanley Baxter in drag. Outside the house, the front garden was as potty as Mae herself. It had even grown to encompass a bit of grass on the far side of the road, sprouting gnomes, wheelbarrows and a glorious profusion of flowers, from daisies to roses. A plastic frog croaked as I walked up the path, another of Mae's little jokes. Roland hid from the cameras but thankfully made me a cup of coffee that I drank in their living room, crammed with furniture and overflowing with bric-a-brac – I recognized the signs of compulsive collecting only too well. It had taken me 30 years to shrug it off and try and learn to love minimalism, saving myself hours of time previously spent at flea markets around Britain. Roland and Mae were still totally enmeshed by collectomania.

In the back garden, Mae's greenhouse stood on the site of the old limeworks engine-room and was full of ripe tomatoes. It seemed the collecting disease was worse than I originally thought. Mae claimed to have eight pet hedgehogs, and one was hiding under a chair. Did I want to see it? Weren't they full of fleas, I said warily. 'Crickey, no!' Mae exploded. 'I've had them de-loused.' I didn't know if she was joking or not. 'And the only thing they eat, Janet, is peanuts. I've got a big bag of them in the front room.

Honestly, it's unbelievable. And I've got a pregnant squirrel. It's a wonder he's not there. Or she's not there.' 'This is like a zoo!' I exclaimed. 'It is a bloody zoo. And Roly's the biggest monkey of the lot,' she replied. Roly was skulking in the kitchen. I got the feeling he was used to Mae's insults. 'He's at a funny age,' Mae sighed. 'You know what men are like when they get older…'

Obviously this was a subject I could talk about for hours, but if I was to walk from Edinburgh to London in 1998, I couldn't get started on the subject of men with Mae Carter. On safer territory, I asked her the route from her house. That turned out to be as big a mistake as getting her started on the subject of men. 'Oh, Janet, I cannae do that,' she cried. 'But you're a resident,' I said. 'I've been a resident for 30 years. I bet Roland doesn't know either. There is a route up the fence outside the house that takes you to the Esperston quarry and right over the hills. It's beautiful.'

Armed with Mae's sketchy directions I picked up a track through the disused remains of Esperston quarry, then got lost by heading too far east. I was going to have to ruthlessly stick to my compass or this could end up a very long journey indeed. Over a flat boggy plain, I discovered that forestry plantations bear no relation to their shapes on the map. Luckily I screwed up my eyes, took off my expensive bi-focal glasses, and managed to spot a little rectangle on the map corresponding to a deserted barn in front of me. I toiled up the slopes of Wull Muir, my first real hill and the start of the Moorfoots, a huge empty expanse of rolling heather. It was pouring with rain and every now and then Tornado jets would scream overhead, only a few hundred feet above.

I looked back in the direction I'd come. It was my last glimpse of Arthur's Seat, 20 miles away. At the top of the hill the fence marked the end of Lothian and the start of the Borders. This was sheep farming country and on the hill in front of me, working with his flock of 450, was Andrew Welsh, a hardy character in a tattered waterproof, who'd been the shepherd at nearby Carcant Manor for three years. Born and raised on a farm, Andrew had rounded up sheep all over Scotland and even worked in the Australian outback. He and I walked and chatted as his two black-and-white dogs kept the flock well under control. I could see he was a sheep dog trials veteran.

It was like Armageddon over our heads, jets thundering over every few minutes and the clouds threatening to soak me for the fifth time that morning. I asked when the sheep had been sheared. 'They finished on 3rd August. That's the latest they have ever been, because of the weather. It was a Sunday and we had to wait till it was sunny in the afternoon before we got them sheared. We finished at a quarter to nine on Sunday night.' I asked if Andrew ever saw good mushrooms on this lush patch of grass. All the ones I'd spotted had been full of maggots. Andrew said the best of them were over now. Too bad; I was just starting my walk and one of my major collecting passions – mushrooms – had been denied.

Andrew explained that he had been brought up to be a shepherd as his father was a farmer. He'd never thought of doing anything else. He'd worked in Australia for four years, in the shearing sheds and then as a field supervisor for a mining company, up in Mount Isa for three years. I'd worked in Australia and loved it, and so had Andrew. He'd gone on to New Zealand as well but the lure of the Borders was too strong. He'd spent 12 years working in Argyll but thought the Borders were more beautiful, with their rolling green hills. We stood and looked to the south, unspoilt scenery and sheep as far as you could see.

I asked Andrew how bad the crisis was in sheep farming here. He said the lambs were fetching the lowest price in 30 years. Why did he carry on? Surely this way of life was doomed? He shrugged his shoulders. 'I'm a shepherd, but I agree with the farmers. It's really terrible but it's my way of life. I can't live in the city.' He agreed that in the end sheep subsidies would be cut and many farmers would go out of business, as had already happened in New Zealand. 'But everything goes round in a circle,' he said philosophically. At the moment even wool was fetching a very low price. Was the situation in the Borders as grim as it is in Wales?

Andrew shrugged again: 'But what can you do, you just have to get on with it and survive in this country, and to me the world's getting over-populated anyway. And I think something will happen. I think there will be another war. I've always said this.' Perhaps the Tornadoes were in training? Andrew laughed – perhaps they were.

And so we parted at the top of the hill above Carcant having discussed how the crisis in sheep farming might be resolved by World War III. I took a narrow track down a hidden valley past a large house where workmen were mending the roof. The flat meadows by the burn were full of cattle and sheep and the odd fir plantation. At a B road I turned west to Raeshaw, the large Victorian shooting lodge which was the focal point of the sporting estate owned by entrepreneur Malcolm Borthwick. Malcolm, like Andrew, was facing hard times. In the last few years grouse shooting had been poor and I'd heard rumours that the estate was for sale.

I sat in the kitchen while two girls prepared dinner, and drank a cup of coffee. The house looked a bit threadbare but well lived in. All the paraphernalia for shooting was visible: photos, game record books, sporting prints, a drying room and a toilet with copies of *The Field* to read. Outside, in the driveway, I met Malcolm, a tall (six foot plus) stout man, with a booming, no-nonsense plummy voice. I discovered he'd once owned a house almost next door to me in London, but had been working in New York, so we'd never met until now. He arranged for me to meet his guests tomorrow, up on the grouse moor.

I headed west through the pastureland by the burn, and then opposite a steep hill (Whiteside Law). I followed a narrow track up Ladyside Burn, turning up above it before a sheep enclosure, and climbing steeply up through the bracken, then heather, heading south-east up Windy Knowe. My aim was to skirt along the tops, avoiding too much up and down. The crew left me to climb, saying they would film me coming down at the end of my day's walk. I contoured round Glenwhinnie Hill before coming down to the track at Trously, my final destination. The crew arrived after me, so no one filmed me on the best bit of the walk so far! Still, I carried it in my head, if not on film. I was beginning to see how hard this walk was going to be to film. And how hard it would be for me physically.

PART TWO

Deaf Heights

to West Allen River

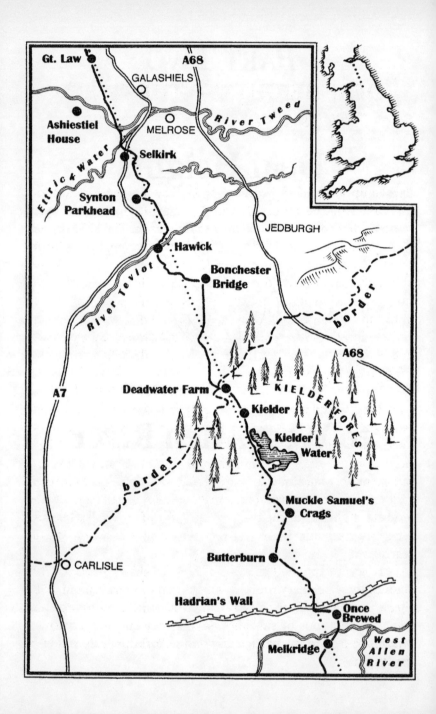

DAY 4

DEAF HEIGHTS TO THE TWEED
Shooting, sphagnum and solitary walking

I woke up in my cosy bedroom at the Ley looking forward to a tramp across the moors. It was 12 August, glorious in every hunter's diary as the start of the grouse season. The blue sky was deceptive as there was a strong chilly wind blowing. I mused over what to wear while eating a delicious kipper for breakfast, although I should have ordered porridge for inner warmth. I was meeting landowner Malcolm Borthwick and his band of rich guns, up at Trously, the junction of tracks I'd reached last night. This southern part of the Moorfoots isn't crossed by any roads, and it took nearly an hour to drive around the hills and down a rough track to the start.

Malcolm was in fine form, surrounded by beaters, gamekeepers and a motley bunch of men (no women!) who were paying £5,000 a week to shoot on his moor. When I got out of the Land Rover I nearly died as the blasts of cold wind hit me. 'You'll need trousers, girl,' said Malcolm, and I got back in the car and put them on. Malcolm was wearing plus fours, socks with feathers on them, an ancient sweater full of holes, an equally aged tweed jacket and a beret adorned with a fine spray of grouse feathers like a badge of honour. His ruddy complexion was testimony to the searing wind.

Malcolm explained that his estate, Raeshaw, covered 8,300 acres of these heathery rounded hills, and they grazed about 1,800 sheep on it. Any more would have damaged the land. Malcolm was contemptuous of subsidies, saying they encouraged tenant farmers to over-graze, particularly on the Yorkshire moors and in the Pennines.

'This moor was run by my great uncle with total disregard to livestock, only for grouse, and when my father inherited it, it was one of the most famous grouse moors in the country. Beautifully burnt and not over-grazed. We strive to keep the balance of conservation – it's very difficult under modern conditions because arguments rage backwards and forwards about predators all the time. We have merlins resting here and they respond to the population of the meadow pipit and the little wheatears and the linnets. This year we had snow in May, then two and a half inches of rain. And it killed the chicks, ruining the grouse shooting.' I'd read in the *Daily Telegraph* that the number of grouse shot on nearby moors had declined because birds of prey were protected. But it seemed the weather was the biggest killer of all.

But getting a word in edgeways with Malcolm wasn't going to be easy. He was prepared to expound ad nauseam about his moors for the benefit of the camera, as they were up for sale. I couldn't really blame him. Changing the subject, I asked if I could meet his guests. Malcolm introduced me. 'Dean's the gamekeeper, Bob's a guest, Ed trains dogs and Dave White trains dogs. They've come to join us and the other guests. Now Janet, do you recognize this face?' 'We met about a decade ago,' the man said. 'You were going out with James Strachan.' I was so embarrassed – he was referring to one of my banker boyfriends, someone I had kept quiet about, bit of an aberration. 'Now you are exposed!' the man said triumphantly.

I asked Malcolm, if his guests didn't shoot anything, did he feel he had to stay out of the room at dinner and keep his head down? Malcolm just laughed. One of the men said, 'He blames it on the accuracy of the shooters, he feels no guilt.'

One of the men had been coming over from New York to shoot for 12 years. They were a mixture: lawyers, a banker turned book publisher, English, American and even a Frenchman, whose outfit was totally different to everyone else's tweeds and long socks. He was wearing deerskin trousers, prepared for all weathers, and a natty flat hat. Trust the French! I asked them whether they considered shooting sport or leisure. Malcolm was immediately on the defensive: 'You call hill walking leisure, don't you?' 'Yes, I do,' I replied. 'I wouldn't call it a sport, it's something that's just enjoyable, I don't think a sport implies you're doing it for a trophy.'

According to Malcolm, the great film director Werner Herzog had a famous quotation about walking: 'It builds something and if you then go off to quarry and hunt it, merely adds to it, so there is a spiritual quality in the pursuit of game which is an extension of your walking.'

I couldn't quite follow all this, but said I hoped they'd have a very spiritual day out on the moors, which raised a smile. The American lawyer said, 'I don't pretend to understand the English mentality on the subject of shooting, with the very strong pros and very strong antis. We don't have as much as a strong or organized anti-hunting element, but hunting isn't as ubiquitous in the United States.' But you shoot anything, don't you? I asked. 'No, only if it moves,' was his riposte, and we all collapsed laughing.

Malcolm introduced me to the head keeper, Robin, and I asked if anyone had shot so appallingly that he'd said to Malcolm, 'Can we not have him back next year, this man's dangerous?' Robin was suitably diplomatic. 'No, no. We have the odd boy who has given us a close call but usually if you have a quick word they soon sort it out.' By that I think he meant they were ostracized, but it might have meant left all alone in the middle of the moor where they could cause no damage.

Malcolm and I said goodbye to the others who were being taken by Land Rovers up to shoot on a hill to the north. We set off straight up a hill through deep heather, heading for Deaf Heights, just over 1,500 feet high and right on my line. Our hike was punctuated by Malcolm stopping to call and whistle his dog Bob to heel. He was fascinated by my idea of walking from Edinburgh to London in a straight line. 'The thing is you go through communities, different cultures, parts of the country that are better managed than others,' he said. 'Country that's been lost to forestry. At the time it seemed a sort of good idea. Now I think people are regretting it.'

Malcolm then digressed into a homily about the evils of bracken and its intrusive root system that blocked good grass and heather from growing, not to mention harbouring flies and being generally poisonous: 'It's carcinogenic, which animals know about. They won't eat it.' At this point I started to glaze over...

Malcolm explained why he was selling for £4 million the estate he'd inherited from his father: 'I took it on really as a venture capitalist...but I inherited a very big tax bill. I knew I would never be able to live for the rest of my days doing this as there's a very big downside when the place doesn't work. If you think of it as a crop, over the years if you can wash your face then you've probably done well.' I think he meant grouse moors ate more money than he was prepared to invest.

But how many people did it employ? 'We've got two keepers, their families and two shepherds on one part, and one on another, and then there's a trainee, so you've got a little nucleus of a small business, that helps to keep the habitat right, and is providing some economic wherewithal. It's a difficult question how much these communities should be subsidized. New Zealand took a very radical step and removed all their subsidies, and it's generally thought that it was a good decision in the long haul, painful in the short term. Britain can't do that because we are part of the European Community and of course then there are political agendas to do with farmers. It's a year-round business, running a grouse moor. You have to walk right over it all year round. It's not just looking at birds, you look at the condition of the heather, the growth or lack of, and a whole host of sort of little things that one stores away in one's mind.'

Now quad bikes and fences keep the sheep under control, reducing the manpower needed. I asked Malcolm whether many intrepid ramblers roamed across his moors. 'Oddly enough we don't have many walkers and the reason is that you aren't going anywhere here. It's so isolated. You end up here and have to be picked up by somebody. It's not like a Munro, you know, a hill you can tick off. And the other reason, which you'll find out as we get higher up, is that the going is very wet. Unlike in the highlands where you're on comparatively firm terrain, here it's quite soft.'

Now I was slightly dreading the next part of my walk when I left Malcolm's boundary fence! We stood on the brow of the hill and looked at the lovely views in every direction. There's the Southern Upland fault that runs from Dunbar right the way through to Clydesdale and these hills, which were the Moorfoots. Over to the east were the Lammermuir Hills and in between were the farms and valley of Gala Water running north to south. Malcolm told me Walter Scott used to ride down it from Middleton which was just east of Esperston to Fountain Hall. The A7 was built as a private toll road by him and his friends in the 19th century, and shortly after that they built the Waverley Hall railway line.

I asked Malcolm whether the Americans who came to shoot were buying into the mythical Scotland which they'd seen in movies like *Braveheart* and that's what they wanted to be part of. Did they have a rather romantic view of Scotland? Malcolm disagreed. 'It's not to do with *Braveheart*. It's a bit to do with Scotland – you introduce them to something and say why am I different? Well, look, there it is. And here we are 25 miles from Edinburgh as the crow flies, marvellous.' Now he launched into a sales pitch and there was no stopping him. 'And it's all kept well – virtually no trees, beautifully burnt, not over-grazed, benchmark. That's why they come here.'

But as far as I could see they could come here and pretend that they have been very brave as well, couldn't they? They'd been out in all weathers with no air conditioning. They could go back home and say to their American friends that they were in the wild. 'Oh yes, they do,' said Malcolm. 'That's how you market somewhere like this – on testimony.' Testosterone, more likely, I thought!

Now Malcolm turned his attention to a wet, spongy-looking substance growing on the muddy bog we were ploughing through – I could feel a factoid or three coming on. 'Did you know that this was used in field dressings in World War I?' No, I replied, truthfully. 'It's sphagnum moss, and there was a family who lived in Moffat called Foreman. Now you might know Denis Foreman of Granada Television. In World War I his grandfather organized a little railway, built it himself on the estate and got all the ladies out in their long skirts and they dug up the sphagnum moss and it was used to put into the field dressings because of the iodine quality, and so they didn't get infection or gangrene. Mr Foreman Senior got a civil award for it like a CBE or something.'

At least now if I scratched my arm or leg on rusty barbed wire I'd be able to dab it with moss. A useful piece of information. Possibly more useful than knowing how to burn a strip of heather, which I'd managed to stop Malcolm explaining in inordinate detail earlier. More grouse moor information was at hand, though. 'Shortly, as we get up you'll come into some cloudberries. It flowers in May and has a berry that looks a bit like a loganberry, not as big, but of that raspberry family. See, here the heather doesn't flower as much.' (I agreed.) 'Its roots have to go right the way down the sphagnum moss and the weather up here is very windy with a big chill factor.' Sure enough we found some cloudberries, and a patch of frost, even though it was August. Malcolm said it had been –25 centigrade at Raeshaw at Christmas 1996. Wow!

At last we reached the boundary fence on the top of Deaf Heights. I looked south-east, in the direction of my line and saw the radio mast at Selkirk. That would be my marker. Now I had to drop down the hillside, skirt the eastern side of Mossy Rig and pick up a shooting track for a while, following Caddon Water. There wasn't a building or a person in sight, just sheep munching away. Very few grouse had flown up during our tramp although I could hear the sporadic sounds of gunfire from Malcolm's guests in the distance.

The next property was called Bowland. We were at about 1,800 feet, so I'd already almost doubled my altitude in four days, as Arthur's Seat was a mere 950.

As a parting gift and because I'd been such a good listener (I'd like to think), Malcolm gave me a chocolate bar, and a drink of water. I'd earned it. I hadn't fallen in the bog once and I'd climbed up through thick heather. I told Malcolm I hoped he got his £4 million for the estate, and we said goodbye. Just think, we'd been neighbours in London all those years ago (25!) and never met then as he spent most of his time in New York. Malcolm waved me off, promising, 'It'll be downhill all the way now,' as he strode away with the faithful Bob to join the shooters for lunch. Somehow I doubted him.

I found the little track down the idyllic valley without any difficulty and followed it to a turn off by a hut that took me up towards the rounded summit of Great Law, before petering out. There seemed to be a lot of grouse cackling away as I toiled through the heather – they probably had heard that the guns were out in full force on Malcolm's side of the fence. I got out of the wind by a wall on Nether Hill and ate my sandwiches. There was a car parked by a building below by the burn, and I walked down to it. A stone shooting hut was being restored, and the gamekeeper laughed and laughed when I told him all the grouse seemed to be on his side of the fence. Even he admitted there would only be a couple of days shooting this season, the number of birds being so low.

I made a slight detour up the stream to find a bridge, cut over the heather of Craig Head and eventually rejoined the road by the deserted hamlet of Blackhaugh, with just a couple of farms; the phone box marked on the map no longer existed. Further on, at Newhall, I turned right over the burn and passed a group of men mending a gate at Laidlawstiel Farm. I asked them if it was OK to follow my line over the hill and they told me to go right ahead. We stopped and chatted for a while about my journey, while buzzards circled over the hilltop. I crossed the pasture which was easy going with nice short grass. Then it was back through the heather, past the cairn. The River Tweed lay to my south and my line brought me out by the junction of the A72 and A707. Cars thundered past in a steep cutting. I could find no way down it, scratching my arms and hands on dense gorse. At the end of a long walk you just don't think straight. My map wasn't a large enough scale to solve the problem.

There was a place marked as 'The Nest' (it turned out to be a boarding house for cats!) on the road, but between me and its driveway was an overgrown railway cutting. I inched, cursing, down it, crawled under the branches of beech and fir trees to stumble, like an escaping convict, in front of the rush-hour traffic heading into Selkirk and Galashiels on the A72. Twigs were sticking to my hair, my face was covered in dirt and my trousers spattered with mud. Motorists probably thought I was a mad witch or a TV presenter having a nervous breakdown on a back-to-nature weekend. Still, the horror of the final hour couldn't really detract from a memorable day's walking. And Malcolm was an original, that's for sure.

That night I dreamt I was gathering sphagnum moss and putting it in my rucksack.

DAY 5

ASHIESTIEL TO SELKIRK
The Three Brethren, Plodders and Bannocks

I lay on my bed like a beached whale. I had zero energy. It was 8 am. There was a soft tapping on the door but I decided to ignore it. More tapping. 'All right, I'm getting up,' I shouted. I dragged myself from the bed and threw back the curtains. It was a typical British mid-August summer day, i.e., the entire sky was covered with a thick uniformly grey cloud which didn't quite reach the horizon. From the edge of it you could see a tantalizing small area of lighter grey which glowed with a slightly brighter luminosity. It had obviously just rained, was about to rain and was going to rain all day. It was that irritating fine moist rain which meant I would be taking off the waterproofs and putting them back on all day.

My case lay on the floor semi-packed. My bottle of high-energy drink lay discarded on the floor partly drunk. My notes from yesterday lay on the floor and next to them the notes for today, half read. I began to realize that walking five days, one after another, was doing my head in. I was very, very bad tempered. I knew I was going to be horrible to everyone today and there wasn't much I could do about it, short of having a personality transplant.

When you walk day after day, you hardly have any time to yourself and what happens is that your brain seizes up. Small things become really irritatingly important and anything that goes wrong with your route drives you into a frenzy of Ffyona-Campbell-style tantrums. I would try to do my best but I knew it wouldn't be much fun for everybody else.

I went into the bathroom and decided not to wash, it would take up too much energy. I got a large dollop of thigh reducing cream and slapped it on to the top of each leg. The only difference to my thighs over the two weeks I had been applying this gunk was that they had a smooth velvety feel to the offending area, but then I had spent £22.50 on this green stuff. Whether or not they were actually firmer I couldn't tell. What I needed was a man to stand in the bathroom and tell me I had great legs. More specifically great upper legs. To me they looked exactly the same big lumpy objects that I had looked at in the South of France two weeks before. I cleaned my teeth and pondered the giant bags under my eyes. There was nothing I could do about them. I'd have to try crinkling my eyes up in a smiley sort of way and hopefully make them look like laughter creases rather than the suitcases they actually were.

I had tried to dry my boots out on the towel rack, filling them with bits of toilet paper. It had been a total flop. The toilet paper inside them was really wet but the boots were still wet as well. I had washed my socks out in shower gel but I had been unable to pick out all the bits of fern even though I had scrubbed them with a nailbrush. Thank goodness they were dry so I put them on and decided to wear a pair of sweatpants, as there was no point wearing shorts as there was clearly a freezing wind outside, and stuck on a new-colour T-shirt because today I was starting programme two. I chose a jolly red one, hoping that it would brighten my mood. Over the top I stuck an orange fleece and went down to breakfast. Luckily there was no one around. I ate some fruit salad, half a grapefruit and then had a poached egg and a bit of the mushroom I'd picked the other day, which tasted delicious.

One of the team had come to collect me and, sensing my mood, wisely sat in the car outside in the driveway quietly reading the paper. They knew better than to approach me before 8.45.

I tried to learn my first piece to camera. It was some waffle about Selkirk and bloodshed and the Borders, but in my befuddled state I kept getting bloodshed, Borders and Sir Walter Scott all muddled up.

We drove down the beautiful valley of the River Tweed. The hills were an amazing green. The countryside seemed just so luxurious. I could see why people had fought over it – it was quite simply the most lovely, the most sensuous group of hills one could ever imagine. Big fat rivers full of fish, solidly built towns like Selkirk and Galashiels. What fantastic country to be walking through.

I started my day's walk on the A707 where I had finished last night. Cars thundered past en route to work. The crew were filming me from the other side of the river. I was to drop down, cross over it and make a small detour to Ashiestiel House where Sir Walter Scott had spent 12 years and written *Marmion* in 1808, before he moved on to Abbotsford, another house in the area. I had seen Ashiestiel House surrounded by trees as I descended from the moors yesterday and I was looking forward to visiting it and meeting its owner. As I dreamily walked along the A707 a car halted beside me. A man got out and walked up. I tried to look as friendly as possible but my mind was full of the words 'Selkirk' and 'bloodshed' and 'Here we are in Programme Two.' He held his hand out, 'I just want to thank you for your walk last year and I want to thank you for being President of the Ramblers,' he said. I felt humbled. My whingey mood suddenly lifted and soon I was chatting away to this man about walking and all the joy it gives you. Then he got back into his car and drove off, and my foul mood returned.

I crossed over the Ashiestiel bridge, putting a jolly face on for the camera. I walked towards it and started to mouth the bit about Selkirk and the Borders and bloodshed. I did it perfectly well, I thought. 'Cut,' said the director, 'you seem to have a rather miserable expression on your face.' 'Ask yourself why,' I started to say, and started shouting about being sick of being ordered around like an automaton and who the fuck did he think he was and I was sick of getting up early and I was sick of walking and I was sick of everybody not knowing what they were doing. It was a full-blown Street-Porter rant. At that very moment a maroon car drew up alongside me and inside a charming elderly lady leant out of the window and said, 'Good morning, Janet, I'm Ann, Sebastian's mum.' It was my friend's mother who farms locally who had come out specially to say good morning to me and invite me to lunch the next day. Chastened by this sudden intrusion of gentility and good manners and the real world, I resumed my piece to camera and did it for the second or third time.

I walked down the driveway to Ashiestiel House. It had clearly seen better days. It was a charming, E-shaped house, the centre part of which had been extended with two wings at the end of which were the Celtic swastikas. It was built in the 1500s and owned by a relative of Sir Walter Scott when he lived there. The present owner had lived there for just over ten years, a jolly woman called Jilly Barnard. Well spoken, she had blonde hair and a rather horsy manner. A small boy with red hair ran across the lawn and into the front of the house. He then appeared at the end of it, leering. When I walked up to the front of the house to talk to Jilly (obviously his mother), he started hissing at me. 'Hello,' I said in quite a friendly way. 'You can all bugger off,' he said. 'We hate you. We hate you television people, you're a load of shit, you are, you're crap. You're not paying my mum any money and we don't want you to be here.' Not letting anyone hear me, I walked up to him and said, 'Look here, you load of rubbish, you look completely stupid anyway running into your front door, we've already filmed you, so I don't care what you say. You're in my programme, you look pretty stupid and if you carry on like this you'll look even more stupid. There's nothing you can do about it, so sod off.' He slunk off behind the building.

Then I had a very charming chat with his mother as if nothing had happened and we talked about the twig from Elba that Sir Walter Scott had brought back (he was a great friend of Napoleon) and it was still flourishing in the garden. According to Jilly, Sir Walter Scott's three great obsessions were: (1) Napoleon, (2) the Tsar of Russia, and (3) King George IV. Joseph Turner adored Ashiestiel too and painted it often between 1810 and 1811.

I could see why – the setting by the Tweed is sensational and the house has a mysterious romantic feel to it.

Jilly and I turned the corner towards the stables and I said to her, 'Was that small boy your son?' 'Yes,' she replied. 'Well,' I said, 'he's a bit of a brat, isn't he?' When I told her what he'd said, she looked stricken and said, 'He's at that difficult age.' I agreed but secretly I thought I'm glad he's not my brat. As we returned to the front of the house he leered around the end of the building again, this time sticking his tongue out and making disgusting faces. I decided to ignore his attempt at TV stardom.

Walking back down the driveway, I headed for the Ashiestiel bridge. My notes had told me to follow a footpath along the edge of the river. I found myself in five-foot nettles – what in-depth research I had been given again. I retraced my steps up the road and found a couple exercising their dogs. They pointed me in the right direction and I followed a broad track through woodland and then meadows heading east along the Tweed. The river was in full spate, it was roaring past, which wasn't surprising because of all the rain lately. Nobody was fishing. I didn't see anybody, just a couple of herons and that was about it. I passed a pleasant 45 minutes walking along swatting at the occasional midge, and reached another lovely mansion, Yair House, standing in immaculate grounds above the river.

I had a cup of coffee before joining the Southern Uplands Way, which I was going to use for the first part of my journey to the top of the Three Brethren, the hill that marks the boundaries of three large estates – Yair, Buccleuch and Selkirk, topped by large stone cairns. I was going to meet a group of elderly walkers, the Selkirk Plodders, and I had rather imperiously ordered them to start ahead of me as I expected it would be easy to catch up with them. (How wrong I was.)

The first part of my ascent involved a dreary climb through the most boring forestry you could imagine, an over-walked muddy track to Hareshaw Hill. Now I discovered that walking five days consecutively was a mistake. This wasn't even a steep climb –

after all the Three Brethren was only just over 1,300 feet – but my legs felt like lead. I dragged myself up, cursing and moaning and swatting midges, sweating profusely when out of the wind.

There was a brief respite through an open clearing where the ground was sandier. Then at last the path curved round and there were my Plodders sitting waiting for me and picking bilberries. What a jolly threesome they turned out to be, quite the best companions I'd walked with for ages. There was Ross aged 80 who started plodding with the group in 1945, 72-year-old Hazel who had been walking for 50 years, and Billy who was 67 and God only knows how long he'd been walking. The Selkirk Plodders have been in existence since the end of World War II. You don't have to be old to be a member but clearly they were in the majority. From eight to 15 Plodders meet once a fortnight for an eight-mile plod, and to join the club and get their badge, you must have walked from Selkirk to Traquair. What a fine embroidered badge it was, and I could see it adorning their rucksacks. I was going to be as grovelly as possible in the hope of being awarded one of these prizes, I decided. I apologized for being an hour late and saw that the way up to the summit was mercifully out of the forest, through heather-covered moor on a wide track with an easy gradient.

We started off and the weather immediately changed from being hot and sultry to the total opposite with a piercing freezing wind. I put on more clothes and just decided to be wet and warm rather than wet and cold. We started up the path. They all entertained me with endless stories about their walking exploits and the history of the area. Billy had a fine stick with badges all the way down it. Hazel had her own stick and had moved to Selkirk from Hampshire. (A white settler, according to Ross.) The other two were locals through and through, regaling me with anecdotes and sayings like 'A day out of Selkirk is a day wasted', which soon had me in fits of laughter. Not a day seemed to pass without one of these three picking up their walking boots and knocking off five miles or so. We made a cracking pace up to the summit, where the white trig point was (as Ross pointed out) redundant as all map readings are done by satellite. It was far too cold to sit on the top and have our lunch so we photographed each other by the huge cairns. I signed the Plodders' membership book (going back to the 1940s) and was thrilled to be given a badge. There were an amazing 511 Plodders in the book. As the rain closed in we started our descent south towards Selkirk.

We rounded a hill and dropped down towards the reservoir. On the way down I got completely drenched. Billy kept waffling on about 'Don't put your waterproofs on, it's just a passing shower', but I think that was an example of ironic Selkirk wit, as a passing shower seemed to mean a heavy shower which would eventually pass when it had entirely soaked you. In places the track was muddy and we slithered about but these three were like mountain goats, they simply kept going. I did put my waterproofs on in spite of Billy but by then I was wet through. At the reservoir we ate our lunch. I'd sat on my sandwiches so they were two completely misshapen objects that once had been delicious smoked salmon and cream cheese but now looked a bit like an accident. I shovelled them down and in spite of my determination at 8 am to have thinner thighs I then ate a third sandwich. How was I ever going to be lean and gorgeous?

The weather looked terrible again so we decided to continue on down the track by Long Philip Burn. At this point our route became quite a wide track through a forest of pines that seemed to be hundreds of feet high. According to Ross and Billy the local landowner regarded them as the finest trees on all his land and they certainly were, standing straight and proud. A spooky child cycled up the track towards us dressed all in black, looking like something from *The Omen*. Then the only walkers we'd seen all day emerged from the car park, a woman in a rather fetching white sun hat (that will be totally redundant, I thought) and her husband.

We had no views of Selkirk to speak of as the track was pretty enclosed with trees. Finally it met the A708 by Philiphaugh Farm and I decided to make a quick detour to my hotel to dry off before continuing on my way. At this point the heavens opened and there was a downpour to end all downpours. I said goodbye to the three Plodders and I knew I would walk with them again. I had promised that I would complete the required trek to truly earn my badge.

The hotel was on the road into Selkirk, right on my route. There I dried my hair, drank a cup of tea, and wondered how on earth I could continue with the day's filming and walking. It was 3.15 pm and I was totally knackered. I lay on the bed. I was trying to read the notes about Selkirk and learn the entire history of the town in ten minutes when there was a knock on the door and it was time to start walking again. I hadn't been able to dry anything and try as I might I hadn't been able to get the heated towel rail in the bathroom to work so I put my wet clothes back on with some dry socks, combed my hair and crossed the bridge over Ettrick Water into Selkirk, past the rugby club. It had temporarily stopped raining but the town was under a grim grey cloud. You'd never believe this was August as it looked more like March or October.

Selkirk traditionally was the town of the shoemakers (souters), who provided the Jacobites with footwear throughout the Risings. The town has a proud and distinguished past, with much of its wealth coming from the textile mills. Now I walked past mills closed for decades. With mechanization the numbers needed in the mills had declined and hundreds of townspeople had emigrated to Canada, New Zealand and Australia right through the 1950s. Then an electronics factory (encouraged by local MP David Steel) opened and Selkirk became the silicon valley of the Borders. (Since I walked through the town this factory has closed and now Selkirk faces a gloomy future once again.)

Land Rovers scuttled past me; this is an area of the countryside where everybody has a battered old Land Rover with a trailer and a couple of cattle in the back or building supplies because, it seemed to me, the two main industries were farming and doing up houses. I slowly walked up the hill into town past a grand classical arch, and a plaque telling me Robbie Burns wrote an epistle here. As I toiled up the hill a car would toot occasionally and people would wave. I tried to be jolly happy public Janet but inside I was absolutely shattered.

As I entered the market square I could see the statue of Sir Walter Scott, who served as the town's Sheriff for 33 years. I was dying to go in the chemist and buy a bottle of relaxing bubble bath but for filming purposes I had to look astounded and interested and deeply involved in Selkirk for the time being.

I crossed over to the tea shop. I went inside and ordered a tea and a Bannock cake, the currant bun that's the one famous export Selkirk has to offer. The tea shop had already closed at 4.15 pm but graciously had decided to stay open for my visit. Why does every tea shop in Britain close at 4 pm which is exactly when people want a cup of tea? Can somebody please write in on a postcard and tell me the answer. I suspect I know why. Tea shops close at 4 pm so everybody who runs the tea shops can have a cup of tea, because after all they aren't really in the service industry, are they?

Anyway I was grudgingly brought a cup of tea and a Bannock cake. Three ladies had been sitting waiting for my arrival. I asked for some jam for my Bannock cake. It was like a tea cake made with a paler sponge mixture, a kind of cross between the Welsh Barra Brith and the English tea cake. It was full of sultanas and tasted delicious. The three harpies were eating it with butter but I couldn't face that. I asked for some jam. There was a stunned silence. 'You'll no' be eating that with jam,' came a cackle from the back of the tea room. 'What's wrong with that?' I asked. 'You don't eat it with jam, I've never heard of anyone eating it with jam, you eat it with butter.' 'Well, I'm eating it with jam,' I said and they just looked at me as if I was a Martian. 'How else do you eat a Bannock?' I asked. 'You can fry it,' said the woman. 'For what meal of the day exactly?' I asked. 'Well, tea obviously,' she said. I drank three cups of tea and looked out at the market square in the rain, scene of the annual Common Riding, a local tradition where hundreds of riders follow a young man elected as leader, commemorating the town's rich history. The Plodders had given me a book of the Common Riding songs with names like 'Pride O' the Borderland' and 'Up wi' the Souters'.

I crossed the square, went in a chemist and bought a bottle of aromatherapy relaxing bath oil, hoping that it would lighten my mood. I also bought some face cream and resisted the temptation to buy yet another tube of thinner thigh cream. Then I went up to the Border Bakery that rather worryingly smelled of very strong disinfectant or bleach. There was no point in buying a Bannock cake if I wanted thinner thighs so I resisted temptation and took the leaflet that gave me the history of the Bannock cakes. Apparently Bannock cakes starred in the novel and film *Mrs Miniver* and are now exported all over the world. A Japanese government official was a devotee, and ordered them by post.

I walked back out of town in the direction of my hotel. En route I bought a couple of local newspapers to try and get the flavour of Selkirk beyond the world of the Bannock. Three little boys aged about 11 followed me down the hill. 'Are you the woman off the telly?' one of them asked. 'Yes, I bloody well am,' I said rather crossly, 'what do you want?' 'Can we be on the telly?' they said. 'Tell you what,' I replied, 'you can be on the telly if you go back to the rugby pitch and kick a ball around for the crew because they're going to film there now and there's no one on it.' The boys rushed off in a state of high excitement and returned five minutes later with a rugby ball. Two were wearing Celtic strip and one was wearing Chelsea kit. 'Don't you get laughed at supporting Chelsea up here?' I asked. 'Not a bit,' he said, 'and, guess what, my jacket cost £42.60, and I've got another one.' 'My shirt cost £39.80,' said the other boy, 'and my mum's bought me another one.' I was just astounded at the price of these rather ugly nylon clothes. Thank God I'd never had children and thank God I never wanted to wear this rubbish. They were clad from head to foot in logos, and not an inch of their little bodies didn't have some bit of writing on them.

I left my three junior rugby players happily kicking a ball around for the benefit of the camera. Back at the hotel I drank more cups of tea, lay on the bed and tried to read the local papers which seemed to have nothing of any interest in them other than the results of a Mr and Mrs golf tournament and a story of a man whose pond was causing a planning furore. I turned the television on and knew I was in the middle of nowhere when the only thing available to view was Border Television sports report. I turned the sound off. I was better off watching *Star Trek* with a load of people with blue faces, than anything about rugby.

I went down to the hotel restaurant. For some unknown reason it had a bizarre Tyrolean style; there was wood on every surface, a nightmare of joinery. Perhaps it was a tribute to all the wood I'd walked through, who knows. Perhaps the owner had been to Austria for a holiday but he'd decided to turn a perfectly nice stone building on the outside into a kind of Tyrolean hunting lodge on the inside. Even my room had a whole succession of bizarre archways. One little archway cut off the corner of the room and was like a little shrine in which my suitcase was placed on a table and it had its own special suitcase light. Forty-five minutes in the Tyrolean restaurant was all I could bear. I slunk back to my bedroom and the specially lit suitcase alcove.

The manager of the hotel, Kevin, had made me a present of a particularly fine walking stick made by his friend down the road in Ettrick Bridge. I was extremely touched. It was a fine slim piece of willow, a long stick, with JSP carved on the handle. It made the whole day worthwhile. It was absolutely superb. If only I'd had it when I'd toiled up the Three Brethren with the three Plodders. They had all had their own sticks and I was the odd one out, but now I had a stick. When I met David Steel the next day I would be fully equipped.

It only took one page of *OK* magazine and a picture of Catherine Zeta Jones to send me off into a deep sleep. It was only 10.30 pm. I awoke at 7 am totally refreshed, to find the picture of Catherine Zeta Jones lying by my pillow a bit screwed up where I'd obviously tossed and turned a bit in the night.

DAY 6

SELKIRK TO SYNTON PARKHEAD
Let's tax caravans!

I walked back up the hill into Selkirk and turned right underneath the beautiful classical arch. It was a fine sunny day. Selkirk looked completely different to the day before when it had been raining heavily. I walked down a long grand driveway. Ahead of me lay an imposing four-storey villa in the Italian style, the Haining. It was certainly the grandest building in Selkirk and looked completely out of place. But here it was tucked away outside the town apparently now owned by a reclusive old man who had come to the door the previous day, when we'd asked if we could film, clad in pyjamas, clearly ill. I skirted round in front of the house and followed a track south-east along the side of Haining Loch. Lord David Steel was waiting for me at the gate. He was immaculately dressed in country clothes as one would expect. I had my shorts on, hoping to restore a bit of the South of France suntan that had been eradicated in the previous two days walking across grouse moors in the pouring rain.

David Steel proved a fine walking companion and knew the area intimately, having been the local MP for 32 years. We walked for about the next hour or so with his dog, Lucy, across rolling farmland on a broad grassy track. David's home, a converted medieval tower, was about four miles to the west. We passed an imposing ruin in a field which turned out to be the remains of a palace for doves. According to David Steel all the big houses had these dovecotes, and I looked inside and saw all the partitions where they had nested. Apparently a friend of his in Firth was restoring one – this one was certainly as grand as a cottage.

I told David I'd been reading his book about the Borders; it seemed to be an area full of bloodshed and so many battles had been fought in it. Yet when I walked through it, it seemed a very sensuous kind of landscape. According to David, the Borders were really wild territory, and just over the next hill was known as the 'debatable lands', because it was constantly changing hands between England and Scotland. There was inter-clan rivalry too, with people stealing cattle and sheep from each other as well as from the English. It was a pretty lawless area, and it didn't come under proper control of either crown.

Our discussion about Borders' history was interrupted by some ghastly noises coming from a cow lying by the path. David assured me all was normal; the animal was just about to give birth. I wish I hadn't had all that toast now for breakfast as I felt quite squeamish. After all, I was born in Fulham.

David Steel claimed I wasn't used to the realities of life, to which I replied I didn't want to get too close. I was sure he'd staged the birth deliberately. I called the crew over and told them to be ready in case any complications set in. I continued along the path before any calves appeared.

David's history lesson continued: 'This was Ettrick Forest, the hunting ground of the Scottish kings and queens. When James IV led his troops down to Flodden to fight his brother-in-law, Henry VIII, in 1513, he took 80 people from here and only one came back to Selkirk, clutching a captured English flag, and he threw it down in market square, unable to speak. The story is re-enacted every year, and they have a minute's silence. The whole square is absolutely packed with people and horses, and you cannot hear a sound. And that's commemorating what happened in 1513.' I found it moving that history still meant so much to people today.

Then David showed me his walking stick: it was carved from a sheep's horn, in the shape of a trout, curving into his hand. At the annual agricultural show there were stick-carving competitions. Mine would win no prizes, but it meant a lot to me.

I asked David about the right to roam – Scotland, as I'd discovered on my walk here, has no law of trespass. People had been very pleasant to me as I crossed their land, and I thought at first that they were just being nice, and then I realized I wasn't breaking the law. David said, 'It's fine as long as you cause no damage to crops or animals, or leave gates open. You can walk wherever you like. And you know, there's so much nonsense talked about the right to roam. If you look around here, there's miles and miles of places that you can walk without causing any disturbance to anybody.' But how could walkers persuade the landowners of England to alter their attitude, because it seemed to me that a large proportion of them are implacably opposed to the right to roam? David disagreed. 'There's a small proportion of them who are opposed, but if you look at the report that the Country Land Owners Association, which is a purely English and Welsh organization, produced, many are very keen on opening up public access.'

What really annoys me is that when the water companies were privatized, with that one move we lost access to a lot of land which went into private ownership. David Steel interrupted my rant to have one of his own. He spotted a caravan in a field. 'One of the things I think the Scottish Parliament should do is have a tax on caravans.' I agreed – what a brilliant idea. According to David, caravans pay no tax at all. They don't pay council tax, as you do for a house, they don't pay motor tax as you do for a vehicle, so they get away with nothing. And I think an annual tax on caravans, and a visitor's tax for a month, would bring in quite a nice little bit of revenue for the Scottish Parliament. Obviously we'll tax those Scottish caravans when they come south too, I thought.

I was getting to enjoy David's company more and more. Here was a fellow caravan-hater! He told me there was a move at one time to get them all painted green. One or two of the manufacturers started to produce them in a sort of pale green, and then they went back to the ugly white boxes we now have to endure, desecrating our gorgeous countryside. But then, spookily enough, David confessed to actually owning one: 'We've had three different motor caravans over the years and we used to trundle all over the country, when the children were small, and all over Europe. It's quite a cheap way of having a holiday.'

As far as I can see caravans don't bring anything into the economy. Loads of caravaners arrive with their own food and just sit in them looking out. So if David wanted a caravan tax, why not go the whole hog and have a tourist tax, as everyone crosses the border into Scotland? He laughed, and said, 'No, we want to encourage people. We don't want to put them off. A caravan tax would be an environmentally sound idea – perhaps we could exempt green ones.'

As we walked down towards Hartwoodburn, David admitted he'd never taken this track before. 'I pass by the end here very often, but I've never actually walked down this little bit we're on now. So it's a first for me. There's a lady in one of these houses who has little Shetland ponies pulling her around in a cart.'

As we reached a B road David opened the gate for me. We stopped and drank a coffee, and said goodbye.

I continued on alone on a path through tall nettles, to the excitingly named Big Wood. Big Wood wasn't so large any more as they had hacked a huge section of it down, and my track took me through a rather unattractive, denuded part. I reached the A7 and a lay-by. David had told me there were many Roman forts in the area and I saw one on the other side of the road, although it was just like a raised earthwork. I crossed over by a sign urging me to eat Scottish meat. It was a home-made affair and a bit wonky but I agreed with its message if nothing else. I then followed a charming road south-east over rolling hills with isolated farms and the occasional small plantation. Where it veered off to the east I carried on in my straight line, along a section of the road they'd simply not bothered to repair. It was a wonderful walk, and all I could hear were the birds and the occasional sounds of cattle. I continued in my ruthless straight line, rising up over a hill and dropping down to a stream called Ale Water. According to my map, a ford lay at the bottom of the hill by Synton Mill. I had asked my researcher to find out the day before how deep the river was. I'd even asked David Steel but everybody was incredibly vague.

When I got there I soon found out that the ford didn't exist any more. My track simply petered out. So I took my shoes and socks off and used my walking stick as a crutch. I slowly made my way across the stream over slippery rocks. This was the first time in my walk south that I'd forded a river – and where was the crew? Not here of course, they were having a cup of coffee sitting in a lay-by by the A7. My phone didn't work so I couldn't call them, and quite frankly I couldn't be bothered. It did make me mad though as I was very worried that people would see my walk on film and think that everything had been so easy to achieve, that I'd never had to climb through six-foot nettles, go over barbed-wire fences or paddle through icy streams.

I dried my feet off with my socks on the other side. The water had been absolutely freezing so I decided to walk on a little further to warm my feet up. Following a little B road I walked up the hill to Dimpleknowe. This was charming countryside, domestic in scale with a succession of small farms and stoutly built stone cottages. Now I followed the road around south-west until I came to the farm at Synton Parkhead. Here the farmer was mowing the grass in front of his house and grilled me about my journey. Why was I doing it? Was it for charity? I suddenly noticed that he didn't have a Scottish accent at all. It turned out that he'd moved here from near Newcastle 25 years ago. I decided to enlist his help. I didn't want to follow the dreary A7 into Hawick, so what was the best route? He directed me over the fields of his farm and said he had no problem with me walking through them as long as I understood which field the bull was in. It takes more than a bull to force me into a detour, I can tell you, so I listened to what he had to say and decided to ignore the second part of it.

I walked down the road a few yards and there was his son and a couple of farm labourers separating the sheep from the lambs. In a few pens hundreds of sheep were crammed in, their heads looking anxious. Weaning, they called it. It seemed a bit unkind but on the other hand there's no point in getting too sentimental about sheep. From now on these lambs and their mothers would be placed in separate fields for the rest of their lives. And with that gloomy thought in my head I got a lift to Galashiels to have lunch with my friend's mum, an organic farmer.

That night we went into Edinburgh to catch some comedy. I saw two shows back to back. The trouble was that the owners of the Pleasance Theatre have divided the building into many small venues, with no air conditioning. Halfway through an Irish comic's interminable drone about his schooldays, I fell asleep. A snore woke me up and, as luckily my seat was at the end of a row, I stumbled to the exit and oxygen. My bed beckoned.

SYNTON PARKHEAD TO STONEDGE FOREST
Hawick – a town in crisis

It was a fine sunny day as I climbed up the first of many rounded rolling hills of the day. This ran off the narrow road by Synton Parkhead farm, up to a small copse of trees. Then I followed an undulating landscape through fields of stubble where the farmers had taken advantage of a break in the weather to cut the hay after the wettest August on record. I struggled through some waist-high nettles, beating them down with my stick. There were no paths here, and it was just a case of avoiding the boggy bits in the valleys and watching out for bulls. I passed under a row of pylons, headed south-east, crossing an old drovers' road.

These ancient tracks which criss-cross the Borders were extremely important in the early 18th century. Cattle and sheep were driven along them to the annual markets in Crieff in Perthshire (80 miles away) or at Stenhousemuir, near Falkirk. English farmers would drive livestock bought at these markets down south to northern England, on another network of tracks. Drovers' roads enabled farmers to avoid paying the new turnpike road tolls on each score of livestock. As the drovers' roads were grassy, cattle were ensured free grazing and soft going underfoot. With the introduction of railways in the 1840s the drovers' roads declined and within 20 years they had virtually been abandoned. Now they're great routes for ramblers and I love walking on them.

I clung to a wire fence that ran along the edge of a bog, trying to keep my feet dry, then headed up over another field to Muirfield Farm. There I picked up another drovers' road, heading south. It had been well ridden and the first part was so wet that progress through the mire was painstakingly slow. I began to regret my decision to take the scenic route rather than tough it out along the A7 straight into Hawick. Eventually the grass between the high hawthorn hedges dried out a little, and after Clarilaw Farm I turned right on a narrow tarmac road, then took the footpath off it to skirt the lush green slopes of Clarilaw Hill, an ancient fort.

My next road skirted round Courthill, a large collection of stone farm buildings, and then I followed alongside a disused railway line to the outskirts of Hawick, by the Burnfoot Industrial Estate. Now I took another bridle path over a beck, through a wood and out on to a flat grassy area by the River Teviot. I was beginning to realize just how many people rode horses in this area. I'd seen many bridleway signs, and images of horses were everywhere: on letterboxes, little figures in gardens, on metal gates and on weather vanes. I sat on my waterproof jacket on the grass by the river to have my lunch. People were out walking their dogs, enjoying the sunshine. It was clear how bad unemployment is in Hawick as there were a lot of men walking large dogs. One surly fellow walked within two feet of me with a particularly revolting Alsatian. When I asked if he could pull his dog off my jacket and away from my sandwiches, he told me to fuck off! It never fails to amaze me how when men are on the dole, they often invest in large aggressive dogs, which must cost a fortune in dog food. It's obviously a small price to pay for maintaining a macho image.

Hawick is a town in crisis. Obviously the surrounding farms were suffering financially but now its traditional source of employment, the woollen industry, is in trouble too. I'd seen teams of Japanese executives at my hotel who were considering whether to bale out one of the famous sweater factories. Pringle – the household name for woollen twinsets – was in serious financial crisis, having laid off 300 people in the last eight months. John Laing had laid off 24 the previous week, and Peter Scott, another factory, was working a four-day week. And yet some of the smaller factories, which had invested in new digital machinery, were doing plenty of work at the very top end of the market, making cashmere sweaters for international designers like Calvin Klein and Yves St Laurent. Unlike Selkirk, no electronic factories or major new businesses have opened in Hawick.

I finished my sandwiches, hissed at another nosy dog, and walked along the banks of the Teviot past Hawick Rugby Club's Mansfield Park stand, the biggest one in the Borders. Rugby is the most important sport round here. This club, 'the Greens', was established in 1872. The modern versions of the burly front-line troops who fought for Scotland's Borders are found on the rugby pitch, and a high proportion of the Scottish team is made up of Hawick rugby players. Sadly the team was suffering of late, as so many good players had left to play for national teams and it had been forced to take on younger inexperienced players, and their sponsor, Pringle Knitwear, was less able to give financial support.

On Mansfield Road I walked past some closed-up factories and a gasometer, past Eastfield Mill (now offices) and over the river by a narrow footbridge. Mills lined the river, interspersed with stone three-storey terraced workers' cottages. I passed the Hawick Cashmere company and could hear the sounds of steam-pressing through the open windows.

Now I turned away from the river and up Bridge Street, past the public library, with its 1904 plaque, tower and leaded windows, and past the supermarket and the job centre. At a junction of roads at the end of the High Street was the proud statue commemorating the Common Rider. Hawick itself seems to have a very masculine air about it, with its no-nonsense solid grey granite buildings. Hawick's knitting traditions started in the 1770s when it made long woollen socks for men, the business peaking by 1900.

But nowhere is the masculine side of the town more apparent than in the event the statue I'd just passed glorified – the Common Riding, which started in 1514. This event, involving over 250 horses, comprises a series of rides and parades marking the boundaries of the town, where riders follow a 'cornet' (a young man elected each year who carries a flag and leads the rides). Women had been excluded from the Common Riding in Hawick since 1931, but a couple of years ago two local women went to the European Court to take part. They won their case, but the episode split the town and the number of women participating has dwindled since 1996. Both the women who went to court moved away from the town after suffering verbal abuse. Hawick is a town with a lot going on beneath the surface.

I walked up the High Street, past the newsagents, the Border Bakeries, the butcher's and the Town Hall with its fairytale clocktower which would have looked equally at home in the Rhone Valley. I climbed up Cross Wynd, a steep hill, past a disused mill and a cemetery with grand stone urns and fine stone memorials. The souls had a good view right over Hawick, spread out in the valley, with its terraces of stone houses strung out in tiers. I slogged on up, saying hello to people strolling with their dogs and heading for their allotments (firmly fortified with barbed wire), gradually shrugging off the last vestiges of the town up Wellogate Brae, passing a riding stables, and at the top, a radio mast. I mused that the future for Hawick probably lies in tourism as the countryside it lies in is so very unspoilt and pleasurable. But can Hawick lose its rather grim image?

Waiting to walk with me a little further down the hill was a local young woman, Claire Tate. A keen rider since she was 12, she had participated in the Common Riding since 1996, even though her own father was opposed to women taking part. As we strolled south along a series of green lanes, Claire led her horse and chatted, explaining that riding was central to Border life, and nearly every family in Hawick had a horse. Although Claire was attractive and vivacious, I could see that she was extremely strong-willed underneath. The issue didn't seem to be one that divided people on gender lines, it seemed.

According to Claire, 'There will still be men and women in Hawick who will say they prefer that women don't take part in the Common Riding, because people don't like change. That's true of every sphere of life, isn't it? People don't like change, they find it hard to adapt.' I found her comments particularly poignant in a town like Hawick where the mills are closing and change is inevitable.

Claire said she hoped people would see that they had to work together as a town to get things back to rights commercially. 'It's a small community and people have to live here and if they have a husband who isn't quite happy with the situation, then to keep the peace women won't say anything or won't participate either. Born and bred and brought up with the tradition of the Common Riding, we feel very strongly about it and as an outsider it's hard to realize the feeling that's running high in the town.'

It seemed to me that Hawick will have to move with the times if it's to face any kind of future. Women like Claire have a spirit that was quite inspiring. We said goodbye and I wished her well. Trained as a teacher, she is running a shop in Galashiels, which seemed a shame.

I took a path over a hill and dropped down on to a tiny road, passing Kaimend Farm. Ahead lay an increasingly uninhabited series of grassy hills, eventually flattening out to a rolling prairie. I tried to skirt around a couple of hills but frisky cows and a bull made me detour. Eventually I climbed White Hill, struggling through clumpy tufts of grass. At the deserted ruined farmhouse of Adderston Lee I drank a cup of tea, ate a couple of biscuits and wished the cold wind would stop. The sun, miraculously, was still shining. It was 4 pm. I'd been walking since 9.30 with only one 20-minute stop. My researcher had estimated I'd get there by 1 pm for lunch. What planet was she on? My legs were weary from the heavy going, and the succession of rolling hills was tiring. Nevertheless I'd enjoyed meeting Claire and the landscape ahead – empty of all people and buildings – was inspiring.

There were no paths, so I followed dry stone walls and wire fences over Hoggfield Hill and down the other side to a small road, where I crossed a cattle grid and entered the Stonedge Forest, clutching a Xeroxed map of how to negotiate my way out of it. The forest was eerily still in the late afternoon and I hadn't seen a soul for hours. The only sign of life was the odd squirrel and occasional hoot of an owl. I was tired but feeling proud of my progress, until I tried to leave the forestry track by the route marked on my paper. It didn't exist! There was a green expanse about 20 yards wide between two rows of trees, but it was a series of deep furrows, ditches filled with water, overgrown with grass three feet high. I could have wept. It took me 30 minutes to get to the field at the edge of the trees, 300 yards away, and then I had to negotiate double barbed wire around a field of turnips. I emerged on the track by Lurgiescleuch Farm at 6 pm, covered in scratches and mud, with my feet soaking wet.

I couldn't speak on the drive back to Hawick. All I wanted was a hot bath and supper on a tray lying on my bed. And that's what I got! I washed out my socks in shower gel and cleaned my boots with an old flannel. These mundane tasks restored my sanity.

DAY 8

LURGIESCLEUCH TO DEADWATER
Bog, border and bilberries

When I looked out of the window I couldn't be sure which way the weather was going, but mindful that this is the wettest part of Britain I packed a thick waterproof jacket and trousers. At 8 am the cloud looked pretty set in although it was relatively warm, but it had rained in the night. After a kipper I had decided to pay a quick visit to the cashmere factory in Hawick I'd passed the day before. There was much excitement in the Mansfield House Hotel where I was staying because an emissary of King Hussein had phoned up and said he was coming for lunch the next day. Apparently the King knew the people who own Jenners department store in Edinburgh and after shooting trips he frequently stops in Hawick on his way back home. The owner of the hotel assured me that although there was a knitwear crisis in some of the factories in Hawick, the small companies were doing very well, especially the ones who made for top designers, and were very adaptable. One of the best companies to go and see, he said, was the Hawick Cashmere Company whose owner David Sanderson was a real go-getting type. As I'd walked past their factory by the river the day before I was intrigued. After a telephone call I arranged to go down there that morning.

David Sanderson turned out to have a very slight Scottish accent, the upper-middle-class businessman's outfit of blue-and-white striped shirt and a very thin black cashmere sweater. He was a likeable fellow and told me that Hawick was suffering an identity crisis. It's a very small town, he said, and the people have exceptional skills, being clever with their fingers and very good at assembling sweaters and weaving. So if people in his factory have relatives that work in other factories and they get laid off it makes everybody depressed. His workforce was about 150 people and he took me on a whistle-stop tour of the factory.

In the main weaving room the crisis facing Hawick was immediately apparent. On one side of the room were rows of the old machines. Eight in a row can knit the same piece of a sweater but only in plain stitch, the fine stitch most cashmere sweaters are made of. They can knit at the same shape, in the same stitch and in different colours at the same time and be watched by one man or woman. On the other side of the room were the new digital machines. These were encased in plastic and ran off a bank of computers in another room. Computer disks were fed into each machine and then it knitted a sweater in a whole variety of stitches. It was exactly the same difference as you see in the television industry between film editing and digital tape editing. 'Well, there you see it,' said David Sanderson. The new machines, invented by the Japanese of course, cost £70,000 each. He had about ten, almost £1 million worth of investment to upgrade his factory.

He made sweaters to order for people as diverse as Americans Calvin Klein and Michael Kors, and British designer Jean Muir. Elsewhere in Hawick sweaters were being knitted for Chanel, Yves St Laurent and young designers like Clements Ribiero. All these designers would frequently visit Hawick and discuss the designs of the sweaters, working nine months in advance. The beauty of Hawick is that the factories are relatively small and so people like David Sanderson can respond to small runs of highly priced well-finished knitwear, and as we went through the factory it became clear that the more complicated designs could take up to an hour to hand-finish.

He showed me a ball of yarn. Each ball of yarn cost about £60 or £70. A sweater might not take too long to knit on the machine but the process it went through would take all day. There was the washing room where, after all the pieces had been knitted, they were then washed to make them soft, various assembly rooms where all the parts were knitted together, and then, finally, the hand-finishing room. It all seemed an incredibly complicated process.

The factory was light and airy with light streaming in on both sides through large windows in all the finishing rooms. Some of the women wore stereo headphones, read books and had music playing. They ranged in age from girls in their 20s to women in their 60s. It was only the second time I'd ever been in a knitting factory, the previous time being a Marks & Spencer factory in the Negev desert in Israel. That was a completely different situation: raw fleeces went in one end, were spun, got processed, went through the whole process of being turned into wool and came out as boring twinsets at the other end. Here the yarn was shaped into a small number of highly designed short runs of very expensive knitwear. In the shop I bought a beautiful cashmere sweater with a collar for £100. In London it would have been £300 at least. I bought a little pair of black cashmere gauntlets (they were only £12), and then I saw a wonderful sweater shaped like a hooded sweatshirt. Unfortunately it was in a very tasteful shade of grey but David rose to the occasion by offering to knit it for me in shocking pink with longer sleeves. I was hooked. I was starting my day's walk with a carrier bag of bargain cashmere and I'd been privileged to see an inside view of Hawick, gaining an insight into the close-knit (pardon the pun) community it is.

Hawick is a complicated place. It's got a strong masculine feel about it but then when you go inside the knitwear factories and see the refined work done by women you see what an important part they have to play.

Now I was going to walk from Lurgiescleuch Farm in Scotland to Deadwater Farm in England, both in the middle of nowhere. The southern part of the Borders really opens out into a magnificent landscape; if only the forestry hadn't got their hands on some of it. These are huge open fells, the scale of which is magnificent. Interesting rounded hills every now and then just to perk your interest up. Well-built stone farmhouses. Beautiful pink stone churches. Fine gardens. Interesting porches and woodwork. All the legacy of the rich heritage of well-run estates.

From Hawick the drive to Lurgiescleuch was most enjoyable, following the river and then a bleak section over some exposed moors before dropping down to Bonchester Bridge, home of Bonchester cheese and a fine herd of highland cattle. From Bonchester we took even smaller roads through a delicious hamlet called Hobkirk. Here were estate cottages with fine gardens solidly built of stone with a fine church of pinky-grey granite. We followed a valley passing through a grand estate until we came to the edge of the moors. This is where I had ended yesterday.

I got out of the car at the cattle grid and walked along a road to Lurgiescleuch Farm. I waved to the farmer. I couldn't imagine living or working here, it was so isolated. From the farm, which was at the end of a track, I dropped down through a field of sheep, crossed a burn and a plank bridge and headed up a long slow slog on a piece of rough ground by the plantation opposite. Forestry plantations annoy me. For a start any maps you own are redundant as the trees are continually cut down. I climbed up several hundred feet between a wall heading south-east, clambering up and down ditches. My map of Wauchope Forest (supplied by the Forestry Commission) bore no relation to what it was like today. Even on the Ordnance Survey map Pathfinder 497 the forest is shown as much smaller than it is. I aimed to enter it and then turn right at what looked like a nice easy-to-follow trail, go down for about a mile and then pick up a road. After two or three hundred yards the track had grown over and obviously nobody in this particular forestry HQ had ever walked up to this little impassable corner of it.

Dave, a forestry expert, had turned up to help, but he turned out to be an expert from the next load of dreary trees, the Fanna Hill Forest. This nightmare was nothing to do with him and he claimed no special knowledge here. We made painstakingly slow progress; something that was meant to take 45 minutes took an hour and a half to travel probably about a mile. At one stage I clung to some chainlink fencing, feeling like an extra from *Tenko* or a prisoner in a camp in Eastern Europe. We weren't just going from tussock to tussock through soaking wet bog, we were walking over ground that nobody had walked over in ten years. At one stage I fell down a hole and found a little frog. We crept along in pouring rain and thick mist. Eventually Dave triumphantly said, 'I can see the road.' What he meant was that we had to turn left and take an even wetter and more discouraging section heading east, where we eventually were very very grateful to meet the legendary forestry road. This seemed like the M1 after what I'd been through. I was wet through to the skin up to above my knees.

Dave and I decided to press on otherwise we would never have made even half of today's planned route. I showed him my researcher's projected timings. According to her it would take exactly 40 minutes to climb up to the radio mast on Wigg Knowe, 491 metres high. Dave laughed. 'If you can do it at that speed,' he said, 'you're better than I am and I'm pretty fit.' He'd been up until 11 pm the night before crawling through his particular bit of the forest on all fours trying to cull the cunning deer who were busy eating the tops of all their fresh young trees.

Apparently German, Belgian and French hunting fanatics pay £500 to £700 a week to come to this dismal bit of the Kielder Forest and shoot deer, and if they don't shoot enough deer then the people who work for the Forestry Commission just have to get down on all fours like Dave and try and kill off the required number if any of the young trees are going to survive. Had Dave got a result the night before? 'Sadly not,' he replied. Dave was an endearing chap who – like me – spent most of his time polishing his glasses in the pouring rain as we were both extremely hot and sweaty from all our efforts (it was a very muggy day).

We trudged wearily up the track to Fanna Hill. Of course, being a Forestry Commission track, it didn't go in a straight line but looped about in an irritating fashion at one of the most uncomfortable slow gradients, the prerogative of all forestry reserves. I would rather climb a 1-in-3 hill than this grizzly slow climb in the driving rain. The mist was now well down and Dave was reduced to describing the views I might have seen. If it's pouring with rain, forestry workers are allowed to go home at lunchtime because they don't work in the wet. Given that this is one of the wettest areas in the country I wondered how many of them actually did a full day's work. 'There's another problem,' Dave said, 'the midges are totally evil, you don't want to try doing any work when they're about.' Working in the forest in this part of the country by now sounded to me like one of the least enticing jobs going in Britain. But there isn't any other work round here so I suppose people don't have too much to choose from, and as most of the farmers I talked to rented their land from the Forestry Commission I couldn't get any of them to badmouth their landlords either.

We eventually reached the mast on top of Wigg Knowe. It was completely melancholy. Visibility was 25 yards. Trees in every direction. I was soaking wet, out of breath and extremely tired. I drank a cup of black coffee and ate a Kit-Kat. Dave said that my projected route down to the south of this forest was stupid as it involved a long trek over open moor, climbing even higher to the top of Fanna Hill, 514 metres. He said, 'I'm asking you this, Janet, do you want to climb upwards in thick driving rain and mist to get to another hill you're not going to see anything from and then walk down another forestry track?'

Of course my answer was no. So Dave assured me that the route he was showing me would be both shorter and easier, and closer to my line. He stepped off into the mist. I followed him and fell flat on my face in a huge patch of bilberries. It was captured on film much to the delight of the crew. The bilberries tasted great though because as there were no sheep in that part of the forest they were nice and juicy and fat, and nobody had managed to get to them before me. 'Don't worry, it's character building,' Dave nervously croaked. I didn't want my character building, I screamed, I liked it the way it was.

I lay in the bilberry patch and wondered why I had bothered to wash my hair that morning. It was now plastered to my head like streaky bacon. Lying there was infinitely more comfortable than the next half an hour descending between two blocks of forestry, down a hill known as Dog Knowe. Why was it that all the placenames in this forest are so ugly? When I looked on the map more and more unattractive names seemed to leap out at me – Black Cleuch, it should be Black Squelch as far as I'm concerned. We slowly made our way down through what seemed like five miles, but was probably only one, of thick bog, reeds, tufty grass. There was no path at all, although Dave kept saying to me in a feebler and feebler voice, 'I think I've found a track.' All I found was a small frog, which I photographed. Eventually after 45 minutes we dropped down on to the B6357 which links Jedburgh to Kielder. I walked down it and only about two cars passed me in 45 minutes. On either side the gently rounded hills were completely covered in serried ranks of exactly the same kind of pine; relentless, unforgiving and depressing scenery.

After a few miles the landscape began to lighten up slightly. I passed a couple of cottages but there were no signs of life. This seemed like one of the loneliest places in the Borders. I was descending gradually. As the forest gradually receded Saughtree Fell rose up on my right to the west. I crossed a cattle grid and the road dropped down to follow Dawston burn. I took an old track off it going over the top of a hill. Sheep stared at me in astonishment. It was clear that no one had walked on this track in years. I contoured round the aptly named Barren Hill. Following the stream I saw a stone bridge below me and took a disused railway line. Some frisky cows momentarily stopped me in my tracks but they were more frightened by me than me by them. They scuttled off. I couldn't believe that there had ever been a railway in such a godforsaken place.

The line was built in the 1850s by a group of landowners from the North Tyne Valley in Northumberland, and was over 26 miles long, serving local iron works and carrying agricultural produce and passengers. Eventually the line went from Hexham all the way up to the border, but it was closed in 1963. There's a campaign to get it re-opened, so reducing the number of lorries taking felled trees out of the forest, but somehow I don't see it happening.

After another half an hour the railway track met the road by a little burn. A family were picnicking and they looked stupefied at the sight of me appearing along the top of the track high above them. It was a sweet picture; they had erected a little windbreak, and the children were playing in a small rubber dingy in the burn. I was heartened by this scene. It seemed to reinforce an idyllic view of family life, a happy holiday with no gadgets, no Gameboys, everybody getting on playing with their toys and just enjoying nature. They hadn't had to get on a plane, go to a beach, squabble with the other kids. I was sorry I was even intruding by walking past them.

I rejoined the road and spent another mile trudging through the edge of the forest until I reached Myredykes Farm which was a lonely cottage and not much else. The burn to the south of the road babbled along beside me and a heron rose and fell every now and then, following my path. Very occasionally a car would go through the forest, generally travelling at high speed as if to leave it as soon as possible.

I reached the border of Scotland, finally agreed on in 1551 after 500 years of wars and bloodshed. Mysteriously the sign announcing the border of England was 15 yards further on. What happens in that bit of no-man's land in-between? Is it a midge breeding ground? They certainly seemed to be out in force as great waves of them rose up to greet me with every step. I had to keep my mouth closed and flap the map a lot.

At Deadwater Farm a blond-haired child was playing on the gate of the holiday cottage by the road. I walked up the path to meet Jim Hall, the first tenant farmer on the English leg of my walk. Jim had a strong Northumbrian accent in spite of living a quarter of a mile from Scotland. He was a rugby fanatic born two miles down the road. His wife came from Hawick and therefore was Scottish. His sons were educated in England and he was very witty about the difference between being English and Scottish. It turned out that he had only ever really taken a long journey south twice in his entire life, the more recent to Birmingham for a funeral. Before that the only other visit he had made south was to Middlesbrough, and this was a man probably in his 50s. He loved the valley and couldn't speak more highly of it. At least it's got one fan, I thought, as I trudged back down his driveway and resumed my long slog down the road towards Kielder Water.

Now I was to spend the next two days really getting to know trees, I mused, as I attempted to make my way through the forest and out the other side on tracks and trails, trying to keep to my straight line.

DAY 9

DEADWATER TO WICKHOPE NICK
I can't keep up

A few days after this stretch of my journey, I was looking at a map of the Kielder Forest and quite honestly I couldn't tell you my route. I started at 11.30 am on Bank Holiday Monday morning. Opposite Deadwater Farm a forestry ranger's car was parked. It belonged to Mike Sanderson, the forest ranger I was to walk with. He was tall, maybe over six foot, possibly a little taller than me, but very thin. He was one year short of retirement and far fitter than me, a fell runner who still ran two or three times a week.

I'd been reading up on the Kielder Forest so I'd have conversational material for my day with Mike. Covering 200 square miles, it was Britain's largest forest, started in 1926. Sensitive to the criticisms of environmental pollution, Kielder Water was encouraging leisure activities like fishing and sailing. And the forest was being improved with mixed planting and broad-leaf trees. Cycle tracks and trails were being established. But there is no getting away from the fact it's a giant, cost-effective tree factory. With trees constantly being felled, maps are confusing. Mike was to make sure I didn't get lost in this monotonous landscape.

The only time I'd ever been here before was when I made a series about Ffyona Campbell who walked around the world. I walked with her from Bellingham into the Forest and she did the whole route along main roads. Giant log lorries whizzed passed us, pinning us against walls. She was marching at a cracking pace. At one stage I wanted to go to the toilet and she wouldn't even wait. I hopped over a wall, hopped back again and had to run up the road. What a cow. Most of the young people who were supposed to walk with her from the Operation Raleigh Charity couldn't match her pace but I managed to keep up for about 15 miles, which we covered in just over four hours; she didn't stop to look at the landscape at all.

Now I was prepared to give the forest a second chance, although it had to be said that if not an environmental disaster, it's possibly one of the most unattractive pieces of landscape in the British Isles, as it doesn't go up and down enough to form any natural features. Kielder Water is a reservoir that has been artificially created and around it there are various islands and inlets but it seems woefully underused in spite of everyone's efforts to encourage leisure activities. On this particular Bank Holiday Monday the weather was grey but warm. Mike, the ranger, said we wouldn't be walking anywhere near the road because he thought it would be very busy with traffic. After I had been walking with him for about an hour I discovered that he lived on the south side of the forest and had worked there for 20 years, and perhaps what he considered a busy Bank Holiday Monday wasn't what I would. As it turned out, there were very few visitors to the Kielder Forest that day.

We took the track opposite Deadwater Farm to the railway line. At this point the forest opened out a little bit with cattle and grazing land. We walked along the disused line and tried to get to know each other. He had looked at the map at the start and said it should take about four hours but hadn't mentioned the 16-mile distance. Time and time again on this walk I was discovering that macho men set a time and an agenda almost impossible to keep to. I kept my mouth shut but looking on the map it did seem an awfully long way to be doing in four hours. We'd gone about 25 yards when I discovered I was in the presence of a supreme athlete. We were belting down the railway track at a cracking pace, probably about four miles an hour. 'Can we please slow down,' I said to him, 'we aren't being filmed so there's no need to do it in the shortest possible time.' He looked a bit depressed but still pressed on ahead. Coming in the opposite direction were mountain bikers at sporadic intervals, puffing and blowing, and this was a flat section. It seemed to be taxing the strength of most of the people we saw and their crash helmets looked like funny little plastic accessories stuck on their heads. I could see there would be a few family rows later on in the day about this particular choice of activity.

After we had gone about another 100 yards I saw one cow which was pregnant and then another cow with something furry and dead-looking on the ground beside it. Suddenly I realized a calf had just been born (my second birth of the walk), probably within the last five minutes. It was lying there not moving very much. The mother was licking it and it twitched slightly. I was very relieved as I was frightened it might be dead. So that was at least one magical and positive moment in the Kielder Forest, which probably made up for the hours of misery I had spent with Ffyona Campbell. I carried along this straight path somewhat heartened. Eventually the track went into the forest and we then spent the next four and a half hours on a whole variety of tracks. There were cycle tracks, there were horrible forestry tracks (made of very hard, uncomfortable chippings) which are the roads they take the logs out on and there was a straight section which Mike proudly announced to me was used once by the RAC in their all-round Britain rally which had now sadly moved to somewhere else. It's known as the straight mile. And then we circled around in a more confusing route than I could possibly describe to you, and at one stage even Mike got lost. He had been extolling all the leisure activities that it was possible to do in the forest (after all, he was the leisure officer) so he was very worried that I might be giving it a bad press. He told me that the early serried ranks of trees were now being superseded by a new policy where contour lines were being followed, there was a whole variety of trees in the forest, wildlife was there in large numbers, blah blah. They can plant it with different varieties of trees, they can make it look slightly prettier, but the basic fact remains that 50 giant lorries a day leave the Kielder Forest laden with wood for all sorts of purposes, and they want their trees to grow straight so they cull the deer who eat the young trees and make them have more than one trunk.

Even on this Bank Holiday the atmosphere in Europe's largest man-made forest was gloomy. Perhaps it was the monotonous grey sky. I asked Mike if anyone ever had to be found in the forest because every vista looked exactly the same. No, he said, no one ever really gets lost. About an hour later we had done a few nifty shortcuts up cycle paths and through trees to cut off a few corners and we came upon a family of five standing there completely lost. The man about the house had a compass that he didn't know how to use. They were studying a leisure map that had footpaths marked on it but were going in completely the opposite direction to the one they should have taken. Mike pointed them on the correct route and reeled off a whole list of instructions that I could see would lead to a huge row the minute we turned the corner as nobody had a pen to write them down. This involved using cycle tracks that had red tape across, crossing down other tracks, etc., etc. I was very grateful I was with this man, even though I had now heard about the history of the coniferous tree and all the attendant wildlife for three hours and was contemplating making it my next A level. Sometimes we went along relatively soft but easy-to-walk-on paths but always there were the trees on either side of us. Occasionally we'd pass the odd house, a legacy from a previous era. Apparently the wardens that live in these houses find the summer months very difficult as the midges are really terrible.

After skirting round some more hills going slightly up, slightly down, we reached the Cranecleugh outdoor centre, used by handicapped people to enjoy the countryside, which seemed a pretty good use. A woman in a wheelchair had been shooting on the archery range. As we passed some of the log cabins a few people were cleaning their cars. They were the only signs of life I had seen for hours.

We crossed over the burn on a bridge and contoured up some more tracks. I was getting tired by now. I seemed to have been walking for hours and there's a limit to how many facts about a forest that you can assimilate in one day, but Mike seemed indefatigable. He told me that he was going to retire next year to look after his goats, grow his vegetables and keep his bees. 'Why don't you hire yourself out to all these tourists, who come to the Kielder Forest and don't know how to enjoy it, as a guide for the day?' I suggested. All the people we'd seen lost, standing in parking lots, or eating their lunch in their cars, had seemed a completely uninspired bunch. What they needed was Mike to talk about frogs, raptors, adders, and get them really vibed up about the forest. He said he'd think about it.

We stopped for lunch at a designated view point (is the view of Kielder Forest really worth a view point?) when two people came up in their cars, got out, took a look and decided it wasn't worth it and drove off again. Nevertheless Mike and I sat at a picnic table and ate our lunch. He being Mr Macho and super fit, only ate one roll; I ate three, which I immediately regretted when we resumed our cracking $4^1/_2$-mile-an-hour pace after lunch, and I nearly stepped on an adder on the path in my post-lunch bloated stupor.

There were a few yachts out on Kielder Water, but nothing else to speak of. We climbed up now through some land that had been recently felled. The landscape as a result looks grey and even more unloved. Mike had told me earlier that the American artist James Turrell was building an art work called 'Skyspace' high up in the forest, a view point funded with Millennium money. He asked me if I wanted to make a detour of half a mile to see where it was going to go. I couldn't face it. To be honest every view of the Kielder Forest is more or less a variation on the same theme. There are trees planted 40 years ago, trees planted 20 years ago and trees that were planted two years ago.

By now my legs were really tired. Unlike Mike I wasn't a champion fell runner. I was supposed to be walking for pleasure but this seemed more like an endurance test. Just to perk me up Mike told me about his favourite walk in recent months, which was over 60 miles involving various peaks done over 20-something hours. The only thought that came into my head was, Why? Imagine doing a walk that involves three peaks, 60 miles and you do it all day and all night. What on earth for? It's the complete opposite to how I walk.

The final three miles were a long slow slog in a southerly direction up to Wickhope Nick. I'd had enough by now. I'd drunk endless bottles of water, I'd eaten all my food, and all I wanted to do was get in the car and have a hot bath. This road was really unpleasant, made of chippings packed down, hard and unforgiving. My back was killing me. We dropped down over a stream and then resumed the grizzly climb. Mike must have sensed my morale was low because he kept telling me we only had another mile or another 20 minutes to go. Finally we pulled up to the hill and I saw the Land Rover ahead. Thank goodness for that.

The downside was there was no tea. Jane, my driver, took us back to Mike's car. I was furious there was no tea. Any excuses about it being Bank Holiday weren't good enough. I'd been walking for five hours, with only one stop of 15 minutes and I was shattered mentally – there wasn't another fact that I could assimilate about forests. At one point I'd fallen in a ditch as I jumped across, and just slithered in and got my feet slightly wet. I looked down and a large green frog was sitting on my hand. I don't know who was the more surprised.

We drove back in silence. Mike got out at his car and I said goodbye. We drove back southwards towards Blanchland and my hotel. At Kielder village I went to the gift shop and the café and got two cups of tea. The ladies toilet looked as if somebody had peed all over the floor and shredded five toilet rolls. It was thoroughly depressing. I drank the tea going along in the car. Finally we got to Blanchland at ten to seven, over two hours since I'd finished the walk, far too long. My legs felt extremely tired. Luckily my four-poster bed at the Lord Crewe Arms was large. I had a nice big cupboard to put my clothes in and my luggage was already in the room which had a four-poster bed, two televisions, a bath, plenty of hot water and loads of windows. Obviously the honeymoon suite.

I perked up a little bit after a hot bath and I unpacked a few clothes but not many because when you are travelling the worst thing is the packing and unpacking. I was too tired to ring anybody or even to read the Sunday papers. I lay in the bed – big mistake – and fell asleep. I woke up starving. I went down to dinner and tried to read my schedule for the next two days. It sounded too difficult to even think about so I tried to just concentrate on whether to have guinea fowl or whatever. The director tried to talk to me about work but I was brain dead.

I went back to my room, got into bed at 10 pm and didn't wake until 8 am. I didn't dream of the Kielder Forest, but instead of walking over moors, my favourite countryside. No fir trees or conifers, or whatever spruces are called. I had asked Mike during the course of our walk if anyone ever stole the trees for Christmas trees. 'They're welcome to them,' he had said. 'We've got 40 million plus here and anyway these trees are grown for their wood, they are very, very scratchy and if you use one as a Christmas tree your children won't go anywhere near it.'

DAY 10

WICKHOPE NICK TO EDGES GREEN
The Kielder Mires

I set off at noon, again with Mike Sanderson the forest ranger, along the forestry road from Wickhope Nick where I'd left it the day before. Another hour's trudge along the same dreary track but my spirits were better than they had been before. Mike gave me a pot of honey from his garden and the weather was improving all the time, with large patches of blue sky. Soon I felt very hot and took off my fleece and tied it round my waist. There was a stiff southerly breeze keeping all the midges and insects at bay and before long I was slapping on the factor-20 suntan lotion. Mike and I were busy discussing solar energy – he had fitted solar panels on his house on the edge of the forest. It was hard to believe that there was enough sun up here to heat up anything, but apparently there is.

We came to a forest clearing where a large machine was stripping all the trees of their side branches, topping and tailing them and stacking them in neat logs. 'Would you like to look at it further?' asked Mike. 'No,' I said, 'after two days of this I'm sick of the sight of logs in any way, shape or form.' Continuing our debate about solar energy and wood-burning stoves, we made our way for a couple of miles along a variety of tracks – relatively dull scenery – but soon the hard chippings gave way to a softer sandier track which was much more pleasant on the feet. We made a small detour through some rough ground to look at a series of seven waterfalls, quite secret and tucked away, where the river fell down into a gorge. We then followed another long slow track through the Wark Forest heading south until we came to Muckle Samuel's Crags, where we climbed up to have lunch. You could see for miles right across to the Lake District in the west. I perched on a rocky outcrop high above the trees and ate my sandwiches, enjoying the sunshine. This day in the Kielder Forest was much more pleasant than the previous one. Even so, there wasn't much more information I could assimilate about trees but I think Mike sensed that and wisely switched to more interesting topics such as what variety of potato grew best up here and what to do about carrot rootfly.

After lunch we rejoined the sandy track and headed south. The forest opened up in front of us and you could see Butterburn. We were in the Kielder Mires, deep peat areas, where no trees grew, unchanged for hundreds of years, rich in plant life and preserved as nature reserves. Often drained at the time the forest was started, now ditches are dammed to raise the water level again. Facing south on the edge of the bog and tucked down just below the road was a little white-painted house where an elderly man was mowing the lawn. I was astonished as it was miles from anywhere. I couldn't imagine a more remote place. Why would a couple of retirement age want to live here? But then, why wouldn't they? I was attracted to the whole place myself after the claustrophobia of the forest. They didn't see us as we continued our trudge down the road.

Mike had said he didn't think we'd see anyone that day and we had just returned to the subject of solar energy when I nearly stepped on a large adder. It was a young one, grey, about 18 inches in length, and basking on the road. When it saw us it pretended to be dead. Another 100 yards along the same thing happened again, only this time the adder was even larger and slightly browner; probably the first one's partner, observed Mike.

Now we headed along a track that was used by the army when they exercised in the forest on their allotted 90 days of the year. We passed another remote house, with children's toys in the garden and tiny clothes fluttering on the washing line but no sign of people, and then we noticed two army signs. On one it said 'Limit of Army Activity' and on the other 'No Army Personnel to Loiter'.

Obviously the owner of the house had complained that troops had been lingering about when army manoeuvres had been completed.

The sandy track headed south and crossed the burn and then became a very narrow asphalt road going down Butterburn. Mike told me this route wasn't used by lorries to take logs out of the forest because it wound too much and so it was a pleasant walk for us. The River Irthing looked very brackish and brown. To the west lay a large area of forest used by the army. We turned left and headed east just before a farm called Lampert, following the bank of the river in a grassy flat-bottomed river valley known as a haugh. Mike explained a haugh was a grassy river bank. I said it was because it was half land and half moor but Mike didn't really get the joke. This was the best land that these farmers had and was divided into small fields, and the rest was bog. They'd already managed to get in their hay. You could tell it had been wet because there were wheel marks in the fields.

We followed the circuitous route of the river until it started to enter a gorge where we climbed up. This is where ospreys nest and even in this remote place their eggs have been plundered. I climbed above the gorge and headed due east across a flat boggy plain, with the path nowhere to be seen, towards the last piece of forest of the day, thank goodness. The going was reasonably OK across the marshland but the last few yards were indescribably boggy and wet. Here the forest rangers had started sticking up signs marking the footpaths, although I couldn't see what kind of nutcase except me would ever be using them.

But the bog did yield some treasures; amongst all the bilberries were cranberries. Mike found some and ate them and pronounced them delicious, although for my taste they are too bitter without a load of sugar and accompanied by a turkey. That's the only time I'm going to be eating a cranberry, other than in a sea breeze cocktail, which is vodka, cranberry and grapefruit .

We entered the forest at Smallburn Hill. Here Mike proudly pointed out how he had created the exact footpath line through the forest by marking it with tape so that workers could come in and cut all the lower branches of the trees off making a way through. This is known as brashing. I noticed bits of gold foil glinting underfoot. It's called 'chaff', and is dropped by the Tornadoes which screeched overhead every twenty minutes or so. As they enact war games, they drop this stuff to confuse the enemy radar. So much for the Armed Forces' commitment to the environment. It sat there, ugly litter, a reminder of how we can pollute even the most remote places.

It had become very hot and the wind was somewhat oppressive. My face was burning even though I was slapping on suntan lotion every 20 minutes, so I was pleased to enter the cool still air of the forest. I had to whip off my sunglasses and put my ordinary glasses on. The pine needles were soft underfoot, that is unless you had to go from furrow to furrow even though Mike's men had removed all the stumps. There's nothing more irritating than the rise and fall of a forestry plantation furrow exactly graded so it doesn't fit the human step.

We emerged north of Scotchcoultard Farm. Here the farmer was known to be rather difficult about footpaths. We crossed the field in the direction of his house. Sure enough there were footpath signs and one seemed to point right through the lawn at the side of the house. These were farm buildings that had been converted into holiday cottages. Not wishing to seem too intrusive I asked a lady who was sunbathing where the footpath went. 'I've got no idea,' she haughtily replied so I just walked right across the middle of the lawn. I was very tired by now and wasn't looking for a grumpy encounter. All I wanted was to find the footpath and have some soft short velvety pasture grass to walk on, but of course that wasn't how it turned out.

After the farm I scrambled down to a beck, found a plank over it, climbed over a gate and looked back and saw a brand new footbridge cunningly disguised by the farmer. I dragged myself up one last hill, found a stile at the top of it and then crossed another boggy pasture.

All across the hill were stiles at intervals. I'm not quite sure why as there was no fence on either side of them. It seemed like a pretty evil joke. We were still climbing up a shallow gradient but it prevented us from seeing High Edges Green which was our destination. At last Mike shouted, 'It's just over the dip,' and then it was only a few more hundred yards through the bog, the cow shit and the reeds to reach the road. It was 5.10 pm and the walk had taken just over five hours. I'd only stopped for ten minutes for a sandwich. Once again I was shattered. I drank two cups of tea and had a chocolate cake.

I drove south to my hotel, a pretty country house at Love Lady Shield. The owner was a Fulham fan like myself and couldn't believe his luck as we could drone on about Fulham football club's fortunes and bore everybody else. He even served me all my teas and coffees in his Fulham supporter's club mug. I had to wear a rather incongruous outfit for dinner – a chiffon dress with a cardigan – and a pair of sandals I'd got in Tobago made from car tyres because I couldn't bear my feet to be constrained by trainers. The only other people at dinner was a party of men who'd been shooting grouse on the moors. Just before I went to bed they asked me to join them for a drink. One seemed to have shot everything everywhere in the world and they were a pretty motley bunch but pleasant enough to drink with, united only by shooting. They were just thrilled I knew Lesley Ash and had something to do with *Men Behaving Badly*.

I slept like a log, waking intermittently with cramp in my legs. It was very annoying as I'd been drinking all the right health drinks and eating a healthy diet, and yet this cramp had come back. I had first had cramps when I was doing a long-distance walk the previous year. Probably it was just accumulated tiredness. Also, I didn't feel I was thinking straight. Even though I was only walking 12 to 15 miles a day, the terrain was so rough that it made my hips and knees really ache too. My lower back felt as if someone had just kicked it, and my legs were scratched from thistles.

All night long I woke up and saw trees. Rows and rows of pine trees, in serried ranks.

DAY 11

EDGES GREEN TO PLENMELLER COMMON
What did Roman soldiers eat?

I'd already crossed one border and now it was time to traverse the most impressive man-made one in Northern Europe. The Roman Emperor Hadrian visited Britain in AD122 and gave orders that a wall was to be built marking the most northern boundary of his empire. About 73 miles long, spanning the country from Wallsend in the east and Bowness in the west, it took six years to build and every Roman mile there was a castle guarded by eight men, with a sentry turret halfway between each castle. The Romans tried to push further north but eventually had to settle for the border at Hadrian's Wall until the early 400s when Roman power in Britain declined. Even today it has lost none of its power. It's a symbol of aggression and of the desire to keep unwanted people *out* and your people *in*.

I was going to walk along part of it with local man Sting, who'd visited it many times as a child and when he was a schoolteacher in Cramlingham, just north of Newcastle. Sting had always seemed to me a very private person, the model of control. I'd last seen him at a raucous lunch, and he'd stayed sober because he had to go off and shoot a scene in *Lock, Stock and Two Smoking Barrels*. But I can't imagine Sting gossiping and shouting anyway. I first met him when I was working in Australia in 1981. Now he seemed much more open and friendly, but still reserved.

I woke up to tremendous rain. There seemed to be a disagreement about where I should start walking. I'd reached Edges Green but Carl, the director, hadn't got a shot of me leaving the Kielder Forest. We drove a mile past Edges Green and then down a flooded and pitted track, a way I hadn't walked. I got out of the car before it turned over and both my boots filled with water, it was that deep. I walked about 100 yards towards the forest, and they filmed me walking out of it in a storm. It hadn't actually rained during the two days I'd walked from the border through the forest, but as the crew hadn't been there they were just pleased this was more of the gloomy weather I'd had at Fanna Hill.

By the time I got to Edges Green I was wet through and thoroughly miserable. It all seemed so unnecessary. From there I walked down a narrow road in the direction of the wall and Melkridge. I tried to cross a couple of fields but it was like wading through brown paddling pools. Hadrian's Wall never fails to impress me, and today it rose up out of the rain, looking utterly forbidding. There had been grand plans for me and Sting to walk together and then have a picnic on the wall. No one seemed to have considered what to do if it was wet. I didn't think a sandwich in a leaky barn (were there any anyway?) would be quite his style.

At Caw Gap, a junction of the road, the wall and the Pennine Way, I waited, and Sting soon arrived with his brother. He looked brown and very fit after a summer at his house in Tuscany with the family. He'd come back a few days before for the première of *Lock, Stock and Two Smoking Barrels*, and was thrilled at its success. I thought I wouldn't bring up the bad weather or the lunch dilemma, but would go with the flow.

Sting was wearing proper kit – hiking boots, a rucksack with a waterproof in it, a big baggy sweater and combat trousers (Jean-Paul Gaultier). I told him how pleased I was to see him, and suddenly the rain stopped (but only for ten minutes). He said it was 20 years since he'd been here, then as a teacher on a school trip when he worked in a primary school for two years. 'We'd come up here to get out of the classroom and throw a few facts and figures at them. The wall always intrigued me because I was born and bred in Wallsend, at the end of it. The house was built on a Roman camp and my school wall was on top of the Roman wall.'

Had he enjoyed school? 'Yes,' he said, 'particularly running' – he'd been the Northumberland 100 yards champion! No wonder he was having no difficulty scaling the rises and dips on our path heading east along the top of the wall. We returned to the subject of the wall; Sting thought that Hadrian had heard about the Chinese Great Wall and wanted to build something comparable in the Roman Empire. But what about the misery of being posted here? I'd read that the soldiers came from Europe – Belgium, Germany and Yugoslavia – but it was considered a very unattractive posting. In this weather I could see why! What did they live on? 'Stotty cake, man,' said Sting in a broad Geordie accent. He seemed very well informed – perhaps he secretly did supply teaching to keep his hand in – and I could feel a few facts coming on: 'The troops that were stationed here were from central Europe so they were probably quite used to the weather, at least the winters. But there's a great story about the ninth legion who were sent here to quell an uprising; they were sent off from the wall and they never came back and not hide nor hair of them was found. No bones.' 'Eaten by the locals obviously,' I said. 'Well, we still like Italian food,' he countered.

Now the weather had got dramatically worse and we climbed over a stile, avoiding a large bull. Didn't he think it extraordinary that this wall was put up and has lasted probably much longer than the people who built it ever imagined? 'No more extraordinary than polystyrene that's going to be around for millions of years,' said eco-conscious Sting.

I wondered if any of the Roman soldiers stayed behind in Newcastle and intermarried with the locals? Sting thought they definitely did and of course locals had manned the wall as well. 'The Romans were around for 400 years, it wasn't as if they were just an occupying army here for a few years. A very long time. I suppose we are Roman partly.'

The wind was making it harder and harder to have a conversation, we were so exposed. What had made Sting finally give up teaching and leave Newcastle for London in 1976? 'I was a teacher, a musician, and had a little band that played in pubs, a good life. I decided it was time to leave when I was 25 and see what happened. I really had no real masterplan but I gave up teaching. My headmistress said, "You can't give up your job, you'll lose your pension", which kind of clinched it for me, I suppose. It was the Jubilee – God Save the Queen. I moved into Bayswater right in the middle of London. I felt I was at the centre of it all.'

He'd been a bus conductor and a milkman with his dad before turning to teaching. We had even shared one job in common – we both worked in the Inland Revenue, my stint in my school holidays in the Holland Park tax office. Sting lasted about a year after leaving school. 'The most creative thing I ever did in the tax office was I found lots of files of old school friends of mine. So I changed all their files to their school nicknames. So they're probably still getting mail today.' Did he give them big tax bonuses? 'Of course,' he said, laughing.

Now, as the weather worsened, we tore ourselves away from the wall and its glorious view (albeit somewhat curtailed by the mist) and abandoned any hope of a picnic. The isolation and wildness of the place was really captivating and Sting was clearly enjoying it. Getting down wasn't going to be that easy, as there was a very steep slope to the south. There was a turret on the map at the 40A marker, but no one could find it or the track down.

Eventually we joined a track near Winshields farm, and emerged on to the Roman road. 'Let's go to the pub for lunch,' said Sting. It was a completely practical suggestion. So we ate ham salad and chips in the pub while it pelted down. The bar was almost empty and no one asked for his autograph until we were leaving. We had a quiet, undisturbed chat for half an hour, trying to dry out. Sting said he enjoyed walking a lot, and went off on his own, played music and tried to write lyrics – sometimes successfully and sometimes not – 'a bit like fishing'.

After lunch we walked down a series of quiet lanes towards the River South Tyne. Sting loved the green lushness of the valley, and waxed lyrical about growing his own organic food. Who'd have thought a kid from Wallsend would end up talking about bio-diversity and genetic engineering. 'Baked beans and Wonderloaf was what we lived on,' he said.

We were now in Melkridge, a small hamlet, and took a track leading down to the railway line and a large green barn-like structure. This was where the RJB mine had a coal conveyor belt going over the river, with a footbridge alongside. RJB had unlocked the gates so I could cross it. I said goodbye to Sting at the river bank. He said he'd had a great time walking in the rain, and I believed him. He left to catch the plane back to London and then to return to Italy in a couple of days.

I tried to sort out my route on the other side of the river as the map was out of date. Even the bridge over the river was incorrectly marked. In the end I decided to use the coal conveyor belt itself as my line. Encased in a steel pipe, I could hear it rumbling away. I climbed up a steep hill hugging the side of it, then I was out on the wide expanse of Plenmeller Common and the sun came out. It was a beautiful evening. The pipe undulated up the hill, through the heather, and I gingerly walked along a slippery wet tract made from railway sleepers alongside it. Behind me the Tyne valley and Hadrian's Wall ran west to east, looking fabulous in the late, low sun. I wished Sting could have seen it.

At the top of Beacon Hill my track joined the road and I stopped for the day.

DAY 12

PLENMELLER COMMON TO NINEBANKS
Helicopters

Last night I watched a ghastly documentary on the Beach Boys on television. It was the worst pap you could imagine. Totally unopinionated and anodyne, but at least it provided some decent background music as I wrote. Finally I got into bed at 1 am, read one page of the *Sunday Times* and fell asleep.

When I woke up near Alston at 7.30 am, I remembered today was helicopter day. Thank goodness it was fine. The hotel was in a state of high excitement as the helicopter was to land on the front lawn. The owner's little girl had her Teletubbies T-shirt on and couldn't wait to see the giant bird descending from the sky. The idea was to film a couple of shots of me walking from the helicopter.

We flew up to the Kielder Forest by a tortuous route, at one stage stopping on top of a moor because of low-flying Royal Air Force fighters flying into Spadeadam on all sorts of air manoeuvres. It was thoroughly irritating and also somewhat frightening. A lot of these Tornadoes were flying much lower than us and at nine miles a second you didn't see them until they seemed to be almost upon you. I was dropped in the Kielder Forest in the wrong place, so while the helicopter went off to Carlisle to refuel, I got a lift in Mike the ranger's van with him and his wife up to the straight mile and waited a whole hour for the helicopter to return. It was already taking three times as long as I'd been told. At least it was a sunny day and we discussed gardens, goats and so on.

I walked down the track between the trees with the helicopter

Left: With Alan Davies on the Royal Mile in Edinburgh, the starting point of my journey

Below: With Ronnie Corbett on the golf course at Prestonfield, Edinburgh

The Selkirk Plodders on top of the Three Brethren

Fording the stream at Synton Mill; the water was freezing!

Walking in the Borders with David Steel and his dog Lucy

Rounding up sheep at Synton Parkhead

Left: Dave, the forest ranger, and the frog we found coming out of the Wauchope Forest

Below: Helicopter day: Mike, the very fit ranger who walked with me, is on the right

Facing page:

Right: Walking along Hadrian's Wall with Sting

Below right: A proliferation of signs at Burnhope Reservoir

A hawthorn tree cut into a bird shape, Langthwaite

The octagonal building is an old powder house, where explosives were stored for the lead mines. Near Langthwaite

On the bridleway to Ramsgill from Jordan Moss, Upper Nidderdale

On the way from Ramsgill to Pateley Bridge

Right: Vic Reeves outside
his childhood home in
Adel, Leeds

Below: Outside an old
cinema in Leeds

filming me from the air. It was very frightening being followed from behind by a helicopter hovering over you at about 100 feet. At any minute I expected it to dump something horrible on my head or drop on top of me, but maybe I've seen too many war movies. The shot completed, I got back in the helicopter and flew up to the pipeline by the Plenmeller Common coal conveyor belt. I walked up the pipeline really slowly, retracing my steps of the previous day when I'd filmed it in the pouring rain after I'd walked with Sting. Luckily the shot would match as by the time the evening came and I'd reached this conveyor belt encased in a big tube, the sun had come out.

A workman came up on a quad bike. He'd been fixing the conveyor belt lower down and very kindly offered me a lift. So I was bumping along up to the top of the hill on the bike trying not to get mud all over my legs when the helicopter flew by again. I hoped they didn't get a shot of me getting a lift on the film. Anyway I had walked this bit already so it didn't really matter.

Then I continued along the road from Beacon Hill heading for the village of Ninebanks. Luckily the wind was from the north so it was in my back. I walked past the ugly open-cast mine that hadn't been really visible on my climb up from the north as it sits over the brow of the hill. I had been told mining was stopping and the site was going to be returned to its natural state within a couple of years. As I walked along the road, I could see the huge open sore where they'd dug out the coal, and the lorries loaded with it left the site via a weighbridge.

I walked south along an undulating road up Limestones Fell. I couldn't find the white gate mentioned in my instructions, which would supposedly cut off a corner, another black mark for the researcher. I had passed a metal gate but it wasn't white, it was galvanized steel. I trudged up the hill until I reached a T-junction and turned left. After a while I came to a small shooting hut on my right where I stopped, glad for a rest and sat on a wooden bench outside facing south and basking in the sun for 15 minutes eating my sandwiches. What a delicious idyll. I hadn't had many pleasant lunch stops in the last few days. There was no one to hurry me along.

I sat and contemplated the pink expanse of moorland in every direction, then picked up a track south-east over Dykerow Fell. The landowner was obviously completely paranoid about me walking across his moor as now every single gate had got two brand new yellow plastic signs stapled to it saying in large letters 'Please close this gate'. Perhaps someone should tell him that I was President of the Ramblers, that I do close gates and I'm not some kind of monster out to drop litter.

The moor was pretty easy going compared to the horrors of Kielder. The heather was short and it was easy to spot the boggy bits. After crossing a field I came to a plantation and Parkhead Farm where two men were mending a stone roof. 'Which way do I need to go?' I asked them. 'Whichever way you like, "hinny",' he said (or 'honey' – I couldn't make out his Geordie accent). They seemed incredibly nice, and said, 'Why don't you just go through the yard?' So that's what I did. Children's toys were stacked up and there was a crash helmet stuck on a wall. I followed a track east across a field and then another one down to a plantation. The green of the grass was the kind of green you only get when you've had about the wettest summer in living memory. For once the green of my jacket was easily outdone by nature. It was one of those days you get at the end of summer which start cold and shivery at 10.30 am. Now it was sweltering and butterflies were everywhere.

I took a track through the woodland where someone was burning rubbish, crossed over a footbridge and reached a T-junction. I cut across the field until I reached the A686. After 100 yards I passed a sweet pair of stone cottages, one with a front garden full of yellow daisies. The next little detached cottage was by the bridge and was called Toll Cottage. Just afterwards I took an absolutely straight B road over Blackett Bridge and the West Allen River, to Ninebanks heading south along the dale. At the bottom of the valley pastureland rose on either side of me.

It was a short day's walking as I'd spent the morning flying about in a helicopter. Although I hadn't enjoyed the flying monster hovering over my head, the view of the Kielder Forest and these moors south of Hadrian's Wall had been superb. I'd gained a perspective on my straight-line route I'd never have got from the ground. It did reinforce my prejudices, however. The forest seemed like a forbidding, unwelcoming uniform blanket. Man-made – disguising and enveloping the landscape, with its own micro-climate and secret paths – it often turned out to be impassable when you were on the ground. The moorland was the opposite. Pink, sensuous, with velvety, bright-green wet patches where springs rose, and full of tracks used only by hares, foxes and sheep, who scattered at our approach.

PART THREE

Ninebanks

to Ramsgill

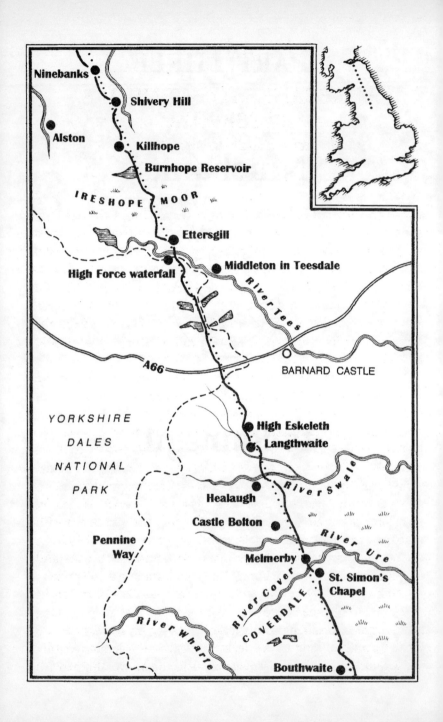

DAY 13

NINEBANKS TO BURNHOPE RESERVOIR
Giant leeks, Buddhists and Weirdodale

I looked out of the window and it was raining. It was that irritating fine rain, not really cold but with a brisk wind nevertheless and a threatening sky. The barometer in the hotel hallway read changeable, not a good sign. I started my walk at Ninebanks, a tiny village almost unchanged over the last 150 years. At the end of the village is a Peel tower built to keep a lookout for the border bandits who used to come over from the north side of Hadrian's Wall and rape and pillage. Villagers would hide in it with their livestock.

I met Geordie Brown who lived next door but one to the tower, a jovial man who proudly showed me his collection of prize-winning leeks. These enormous if not gross specimens were housed in a special plastic tunnel at the bottom of his garden. Next to his greenhouse was a washing-up bowl full of rejected specimens, all of which were thicker than my arm and about ten times larger than any leek I'd ever grown. They seemed to fail on all sorts of mysterious counts; they were either too short, too fat or too long, but all were enormous. Geordie had me in fits with his stories of leek growing. Apparently there are all different classes, including six-inch ones, seven- to nine-inch ones and intermediate ones. Each winning leek could snap up a £50 prize.

Next to the leeks was his vegetable patch, a sorry sight compared to the one I used to have. It was clear that all his waking hours went into talking to his leeks, combing his leeks, breeding his leeks and perking up his leeks. Cabbages and lettuces hardly got a look in. I was to discover that if Geordie worshipped his leeks, he wasn't the only religious fanatic in West Allendale. It turned out to be a most unexpected hotbed of belief.

I walked south down the narrow road out of Ninebanks following the bank of the river, climbing all the time. At Limestone Brae was a Wesleyan chapel (I'd just passed a house with the name of Ebenezer, a chapel name if ever I'd heard one) which had the Sunday school section and was obviously still used. Just next to it I saw a sign for the Throssel Nest Retreat. Intrigued, I walked up the driveway and discovered a new Buddhist monastery housed inside a traditional stone building which looked just like a farmhouse on the outside. Men and women with shaved heads in brown robes and black robes were going about their business. The Buddhist abbey was owned by the order of Buddhist Contemplatives who follow the Serene Reflection and Meditation Tradition, a branch of Japanese Zen Buddhism. Working in the kitchen garden I met Vice Abbot Saido Kennaway. He was extremely friendly and explained that he once worked for the Water Board in South Wales, dealing with sewage. Saido used to travel a lot and had started coming here in his early 20s. At the age of 26 he finally joined as a postulant (trainee monk) and had now been here for 20 years. He didn't look 46 to me with his unlined face, twinkling eyes and ready smile, but I suppose that a life of reflection, meditation and a lot of thinking does stop the wrinkles. Judging by the monks, the abbey seemed a stress-free zone. Saido showed me round the elaborate garden that they had made. Apparently two of the monks had been landscape gardeners in an earlier existence. The house itself had been extended and was being enlarged further. About 37 monks lived there as well as devotees who were in America and those who were currently travelling. It was a retreat for people who wanted to come and stay there and that was mostly how the monastery got its income. I went inside, taking off my walking boots, and passed through the dining room where long tables had rice bowls in serried ranks with white napkins over them ready for lunch.

Upstairs Saido proudly showed me the temple, a large room with a shrine at one end, a beige carpet and a prayer mat in the centre. What a calm wonderful spot after the battering I'd received from the wind and the rain over the past two weeks. I could have stayed there all day. Saido explained that they had made most of the furniture themselves. We went to the lecture room and had a cup of tea and a chocolate biscuit. I could have sat and talked to him for hours about Buddhism and all its different varieties but after half an hour I felt the call of the moors and wanted to get ahead and do a bit of walking on my own. Maybe even do some thinking before I felt a conversion coming on! I remembered that driving through Hexham I'd seen the monks shopping, looking somewhat incongruous. I wonder what the local hill farmers make of them?

I walked south towards Carr Shield, following the quiet little road I was already on, climbing all the time, until it joined up with a higher road at Hartleycleugh. Here a footpath was shown on the map but someone had cunningly removed any sign of it. I could see someone that looked like the farmer working in a field opposite so rather than risk his wrath I walked about 100 yards down the road and then legged it up through a field of cattle and climbed over a couple of gates until I got on what I assumed was the bridleway. I spotted a man on all fours on the edge of a pond photographing some bright-yellow spotted flowers. I carried on south-east and started to climb on to Carr Shield Moor high above Temperance Farm. The bridleway seemed pretty indistinct. I pressed forward on a south-easterly route along my line aiming for the aptly named Shivery Hill. As I toiled on up the path enjoying this moment by myself, a farmer on a bike came up on a crossing track with his dog. He had a black knitted hat on and was in his early 30s. I said hello and he started to scowl but then he recognized me and perked up, switched the engine off and was all set for a big chat about the terrible price of lamb, there was no future in farming, etc. The thing about most farmers is they are very lonely and if you bother to talk to them they will chat happily for ages. All they want is a sympathetic ear to the plight of the British sheep farmer. I must have heard the same thing 25 times from different farmers on this walk. This guy said lambs were fetching half the price they were last year and he might as well retire. 'Why don't you turn your farmhouse into a bed and breakfast?' I asked. 'Not a bad idea,' he said before wishing me goodbye and speeding off. Before he left I asked him where the footpath went. 'I don't know,' he said 'but it doesn't really matter where you walk,' so I continued up the hill.

I got almost to the top and saw the crew go past in the Land Rover. When I reached the road they started to film me walking up the road. We then had a screaming match about why hadn't I walked up the footpath. As the last 300 yards of the walk had no track at all and was a thick bog, I couldn't see that it was that important how I reached the top of bloody Shivery Hill, and if they had had any wit they would have dropped down a little way and seen me climbing up it. It was now 2 pm and I was in a thoroughly bad mood. After all that Buddhist contemplation, those good vibes given off by Saido the ex-sewage-plant worker had all disappeared. I sat in the Land Rover and sulked, eating a smoked salmon sandwich at the speed of light. Now I was at the top of Allendale, about to cross into Weardale. But first I had to climb Kilhope Law, a small hike of just over 100 metres to 673 metres. There was no footpath but the top was clear to see as a rather ugly pole stuck up from it. The crew had already set off up there so having eaten my smoked salmon sandwich, chocolate bar and a cup of disgusting lukewarm tea (when will the people supplying my refreshments realize that thermos flask they bought doesn't work?) I set off to slog up the hill.

Providing I kept up a reasonably slow pace I didn't really need to stop. It was boggy but not a bog as I have come to know them. On my scale of bogginess this was about a four out of ten. It didn't reach over the top of my boots and I didn't have to climb up and down too many peat hags. The wind was really whipping up. The reason I was pressing on was that the clouds were gathering and I really didn't want to be caught in a downpour. At the top Carl the director had suggested I might like to say a few words about my journey so far. I'd told him firmly at the bottom that I thought that was completely cheesy and I'd do what I felt was appropriate.

At the top there was a trig point, an ugly wooden mast that seemed to serve no purpose and another cairn, so I visited all three. They were surrounded by the usual over-walked boggy area. I'd been told there was no path down the other side but all I had to do was follow the left-hand edge of two forestry plantations. That was a laugh for a start because they no longer existed, they had been cut down about 10 years ago but luckily their horrid little scarred outlines were still clearly visible. I half ran down the hill to get warm again as I had got quite cold sitting on the top for even a minute. In my haste to get down the hill I tripped and fell quite heavily in the bog. Now my back was really hurting and that was God's punishment for being vile to Carl. I could see for miles ahead down Weardale, tiny white houses clinging to the lower slopes and the ruins of countless mines ahead.

At the edge of the forest I joined the Weardale Way, through a gate and down a well-made stone track down through the forest in a straight line. A huge variety of fungi poked through the trees. It was a pleasant ten minutes out of the wind and I joined the road at the bottom, following it down to the Kilhope Lead Mining Centre, a little bit of tourist Disneyworld here in Weardale. This was a restored mine complete with watermill, tracks, the whole lot. I popped inside for a cup of tea and the purchase of a few postcards. There was the most wonderful one of three miners in a reconstructed cottage, lying on one sad bed of sacking all looking completely sick and tired. I bought a whole stack of them to send to friends and tell them that this was where the crew was staying. I didn't think the crew would find that as funny as I did. Most miners died in their early 40s from lung disease and had a shorter life expectancy than slum dwellers. During the week they stayed in dwelling houses called mine shops, as their homes were often over ten miles away.

Getting a weak cup of tea out of the lady in the centre's café proved a major trauma. She didn't seem to understand the meaning of the word weak. First she served me with what looked like a mug of oxtail soup and then when I asked her to make it weaker she simply poured out half the tea, put the teabag back in and poured more water on it so tea number two was exactly the same colour as tea number one. Finally I simply went into the kitchen, asked her if she didn't mind, and poured half the tea down the sink and filled it up with cold water. Then it tasted halfway decent. She was utterly confused. I sat in the café and read about lead mining. Apparently in the early 19th century the area was known as the 'Klondyke of the Pennines'. I was able to see the evidence of mining since Roman times everywhere I walked in Weardale. When the industry declined in the 1850s because of cheap Spanish imports, many miners walked from here to Liverpool and took assisted passages to the US, where they set up fresh mining communities.

I left the lead mining centre and walked past a man in a red jersey who seemed to be shovelling stones or something across a stream. I couldn't make out if he was part of the building programme or a piece of living history. I didn't want to stop and ask in case he was the owner hoping to be interviewed. The watermill was chugging merrily away and high above us on the moor on Cowhorse Hill I could hear the sound of the grouse being culled.

I now walked along the Weardale Way high above Kilhope Burn. The first section of it followed the A689, and quite a surprisingly large number of heavy lorries (some bearing the dreaded logs) passed me in the mile and a half that I followed it. Then, thankfully, I took a path off to my right heading south crossing Kilhope Burn at a little bridge and then crossing a side burn to rise up to a farmhouse at Blakeley Field. Now I was on the south side of the burn travelling down Weardale. High above me the grouse shooting continued. The landscape looked like it had suffered at the hands of industry, it has to be said, and I found it very depressing. There were disused shafts and spoils and abandoned quarries in every direction. The miners' cottages weren't architecturally of much merit but all had been lovingly restored by weekenders or people seeking a home in the country in this isolated part of Weardale. Perhaps it was just the grey day but I didn't find it particularly inspiring. My path went along the back of several old farms which were being restored.

At last, having crossed a couple of fields, I rose up on to Moss Moor and headed south-east along the edge of it. It was blissful walking on a track through short heather after such boggy fields. At this point I should have followed my instincts and my line and headed south across the moor to Burnhope Reservoir, but I made a big mistake and dropped down on a non-existent series of footpaths through fields that were absolutely waterlogged. I climbed over barbed wire and gates tied firmly by string. There was a vast and confusing network of footpaths marked on the map, none of which seemed to be used. After about 15 minutes' frustration I just headed south and eventually joined the tiny road heading for the reservoir and then irritatingly it climbed back up again, almost as high as I had come down.

The road eventually reached the edge of Burnhope Reservoir. Here was the reservoir keeper's house restored to an unbelievable level of ugliness, its stone cleaned to a hideous yellow colour, bay windows on every side. I wasn't quite sure if it was a fishing lodge or someone's private house but whatever it was, it was an eyesore. I love reservoir architecture and never miss a chance to see a good Victorian or Edwardian edifice. As reservoirs go, Burnhope was low down in the third division, with not enough castellation or turrets for me, but a pleasant spot nonetheless. The sun had broken through in the last hour for maybe five or ten minutes and shafts of light had briefly lightened up the forestry landscape around it. Now, alas, it was back to doom and gloom.

I crossed the reservoir via a tiny road. There were no cars in sight here, not even a fisherman. I reached the other side and decided to call it a day as my legs were really aching. Ahead of me rose up Harthope Head, which I would have to tackle tomorrow, and beyond that Langdon Fell and Teesdale. On the drive back to the hotel, I paused briefly to visit Alston. This extraordinary village is in a time warp, full of tea shops, cobbled streets, cake shops and loads of wholefood shops, a sure sign of a hippy intake if ever I saw one. But everything was closed. Even the fish and chip shop had a posh hand-painted 'closed' sign. Only one shop was open and that was the Late Shop. Inside it was a supermarket with a surprisingly wide range of stuff. I bought Radox bath salts, a hairbrush, a clothes brush to try and brush all the thistles and thorns out of my socks because they were getting washed and returned to me complete with bits of thistle still in them, and a roll of sticky tape for getting fluff off my clothes. My Polartec jacket had moulted over everything leaving orange and green fluff everywhere.

Back at the hotel a wedding was in progress. A lady in a macramé lace dress with what looked like a cake doily and flowers on her head, and who looked about my age, greeted me in the hall. 'Hello,' she said, 'I recognize you, you're famous.' 'It's your big day,' I said and ordered a large gin and tonic and took off to my room to escape the wedding. Sounds of merriment drifted up the stairs. I was shattered. I lay on the floor and put my feet up on a chair. Nothing would ease my aching back. Eventually I ordered dinner in my room, worked on the script and timings, read endless maps, wrote letters, read faxes, watched an hour of television to stop me thinking about walking and (incredibly) could only drink one glass of red wine. What had happened to me? It's unknown – a half bottle of wine still half finished at 11 pm. The shooters returned from wherever they had been killing grouse and I lay cocooned in my room unable to even get off the bed, dreading the next day's walk. This was all wrong. I should have been thinking of the Buddhist monk and treating my journey as a period of quiet contemplative reflection and not an excuse to scream abuse at the director. Today's low moment came when we were coming down the hill to the lead mining centre. At one stage he ran to keep up with me but the path was stony and very slippery. 'Catch me, or I'm going to fall,' he said. 'And break your neck hopefully,' I replied rather cruelly. Luckily he laughed, otherwise I think he might have hit me.

BURNHOPE RESERVOIR TO HIGH FORCE
A lot of weather

It was raining the next day. I undid the gate at the end of Burnhope Reservoir and walked up a steep hill and on to the moor, turning right at a T-junction. There wasn't a car in sight nor another person which wasn't surprising as the sky was an angry grey. I had already experienced a heavy shower before I'd even got out of the car and they were to occur at approximately 20-minute intervals throughout the day.

I followed the Grasshill Causeway up on to Ireshope Moor, rising gradually in a south-westerly direction. At the end of a wall I turned left, and the moor was completely soaked with no track that I could see. It was relatively short grass so it wasn't that hard to navigate. A few sheep stared at me as if I was mad. After about half a mile the wall fell steeply down to a burn. Because of the rain of the last few days it was a surging torrent with an attractive waterfall facing me. As I had dropped down to the burn I had seen the crew filming me from the opposite hill but they couldn't know I was trapped by the raging river. If they had moved 50 yards they would have seen that I couldn't find a way of crossing it. It snaked down the valley, fed by half a dozen or so tributaries. After looking at it and thinking about it for about 20 minutes in the pouring rain, I used my walking stick (the present from Kevin in Selkirk) as a prop and managed gingerly to cross it. The bank opposite at this point was very steep and I toiled so slowly up that hill with my legs like lead weights and my back really aching. This was the fourth consecutive day of walking over rough moorland and now I was really paying for it. I'd only had one day off from walking in two weeks. I inched up the hill cursing slippery grass. The crew asked me if I wanted to stop for a coffee but I couldn't face it. I arranged to meet them at the very top at Harthope Head, and off they went in the Land Rover. Away to the north Weardale was green and pleasant even in this dreadful rainy weather. The lower part of the valley was a patchwork of small fields and white-painted cottages but where I was it was bleak and cheerless with not even a barn or a sheep pen for shelter. I kept on the line of the wall when it ended and headed south-west over Noon Hill heading for the quarry at Harthope Head. This was a really gruesome peat bog, the worst I had encountered since Hadrian's Wall and I was soon slithering and sliding up and down five-foot precipices of black mire. At one stage I climbed all the way up to the brink of a cliff of peat bog only to slide all the way back down again with my fingernails full of this muck. Thank goodness I had my stick. The rain was the least of my problems.

Harthope Head was a spoil tip from a quarry and I inched my way round, frightened of slipping on the wet rock. I sat in the Land Rover by the road trying to dry off, drinking a coffee and eating a bar of chocolate. I dissuaded the crew from walking with me over the next section because the weather was getting even worse, and I couldn't see the point of any more shots of this rather dreary flat-top moorland. After a short blissful spell along the road I turned left on a track through a disused quarry heading south-east. I got to Harthope Bank, a quarry which I thought was disused. I went behind a pile of rocks and had a pee and then to my horror heard the sounds of a digger really close by. I pulled my trousers up, stepped back on to the road and was almost run down by a man in an earth-moving machine. There were diggers and trailers and men at work. I said hello to the workmen and decided not to have my lunch there as I could see really dark grey storm clouds whizzing in from the south. The wind was so fast that the weather seemed to be moving towards me at 20 miles an hour. At the end of the quarry there was no trail so I headed out on to the boggy moorland taking a compass reading and aiming for Church Bowers, a disused quarry. The bog was so bad that I was forced to walk slightly uphill and I ended up at Short Bowers, probably about quarter of a mile to the north of where I wanted to be. Then I had to painstakingly pick my way down through peat hags to the cairn that meant the start of the track down to Ettersgill and Teesdale. Someone had obligingly piled the flat stones up in two towers almost like a broken archway. There was a grassy track which dipped down steeply over the moor heading due south. Reedy and boggy at first, after a mile or so it gave way to grassland although it was still extremely wet.

Now the weather was really dramatic. I was facing due south and looking at the top of Teesdale with rocky outcrops rising through the rain clouds. It was a spectacular scene, worthy of Turner. I didn't even mind the fact that my feet were soaking wet, my shoes full of water and my trousers wet through to the skin. I drank in the magic of this changing weather. It was totally exhilarating. The sun came out twice for brief moments. The wind was whipping around and the clouds scudding through grey upon grey, different shades from almost white to almost black. I eventually reached a gate in a wall, went through it, crossed a field of cattle and then turned left along another track, crossing a whole series of fields until my track became a little asphalt road which led to a farm. Then it became a bigger road and I emerged by a telephone box on the road down to Ettersgill. This pleasant road wound past white-painted farms until it reached the B6277. Here I stopped for a minute to eat my lunch. It was 3.30 pm, I hadn't been anywhere with shelter up on the high moor and I hadn't felt really hungry. I guess I'd just forgotten about everything in the excitement of the weather, the solitude and the screaming wind. I hadn't seen anyone for miles.

There was no point in changing my wet trousers so I dried my hair a bit, turned right along the main road and then took a left well-maintained track down to High Force. This crossed over a brand new wooden footbridge, and then I turned right and followed the river upstream, which was thrashing past, churning up mustard-coloured foam. The peaty dark-brown water looked dangerous and exciting. After I had gone a mile upstream I saw High Force. The water was thundering over the falls. I couldn't imagine the possibility of crossing the river here. The noise was tremendous, it was deafening, although not as deafening as the two Tornadoes that had skimmed over me on the moor.

After paying my respects to the waterfall I turned back, retraced my steps and decided to call it a day at the main road. I'd asked at the High Force Hotel if I could have a room to change in but they had refused so I got in the car wet through and drove to Romaldkirk and the Rose and Crown Inn, passing through Middleton in Teesdale, a town that looked like a set from *All Creatures Great and Small*. My hotel was a charming pub, and at 7 pm my shiatsu masseur arrived (I'd got his number from the hotel), a bloke with a London accent who had lived in Alston for 20 years. He was extremely good and soon I was in a soporific, totally relaxed state. He stuck a magnetic pad under my back and had me lying on a spaceman-type thin mattress full of protons or neutrons or something designed to relax me. I went downstairs and had a delicious dinner with John Bush, the director of the episodes south of Leeds. As he is well known for his organizational skills there was masses of paperwork, lists, charts and everything else. I knew I was going to have a good night's sleep.

DAY 15

HIGH FORCE TO PASTURE END
The Pennine Way

I had slept really badly. I was in a single bed and under the sheet was a scratchy blanket. For about an hour I thought I was suffering with some weird allergy as my whole body was prickly, then I realized it was the blanket so I tore it out and threw it on the floor. I spent the whole night trying to catch the duvet from slipping off one side and then the other. At 3 am I got up convinced that the boots that I'd left in the boiler room were melting as I'd stuck them on the hot water pipe. Although I'd been given a very pretty suite with twin beds, a large bedroom, a sitting room and bathroom, I would rather have had one big bed in a small room.

I looked out of the window and it was raining. The sky was uniformly grey, the same colour as the buildings really, and nothing was happening in Romaldkirk. I had to get myself moving and try and loosen up enough to walk. I sat at breakfast reading maps for next week's walk through the Yorkshire Dales, trying to reconcile filming racehorses on the gallops at Middleham at 8.00 am with dominoes in a pub and meeting coast-to-coast walkers at Healaugh. Eventually I dragged myself into the Land Rover and was dropped by the B6277 in Teesdale on the north side of High Force. The sky looked grey and threatening, with banks of storm clouds being blown towards me by a strong wind. Sure enough it started to pelt down before I'd even crossed the River Tees, which had risen about three feet overnight and was thundering under the footbridge, a brown and churning torrent. I followed a path higher than the Pennine Way, climbing up above the river and heading east along farm tracks.

The Holwick Scars, impressive outcrops of sheer granite, rose up in front of me. Climbing up a small road towards them, I turned past a farm and headed back west and then spotted a gate in a wall high above the path. I went down, clambered gingerly over the river and carefully made my way over the crags between two slabs of rock. Once out of the exhilarating environment of the Scars, I crossed a quiet green area of pastureland, heading due south through a series of white-painted stiles. It was easy going, but then I encountered the first of many burns swollen to a raging torrent by the downpours of the last few days. My bridleway became increasingly waterlogged as I climbed up the fell ahead. After an hour my feet were wet through. I got over one stream by sliding along a thin log and clinging to some rusty old wire, praying my weight wouldn't mean I'd be deposited in the water! I skirted Crooks O'Green fell top and turned south-east, nearly treading on a couple of light-brown frogs – I was obviously going nuts with all this walking as I started talking to them as they hopped off into some reeds. This flat, bleak moorland is normally my favourite walking, but I kept having to wipe my glasses as I couldn't see anything.

The top of the fell had provided some shelter from the wind but now the path emerged on to a flat grouse moor, with heather underfoot. As fast as one shower passed over a fresh set of dark grey clouds arrived to tip their contents over me. By a convergence of shooting tracks I discovered I was heading off on the wrong path, and as I retraced my steps, I could see a face peering out at me from the shooting hut below. To my amazement, two young men were sheltering from the storm and eating cheese and pickle sandwiches. We had a good laugh about how crazy you'd have to be to walk in weather like this – they were doing a circuit from Middleton in Teesdale and had come out from Middlesbrough for a day's walking. Reluctantly I said goodbye to them and continued on my way.

I followed the path over the top of a heathery moor, then it dropped down Collin Hill and I lost it for a while. It seemed obscured by streams and tractor tracks. Eventually I came to a farm, turned right and followed a small track on to the road. For the last few hundred yards I had joined the Pennine Way for the first time in this walk and when I got to the B6276, which was on the northern side of Lunedale, I was sitting having a cup of coffee when I noticed two Pennine Way walkers coming up from the south. I couldn't resist calling out to them as they were crossing the road with alpine sticks and one of them had a broad-rimmed bush hat on, which as it was pouring with rain looked completely ridiculous. When I waved to him it then appeared he had stereo headphones on and was listening to music. He unplugged the earpieces, came over and said hello. When I asked why he had the sticks, he claimed that they were invaluable on slithery ground. 'But you're crossing a road and you're going up a very gentle gradient here,' I said, 'and it's the Pennine Way.' 'Wait until you cross the bit we've come across,' was all he said. We had a good laugh about walking in such appalling weather and then I downed the rest of my cup of coffee, taking advantage of a brief lull in the downpours, and continued southerly along the Pennine Way through some fields of cows and then down to Grassholme Farm where I crossed over Grassholme Reservoir.

There were two reservoirs here, Selset and Grassholme, and there was nobody about at all. It was even too wet for anglers. Then I decided to leave the Pennine Way for a while because it started to pour, and to avoid the bog I followed a tiny B road that snaked around the plantation. This was such an isolated spot, it was an enjoyable walk and the road was obviously never used. I crossed a couple of cattle grids and then at a T-junction turned right along yet another B road.

This part of Baldersdale seemed deserted. Here at the head of the dale, the farms are very spaced out and there are hardly any cars. I knew it was the end of the holiday season but I wondered if anybody ever came here in good weather. After walking west for about a mile I found the Pennine Way again, picked it up, dropping down a track, through some fields to another couple of reservoirs. This time I passed a nature reserve and it turned out to be High Birk Hatt Farm where the famous Hannah Hawkswell had lived and farmed until she retired in her 80s. Hannah had been the subject of a TV documentary that highlighted the isolated and lonely life she led while persevering with hill farming. The fields around the farm had been purchased and turned into a nature reserve and I made my way through them down to the edge of Blackton Reservoir, crossing over the bridge by the still flats of reeds and grasses, with ducks and frogs. Not a human being in sight. The sky was the blackest it had been all day.

High above me to the west was the wall of Baldershead Reservoir rising up like a high grassy slope. My weary legs wouldn't take me much further. I mused that hill farming seemed to have got even less profitable and unrewarding since Hannah had retired. In fact we are at the end of an era for this kind of farming. The leisure activities like water skiing on Baldershead Reservoir seems to be the way this countryside is heading. Leisure, not food, is its future.

I skirted round some more fields and wearily climbed up the side of Baldersdale, heading south to the car park by the youth hostel. I had been walking since 10.30 am. Now it was 3.30 pm and I was completely mentally shattered. I'd been wet through for four hours and there was simply no point in changing my socks. But I still wanted to complete the remaining four miles to Pasture End. This lay over high, bleak, flat moor and would bring me down on to the A66. I looked at the sky and saw it was going to pelt down with rain and it would mean getting wet one more time.

There's not much to report. The track, being the Pennine Way, was wide, well-walked and extremely muddy. I climbed up slowly over Brown Rigg Moss with the odd wooden bridge thankfully taking me over burns and boggy bits. The land was sodden. Four people passed me, walking in the opposite direction, and we stoically said hello and grimaced at each other. From a boundary fence the path wound down to Deepdale Beck, then climbed up to an outcrop of rock, Ravock Castle, from which I had fine, if stormy views over this huge landscape, before descending to the end of a sheep enclosure and the A66, with lorries thundering past.

I called it a day and we drove back to my friend's house in Wolsingham where I was very relieved to have a hot bath, about seven cups of tea and look forward to a good dinner. The next day I got up early and got a taxi to Durham Station and the train to Edinburgh, as I was to judge an architectural competition for a firm of developers in the city. The competition was for an inner-city site in the old town just off the Golden Mile called Tron Square.

Putting my time to good use, I had decided to arrive in time for lunch so that I could have a meal and write about it for my restaurant review column in *Vogue*. I'd tried a couple of new restaurants in Edinburgh already during the Festival and hadn't found them that good. Now I was going to one near the university called the Marque with my friend Antlers who runs a catering company. His real name is Anders and we'd met on a shooting weekend in Scotland a couple of years ago. We were joined by Piers Gough who was there to judge the competition with me and is also a fine cook. After a really good lunch it seemed a real shame to have to go and look at architectural drawings, but once we arrived at the university and got involved in it I was thoroughly engrossed. The competition ended in what can only be described as a heated argument as Piers and I (the English) voted for one scheme and the three other jurors (Scottish) voted for another. We argued and argued, and even with our joint giant egos Piers and I couldn't persuade the others, so we had to give in. When the winner was announced it turned out to be someone Piers knew and thought was very good even though this particular scheme had been pretty uninspiring, so everybody was happy in the end. There were drinks, champagne was served and Piers made a small speech, and I presented the winner with the letter confirming that he had the job and an invitation to dinner. I left the reception in full flow and went back to the hotel. My mobile phone had got so wet the day before that a new one had been delivered to the hotel but it wouldn't work with my SIM card and the phone company representative had gone back to his home in Fife so now I had one mobile phone full of water, useless, and one new phone with no SIM card, so that was no use either, and I was getting up at 5.30 am to go to Llandudno and sort out the belongings of my mother, who had recently died. It was pretty frustrating.

My room had a six-foot square bath which included a jacuzzi and I started to run it. It took about an hour to fill so I was able to make lots of phone calls. By the time it filled up and I'd laid in it, it was time to go out. I collected Piers. I was very pleased with my outfit, a silver Issey Miyake pleated dress that caused quite a stir as we arrived at the restaurant. We were in a private room with a load of already drunk architects, developers and City councillors. I refused to sit next to anyone dull. I've realized that I have to be ruthless in these situations otherwise you're put somewhere simply to entertain some boring old fart they want to impress. So I sat opposite the winner and next to the two partners of the company. The food was absolutely revolting: overcooked pigeon and a dreary salmon. Then everybody wanted to go and party some more so we went in the bar next door, which seemed to be full of graphic designers and architects, and then everybody came back to my hotel, which was a jolly good idea because after one drink I could dump them and finally escape to bed at 1.15 am. At 5.45 am I got the dreaded alarm call but luckily I'd taken the precaution of packing the night before. At 6 am I was in a taxi to the airport to catch the 7.15 plane. On it a breakfast was served which probably had been cooked about five weeks earlier. It was a British Airways special – an omelette baked on to the plastic tray, a weird sausage and a strange piece of fatty bacon. At the airport my hire car was nowhere to be seen and my luggage took half an hour to come from the plane so it was an hour before I left.

I drove to Llandudno and went straight to my mother's flat and spent the rest of the morning sorting through her clothes with my sister. In the afternoon we scattered her ashes on a hill above Llanfairfechan and in the streams and all around the village and on the seafront. It was thoroughly enjoyable and uplifting and not at all depressing. We went for tea with my Aunty Phyllis, who'd made scones specially.

I went back to my hotel at Bodysgallen Hall. I couldn't be bothered to do very much. I lay on the bed and had a large gin and tonic. I felt shattered and should have gone straight to sleep but at 8.15 pm I picked my sister and her husband up and we went out for dinner at Llandudno's answer to Fawlty Towers, where the woman is on personality overdrive and witters continuously while you eat. We had a very, very good dinner in spite of her best efforts to talk us to terminal boredom throughout it.

DAY 16

PASTURE END TO HEALAUGH
A gamekeeper and a game of dominoes

It was another grey and windy day, my last day in County Durham, with the tough unrelenting landscape of the north Pennines. It is a place abandoned by miners, isolated and sparsely habited. Hill farms scratch a living and it is too bleak for most tourists except the nutty long-distance walkers.

I took the tunnel thoughtfully provided under the A66, where huge lorries thundered overhead taking produce for Asda and Sainsbury's from the east coast to the west. For a short while I would be following the Pennine Way and I was curious to see if the foul weather of the past weeks had deterred any walking fanatics anxious to gain this prize. I'm very ambivalent about long-distance paths as they are often over-walked and crowded, drawing people from equally attractive unnamed routes. They don't encourage walkers to be adventurous and devise routes of their own. Too many long-distance walks have become symbols of macho achievement. I prefer to walk for personal enjoyment in out of the way places.

But my intention to walk from Edinburgh to London in a straight line had thrown up some bizarre coincidences. Here it virtually followed the Pennine Way (everything I was trying to avoid) and later it would come within five miles of my cottage in Yorkshire.

Now I dropped down from the road to where an outcrop of limestone formed a natural bridge over the River Greta. Being the Pennine Way, my route was a wide and well-used track. As I climbed up the bank opposite, the wall was being repaired by three men, working in check shirts even though it was cold blustery weather. They said their work – building about 8 yards a day – was funded by grants, another indication that the only future for this area will be tourism and leisure. I asked them how many people took this route. 'A lot,' one man said, 'but you're the first famous person we've seen on it.' I wished them well and continued over Wytham Moor, dropping down to Sleightholme Beck, where I encountered a man walking in shorts, for God's sake, with a garish short-sleeved T-shirt and a map in a plastic holder flapping around his neck in the biting wind. He was carrying a heavy backpack. A Pennine Way walker for sure. (And he turned out to be a civil servant!) I asked him the only question there is – why? 'Because it's the big one, isn't it? You've got to do it,' was his incredulous reply. 'I thought if I don't do it now, I never will, even if it's turned out to be one miserable trot through a long bog.' The last part echoed my sentiments entirely, although we agreed that the stretch around Malham was sensational. But that's Yorkshire, I said – and this is County Durham. But I'm biased, having lived in Yorkshire for years.

A little further up the track I met Paul Wilby, the sporting head gamekeeper for the 11,000-acre estate on Sleightholme Moor. From Essex originally, he'd spent all his 40-odd years working in the open moorland. We followed my line through the deep heather, over a hillock and then across a vast plain. Paul was immaculate, with smartly cropped silver-grey hair, an Essex accent, plus-fours and a tweedy sporting jacket with big pockets, a long way removed from my traditional idea of a gamekeeper but, as he pointed out, shooting is no longer in the hands of the aristocracy. Anyone with money can join a syndicate and buy some days' sport. The cold wet weather during the breeding season had meant that fewer chicks had survived and less grouse would be shot this year. Paul was a passionate defender of the sport, claiming the selective burning of the heather caused new growth to regenerate the moors. The income from shooting kept the land well maintained and in its natural state. I could see plainly that this bleak place was fit for nothing else. It couldn't be farmed and walking across it was extremely heavy going. Paul was against the proposed 'Right to Roam', telling me that he thought people needed to follow paths, and that access should be controlled in wild scenery so you knew where to look for people if they got lost. And he thought dogs should be kept under control. He allowed that many footpaths were out of date, and thought they should be created to follow interesting routes. And he didn't want walkers disturbing birds during the nesting season. We would have to agree to disagree about the right to roam, and there's plenty of evidence that birds are unaffected in moorland areas like West Lancashire where the Water Board has already granted free access. Birds of prey have got more to fear from gamekeeper's guns than any rambler's boots. Paul and I agreed on one thing though – our love of the moors. When he dies his ashes are to be scattered over the heather on a windy day. The crew was having considerable trouble keeping up with us. Operating a camera and walking backwards through ankle-grabbing heather is impossible and before long Dave, the cameraman, had fallen a couple of times.

We struggled up Stony Hill and a dilapidated fence that marked the boundary of Paul's domain, as well as the end of County Durham and the start of my second home, Yorkshire. Paul gave me some advice about the best route over the moorland ahead, invaluable tips about how to avoid the boggy bits and deep heather. Then, with a wave, he and the crew were off, and I struck off alone, heading south-east for Arkengarthdale. I walked over Cleasby Hill and looked down at the delightful dale ahead, a patchwork of small green fields along the bottom of the valley, bordered with endless dry stone walls. A wide valley, Faggergill Moor was full of deserted lead mines and tips. I crossed over it and up the eastern side on to a track which, after passing through a couple of isolated farms, gradually became a tiny road bending east into Arkengarthdale.

Suddenly I was aware of domesticity – a cat in a farm window, black-and-white sheepdogs in outside kennels, chickens scuttling around a farmyard as I walked past. Lace curtains in windows and bed and breakfast signs, even at these isolated dwellings.

By the little narrow road at High Eskeleth, I sat on a wooden bench with a fine view down the dale. On its back was a plaque inscribed:

THIS BENCH IS FOR JOAN, WHO KNEW
THE BEAUTY OF THE DALES.

Joan Merrill was just an ordinary walker who loved the area. I knew how she'd felt. After the bleakness of the northern Pennines this landscape was cosy and welcoming. Before Eskeleth Bridge I turned right, and crossed the river, then right again. I noticed a distinctive octagonal building in the field, a powder house, where explosives had been stored for the nearby lead mines. I passed the CB pub, not named after the radio frequency, but Charles Bathurst, son of Oliver Cromwell's doctor, whose family owned land locally. CB was stamped on the lead ingots produced at the mine. I'd promised to return later for a game of dominoes, but now it was only 4 pm and I had to press on.

There was a grand grey house on the north side. I passed Langthwaite village church. At the edge of the graveyard was a wonderful allotment full of flowers for cutting – sweet peas, dahlias and daisies – and next to it an allotment full of large cabbages and brussels sprouts. On the opposite side of the road was a hawthorn tree cut into the shape of a bird. Where the eye should be someone had put a red round sticker. I laughed out loud and took a photo.

Yorkshire felt completely different from County Durham. Here, everything seemed tidy, in its place, the landscape tightly controlled and the dry stone walls repaired. On my right was a little war memorial, rather plain with green railings in front as if there might be a horde of people trying to stampede it. Next was a fine chapel with two storeys of windows elegantly spaced with curved tops to them. This 1882 Wesleyan chapel is still used and the graveyard had fresh flowers in it. Further along the Wesleyan Sunday School Institute had been renovated as someone's house with a lamp over the gate and a well-tended garden. The village centre of Langthwaite, where some of the TV series *All Creatures Great and Small* was filmed, was a captivating jumble of cottages nestling up to each other.

I was now right in holiday-cottage land. There were 'to let' signs at every large house. A little way out of the village I turned south-west and climbed over Reeth Low Moor on a bridleway. I looked back up Arkengarthdale. It was a homogeneous whole, clusters of little grey houses all with white woodwork, a big argument for having planning control. A completely coherent landscape as beautiful as any in Italy or France. The village lay below the road clustered around away from the traffic. As I'd left the village I'd noticed a pay and display car park, a sure sign of masses of tourists. It was a completely grey late afternoon now. The cloud had closed in and there was that fine, fine rain that doesn't seem worth putting your jacket on for. So I trudged across the moor, trying to take a bit of a short cut rather than hug the velvety green bridleway. A hawk hovered in the sky above.

Between the bright-pink heather were patches of bright-green closely cropped soft, velvety grass. It made a change from the clumpy, tufty stuff I'd been walking through for the last week. As I came over the hill I saw Swaledale rising up in front of me, running from east to west with High Harker Hill straight ahead on the other side of the valley. Now I was about to cross another long-distance footpath, the second in one day, where the north–south route meets the coast-to-coast route which runs across from Cumbria in the west to the coast near Whitby in the east. I'd walked it in 1986 during an August which was recorded as the wettest ever, although I thought this August had probably supplanted it. I found the crossing by Thirns Farm and sat down by a footpath sign. I took a break and read my coast-to-coast book from 12 years ago. It recorded every stage of my journey and was covered in water stains from the rain. Every entry seemed to read 'heavy rain', 'light rain', 'light but grey', 'lovely evening after rain'. It all sounded very familiar. I must be fitter now because I seem to be walking far longer distances more quickly than I did back in 1986.

I cut down the very steep hillside to the little road into Healaugh through some bracken. The village seemed completely dormant. It was full of signs offering rooms and bed and breakfast and holiday cottages to let. Healaugh seems to have very little personality left, unlike Langthwaite clustered round its village shop with not a sign in sight. Healaugh is strung out along the B6270 that is heavily used by tourists heading from Reeth west up to Swaledale in the holiday season. Now it was mid-September and few cars came along the road. I stopped my walk just after the end of the village and the next day I intended to head down to the river and decide whether to ford it or cross by the footbridge.

I drove back to the CB Inn where a dominoes league match was in progress. There I met up with John Hird, whose nickname was Cocker John because he lived at Cocker House. John, an ebullient fellow, and his friends were engrossed in a very determined game. Down one side of the pub there were ladies on one table and men on another. I had a gin and tonic and a good chat. They thought that the dale was being revitalized and that people were coming back to live here year-round. I said I was always worried that dale villages would turn into simply holiday cottages, dead in the winter or alive only at the weekends. They assured me this wasn't the case and that in fact in recent years there were more people living here and retiring here than for decades. I hope that's true because I'd hate to see the dales become some kind of tourist theme park, always a problem with a National Park as beautiful as this one.

I said goodbye, got in the car and drove back to Reeth where I stayed at the Burgoyne Hotel. Twelve years ago I'd stayed in the Arkleside Inn, which had a very uncomfortable bed as I recall, halfway through my coast-to-coast walk. This time I wasn't quite halfway through this walk but I'd got a fine room with a comfortable bed and a view over the green. I ate roast grouse on a tray in front of the television and thought life was good after all.

HEALAUGH TO LORD'S BRIDGE
Swaledale to Wensleydale

It was a sunny day but very, very windy. I walked down the road from the village of Healaugh and headed south across the meadow directly down from the road. I'd been struggling with a straight-line dilemma. I wanted to wade across the River Swale and stick to my straight line, but no one could tell me how deep it was, and because it had been so wet, the river was full and flowing strongly. So I lost my nerve and took a detour of nearly a mile along the bank.

It was a pleasant walk through stiles on a well-trodden path. I saw some walkers going in the opposite direction. I felt in familiar territory as I'd walked in this area many, many times before. Soon I reached a footbridge and crossed over it and followed the opposite bank up through a series of fields. Here there were millions of footpaths and it wasn't quite clear which one to take so I just headed south up to Bleak House on the road. I was mentally fatigued from the long day yesterday so that even this brief climb up from the River Swale was enough to make me feel really tired. I drank a cup of black coffee and then contemplated how to cross the moor over to Castle Bolton.

I decided to head back west a small way along the road, where I picked up a grouse-shooting track rather than a footpath. I followed it up over Low Harker Hill. It was pretty easy going and I'd soon climbed high above the road and had a fine view over the dales to the north. On my way up I was sheltered from the wind but it was really slowing me down. Then I headed off on a smaller track west to the brow of the hill. Now I was struggling hard against a very strong westerly gale and the sky was getting grey and looked as if it might rain at any minute. By Long Scar I took a small footpath south through the heather aiming for the shooting lodge directly opposite. This hidden valley by Grovebeck Gill was wonderful with the rocky outcrops above. I hadn't been here for years, and I'd forgotten how secret and special it was.

By the shooting lodge was an old quarry where I squatted down, had a pee, drank a cup of coffee and decided what route to take next. There was no really easy path here to keep to my line. The next footpath started about a mile south on the top of the next hill but getting there would involve a giant detour of about two miles so I decided to follow a stream up through the heather as far as I could and then just tough it out over the top of Grovebeck Moss. The next half hour seemed one of the longest for ages. Although the wind was coming from the side and the rain held off, the heather was very, very deep. Behind me Harkerside Moor and Long Scar looked forbidding as the cloud thickened. I took a compass reading to look for a wall. Eventually I saw the shooting hut at the top of the hill. I climbed over a wire fence and found the footpath on the other side. Thank goodness. Now I just followed this relatively easy path on an exhilarating drop down heading towards Castle Bolton. The wind buffeted me like mad. I dropped down towards a sheepfold at Dents Houses. The crew were facing me on the opposite hill. Too bad they hadn't filmed me slogging it up through the heather.

After Dents Houses I took another track directly south over Blackhill. The track itself was easy walking but I was so exhausted that I found it a struggle to even climb 100 feet or so. I had no one for company except for grouse cackling every now and then, and as I descended into the meadow above Castle Bolton I was watched by sheep and the odd cow. I'd started walking about 10.00 am and reached Castle Bolton at about 12.30, later than I had expected. I took a footpath to the road.

This is a pretty, if somewhat featureless village. The castle sits at one end of it looking really imposing until you know that down the road is Middleham Castle which is better situated with a more attractive village around it. Castle Bolton has a bit of a chocolate-box feel, not really like an actual village at all, even though it does have a post office. In fact only one wing of the castle is restored as a tourist attraction and it seems more like a fortified manor house than a true castle. Nevertheless, it looks suitably impressive when viewed from across the dale, and Mary, Queen of Scots was held here for six months before being taken to London to be executed.

In front of the castle I followed a B road and was glad to be walking on asphalt after all the heather. Nothing much was happening around here, a few tractors went past but no cars. Then I picked up another road and headed east into Redmire. There was quite a lot of farm traffic. At the end of the village I took an old green lane heading south-east. It was pleasant walking until I noticed that a giant lorry was inexplicably trying to drive down it behind me. I continued on a footpath until I came to West Wood, clearly part of a grand estate. A broad track led through a wonderful wood of well-planted conifers, bringing me out in front of Bolton Hall, which looked very grand if somewhat closed up. In front of the hall I headed south across the stylish stone Lord's Bridge across the River Ure, then up a straight avenue of trees that brought me to the A684, then up a farm driveway, Bay Bolton Avenue, again with fine trees on either side. At its end I followed a footpath directly up the southern slopes of Wensleydale. It was wonderful to be able to walk in a straight line although I was so tired. It took all the energy I had left to climb the hundred or so feet up Capple Bank, then through the plantation, emerging by the gallops at Middleham High Moor. It was about 5 pm. I felt shattered. I'd done more than enough walking for one day. Tea beckoned.

DAY 18

MIDDLEHAM HIGH MOOR TO COVERDALE

Monks and horse racing

Last night I'd had enough of hotels. I'd got a lift back to my cottage in Nidderdale and I spent the night in my own bed. This morning I had to get up early to get back to Middleham. It was a nice day for a change. There was a group of racehorse owners or maybe they were just enthusiasts standing by the gallops. There were several dozen horses cantering up and down.

At the end of the gallops, a broad area of closely cropped grass, I met Deirdre Johnston. She was small, dark-haired and vivacious, looking young and full of energy, clad in riding gear. Deirdre was overseeing the exercising of the horses from the successful stable she and her husband own nearby. In fact they had trained more winners than anyone else in Britain in 1998. While we talked, the horses circled round us, some going on up to the high moor and others cantering back along the gallops. It was a wonderful sight: thousands and thousands of pounds worth of thoroughbreds going full pelt over this beautiful hill with views over Coverdale and Wensleydale.

Deirdre told me that the High Moor at Middleham was the oldest recorded site of a race meeting in Britain. The monks of Jervaux Abbey used to race their horses here hundreds of years ago.

Now about 350 horses were using the moor each day, which was about full capacity. At the edge of the gallops was an all-weather track built with money from Development Challenges. Deirdre and her husband Mark, with 140 horses, were the biggest trainers in the area, having started with just three horses. They spent their first two years in Lincolnshire right on the coast where they used to train bang on the RAF bombing range, but came here ten years ago. I'd seen Deirdre on TV at Royal Ascot in the Queen's carriage. What an honour! 'What we'll do to beat the traffic to get to the track,' she joked, but I could tell she was really proud. 'It was a lovely day. We had lunch at Windsor Castle and then we went in the carriage down the track and spent the afternoon in the royal box, and we nearly won the big race that day with Double Trigger – we were second in the Ascot Gold Cup – but it was a wonderful day.'

I asked her what personal sacrifices this life had meant for her. 'My husband is the trainer but I'm absolutely full-time in the business, that's all I do, and it is a very demanding job. It's seven days a week, 24 hours a day; you've got the owners to look after, the staff to look after, the horses to look after, and it's a real commitment and a way of life rather than just a job.'

Deirdre has two small children – three-year-old Charlie, and Angus, seven. I asked her how she fitted everything in to the day. 'We start work at six and I think I get up about five to, jump into my jodhpurs and I am on the back of a horse by about quarter past six, and I ride out with the horses three times every day. The first few lots are about an hour and a quarter each, and this lot that come all the way to the High Moor are out for two hours. So in general I ride about four and a quarter hours a day. We've got about 70 people working for us. The reason we expanded so far so fast was that the horses won races for us and we spent very little money, and they won more races and then we spent a bit more money, and then they won more races. Last year we had 131 winners and we were the most winning trainer in the country. There's a lot of pressure to keep up all the time.'

I said goodbye to Deirdre, waited until the going was clear and crossed over the moor. At the far side a well-signposted footpath took me south over pastureland, bringing me to another moor which eventually joined a little road leading down into Melmerby, a sleepy dale's village full of cottages that looked pretty quiet. Two men were rounding up sheep in pens at one side of the road and tractors were busy bringing in the hay, taking advantage of a brief warm spell of weather. At the bottom of the village I turned left and then dropped down to another B road and then took a footpath across beautiful pastureland down to the River Cover. Here I crossed by the wooden St Simon's Bridge and walked through idyllic secret woodland glades until I came to St Simon's Chapel which had a plaque on it reminding me that this is a medieval monument. What a magical spot to end the day's walking. Only one more climb back up to the road. Then I turned east again heading along High Lane.

DAY 19

WEST SCRAFTON TO RAMSGILL
A heather mattress and a meeting with Sambo

I had the luxury of sleeping at my cottage in my own bed, so when I woke up at 7.30 am and saw that it was pouring, it seemed quite acceptable anyway. I threw on some clothes and got driven along a lengthy narrow lane up from East Witton, following the south side of Coverdale. We started walking on High Lane, by a bungalow, after East Scrafton. The sky was clearing up fast although there was quite a stiff breeze blowing. We turned off High Lane opposite a farm up a track and ahead lay Caldbergh Moor and West Scrafton Moor. We headed due south-east up the track following the wall. A shepherd was rounding up sheep on a motorbike. He had extremely long hair, and said hello to us. He didn't seem to mind that we weren't walking on a footpath so I asked him if it was OK and he said go right ahead. So we followed the track to where it ran out and then continued along the wall and went through a gate and a marshy area and then up a pretty steep slope veering away from the fence and heading straight up to the top of the hill. We were actually east of Great Roova Crags. Today I was determined to walk as close to my line as possible.

The first hill of the day is always the worst. I was walking with my friends Darryl and Janet and we were sweating like mad. We slogged up through the heather, without a path and it was a long, slow hike up to about 1,200 feet. When we reached the top Darryl and I immediately had a disagreement about the best way to proceed across the vast expanse of moors ahead, but unusually I took his advice and we headed slightly further south than the line in order to avoid coming down too far.

What a wonderful day! I love being in this huge landscape. The heather was deep and hard to walk through. There were no paths whatsoever. Depending on whether the heather had been burnt in the last few years or not meant that your route would take you through knee-high heather or mid-calf-length heather. In places it was pretty boggy but not as wet as it had been in other years. That wasn't the problem. The problem was horrible hidden holes in the deep heather. Pretty soon as we crossed this huge pink plain of heather Darryl had fallen down a hole up to his waist. The minute I laughed at him I too fell forward on my face and then so did Janet. We had to make our way across this vast plateau of pink painstakingly slowly. You couldn't remove your eyes from the ground for a minute. You couldn't see where to put your feet. The heather made a dense thick carpet. It twisted round your ankles. It grabbed on to your feet. It seemed not to want anyone to cross it. Then there were the bits that had been burnt. They just scoured and scratched your legs. Thank goodness I was wearing sweatpants.

Progress was extremely slow and as the day improved and the sky got bluer the wind thankfully didn't let up, otherwise we would have been dripping with sweat. To the west we could hear the sound of shooting. It was Lord Vestey's shooting party high up on Scar Moor. We saw very few grouse although occasionally three or four would fly up in front of us in a half-hearted manner and then come back down and dive under cover.

I imagined that the boundary between Coverdale and Nidderdale which was marked on the map as a nice thick green line would be a boundary fence. How wrong I was. I spent an hour and a half looking for this fence only to realize eventually it didn't exist. This boundary was marked by stones, the minutest bumps in the landscape in the undulating plateau of moorland. We skirted around the top of the old Coal Road up from Colsterdale, a route I had walked up many times from the east. Now we were at the very head of the dale and we had to take care not to go down into it and make our passage any more difficult so we skirted round in a loop to the west.

Then the hill of South Haw was ahead of us and you could dimly make out one or two little fenceposts on its profile. We had to aim to the east of it to the end of Brown Ridge. We toiled our way forward making very slow progress. Janet fell in a stream and hurt her shoulder. Darryl fell down a hole once more and got both feet wet. But somehow the camaraderie between the three of us – such old friends – made it just hilarious, not irksome. I just occasionally slipped down a hole or twisted my leg. My back was aching like mad from the strain of it and every time I slid from tussock to tussock it was jarred even further.

As we got to the end of Brown Ridge I had only crossed one shooting track in miles and we decided to stop for lunch. It was 1.15 pm and we had been walking for just over two hours. We crouched down in the heather at the end of the hill, laid out our waterproofs and made warm heathery nests to lie in. The sun came out and we were rewarded with magnificent views in every direction. After a couple of rolls, a Kit-Kat, a bottle of water and a flapjack I felt sleepy. I pulled my hood over my head and snuggled right down into my heather mattress. I couldn't care less about ticks or flies. Within five minutes I was in a deep sleep, woken only by the sound of Darryl's snoring. An army helicopter chugged overhead. From time to time the only other sounds we heard were low-flying Phantom jets, simulating fighting the Vietcong in Upper Nidderdale and Lord Vestey's shooting party killing grouse. The shots from the party were a bit more sporadic; either lunch was being served or they'd had a lot to drink. They didn't seem to have quite the enthusiasm for culling they'd unleashed that morning.

We lay in the heather and dozed for about half an hour then dragged ourselves to our feet and plodded on. Eventually we made the boundary fence and turned west along it. For a couple of blissful miles we were walking on grass. At Throstle Hill we turned south and the next two miles, although hard work, were worth the entire day. We clung to the fence. Again the terrain was virtually flat but the path itself disappeared by the fence and we walked from heather clump to heather clump falling down, dragging ourselves over streams. It was grizzly slow progress. Every now and then the grouse would rise up and cackle at us.

To the west we could see Scar House Reservoir and Whernside beyond. The crags of Dale Edge were to the south. I got a final lease of life and dragged myself through the heather to the cattle grid at Jordan Moss. I thought that I might as well bash off half a mile down the road to pick up the other track to Ramsgill. That brief ten minutes was the easiest walking all day. Gradually my back relaxed as I walked along on the asphalt. A couple of tourists went past in their cars looking amazed at the sight of a woman miles from anywhere with bright red hair tied up in a funny knot and bits of heather stuck to every bit of her.

We stopped for a cup of tea. My feet were entirely covered with bits of bracken and heather. They looked like brown fur. I took my socks off and tried to pull the heather out. It wouldn't budge.

After tea I put on some fresh socks and continued along the high level track into Ramsgill. After what we'd been through this was a doddle. The wind was dropping and the weather improving by the minute, and it was a fine evening. We walked along the track towards Fountains Earth Moor passing the crags known locally as Jenny Twig and her daughter Tib. There were very few grouse on this bit of land and the well-made track was only occasionally full of puddles. We crossed a beautiful bridge built over 100 years ago and then we joined up with another track back to Kirkby Malzeard. We skirted Helks Wood and took the path over from the east, noting our meeting point for the next morning. We looked ahead and saw Gouthwaite Reservoir, beautiful in the evening sun. We dropped down to the settlement of Bouthwaite and there the car was waiting for us.

It was hard to work out how far we'd walked that day. The first ten or twelve miles had taken four hours of hard going. Then another four miles and it had taken an hour and a quarter. I was ready for a hot bath and a gin and tonic. I got both and then we went to the Sportsman's Arms in Wath for dinner. The dining room was a disaster as 30 people from the American base at Menwith Hill were having a goodbye dinner for someone who was retiring, all sitting on one long table. Then there was Lord Vestey's shooting party, six extremely upper-class people, including an art dealer, a very well-spoken woman from Belgium and Vestey himself, wearing a gaudy striped blazer, looking more like a City trader than a multi-millionaire butcher or whatever he is.

I had to have dinner with an executive from the BBC and it was quite a strain as we were all very, very tired. All I wanted to know was what work I was going to be doing next year. And I wasn't getting any answers. It was very hard to concentrate. After dinner we made our getaway into the lounge for coffee. We had only just sat down when we heard the Americans embark on a series of interminable speeches. A quarter of an hour later Lord Vestey burst into the lounge. 'Thank God we are out of that one,' he exclaimed. 'You did the right thing,' he said to me, 'you got out before the speeches,' whereupon he started to imitate the poor unfortunates on the other side of the wall at the top of his voice thanking all and sundry and behaving like an American hick. It obviously did the trick as the dining room emptied within 15 minutes.

By then we were all feeling pretty friendly in the resident's lounge. The Vestey shooting party was very jolly and enormous amounts of alcohol had been consumed so I felt bold enough to ask him if his nickname really was 'Spam', which I'd read in the newspapers. 'My dear, that's a name that Nigel Dempster made up,' he said. 'Some people call me Spam but you can call me Sambo.' I shall dine out on that line for quite a long time. After a few more drinks he told me he wished his daughter would marry a black cricketer instead of some ghastly white Protestant banker or whatever as it would mean better blood coming into the family. He was an absolutely hilarious mimic, drunk or sober. We ended the evening with me promising to turn up at their next shoot.

I realized the man I'd been chatting to, who shared my birthday, was Andrew Parker-Bowles, Camilla's ex-husband. He was definitely a ladies' man, charming in the extreme. Sambo was a complete turn, with a booming voice and an avuncular manner, a cross between Jeeves and Alexander Hesketh. They told us they'd shot, depending on who you spoke to, 46, 52 or 56 brace of grouse. Whatever – they'd all had a top day out, and Ray Carter, who owns the Sportsman's, had been invited along to shoot as well and at lunch they had given him a birthday cake covered with pictures of grouse.

By now Vestey had gone through a port bottle and we made our excuses and left. Luckily I took two Nurofen before I passed out into a dreamless sleep.

Part Four

Ramsgill

to Brampton

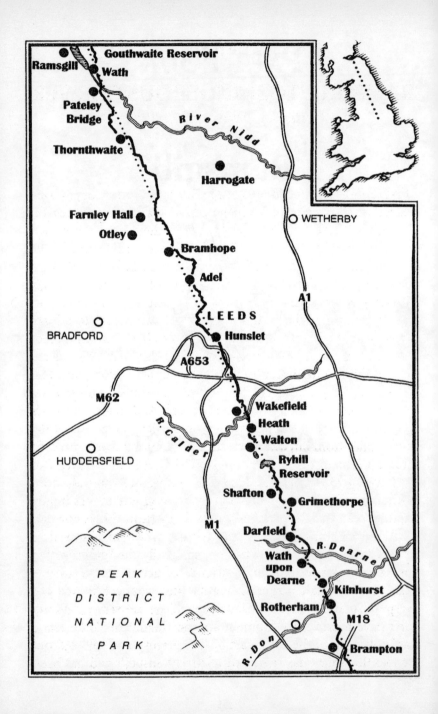

RAMSGILL TO DANGEROUS CORNER
Butter sculpture and Golfballs

I first came to live in Nidderdale 20 years ago. In those days I lived nearer to Harrogate in a village called Darley in a beautiful Georgian house with a fine walled garden. I grew my own vegetables and loved walking. But the scenery at that end of the dale is gentler and doesn't have the dramatic quality that you get above Pateley Bridge. But then my village got expanded, and ugly bungalows were added and the pub underwent a massive transformation, going from one that had two rooms to a huge place with a giant asphalt car park. That was it, I'd had enough of Darley. I can't bear looking at bungalows. They and caravans are the two things I despise most about the English countryside, and although I've mellowed a bit on the subject of bungalows, caravans still drive me into a frenzy of rage. And so over ten years ago I found two ruined cottages in a small village at the top of the valley, miles from anywhere in a tiny community that I could fit into and remain relatively anonymous in, and that's where I've been every two weeks since. It suits me perfectly. I can walk from my house miles in every direction over the grouse moors in any weather. I can walk by myself and everybody treats this as normal.

At the beginning of the century the whole of Nidderdale above Pateley Bridge was owned by one family, the Yorkes, with a huge estate of hundreds of thousands of acres. This history is what gives the dale a special quality, and wonderfully it's not overpopulated. In the upper dale the villages are very small and don't have massive development around them. The Yorke estate was broken up in the early part of this century and sold off, but even so this valley has remained relatively unspoilt and has been declared an area of outstanding natural beauty which is better than being a National Park as it doesn't draw the number of visitors that designation attracts. But over the last 20 years I've noticed that tourism has come to replace agriculture as the main source of income and that has meant more caravans, and it has also meant that house prices have gone up, making it harder and harder for locals to live there. In my own village four small houses were built recently in stone and blended in very well. They were called affordable housing and were to be rented out to locals at a rent of £50 per week, but this was thought by most people to be far too high and they had a great deal of difficulty in letting these houses. Unless the Government introduces a transport policy which is subsidized and which serves these remote rural areas, nobody will live in them and they will become dormitory villages full of weekenders. Who will live in these tiny villages up the dale when there is no bus service and you have to rely on the butcher coming round in a van once a week, the travelling library and lifts into town from your friends? You are really isolated and as most families only have one car, if one partner goes to work the other remains stuck at home with the children.

I walked up the lane out of Gouthwaite. There had been a railway station here in the 1920s and early 1930s on a private railway line running all the way from Pateley Bridge up to the Scar House reservoir as it was being built. This remained in private hands longer than any other railway line in Britain. What a shame it was dismantled. Now the stations have become sought-after houses, and the one at the end of Gouthwaite Reservoir had been rather badly restored with an extremely ugly large greenhouse in the garden. How did that get past the planners?

At the top of the lane on the edge of the moor I was meeting Tom Wheelwright, whose land extends along the eastern section of the reservoir and is owner of almost the entire village of Wath. He was said by locals to be someone from another era. I'd never met him but he was adamant that I couldn't walk across his land unless I walked with him. He seemed to take offence very easily and I was wondering what he would be like. He was waiting by the wall, wearing a hat and with a black labrador called Jack who obeyed his every command. He seemed to have a very intense relationship with his dog. Tom had a booming, well-educated public school voice and we immediately got on well, as long as the conversation was confined to grouse moors, bracken burning, sheep ticks, etc., and after my walk through the grouse moors in Scotland I now feel I could do *Mastermind* on the subject of heather restoration. Our walk was relatively uneventful, and the weather sunny and pleasant. No public footpath passed our route although he didn't seem to be particularly opposed to the right to roam. Tom's big plan was to get rid of the bracken so that the heather could grow back, a process taking up to ten years. He paid a helicopter to spray the bracken from time to time, not altogether successfully, and in his own estate, which must extend to thousands of acres, he only employed one gamekeeper. He and the keeper would walk around with a rucksack of chemicals spraying the remaining bracken themselves. It seemed a very arduous process to say the least.

We went down to a stream where I saw a landslide and then we climbed up the other side. It was the best day for weeks; there wasn't a cloud in the sky and it was boiling hot – slightly too hot for walking. I'd been a bit over-enthusiastic and put my linen shorts on but unfortunately we had to walk through some bracken and I was soon regretting it. We contoured along the north side of the reservoir. It lay like a piece of opal below us with not a ripple on it as there wasn't a breath of wind. Tom regaled me with stories of how aeroplanes had crashed by flying too low over it. At that moment a couple of bombers passed on a low-flying exercise below us. Earlier on we had been bugged by an army helicopter that seemed to be circling up and down the valley in an aimless fashion just wasting tax payers' money. This was a relatively new development. I hadn't remembered seeing these army helicopters flying this low before, although Tom said it had been going on for years.

Sigsworth Crags rose up out of the heather above us, a fine outcrop of rock. All along the valley on the north side lie exposed rocks at about 1,200 feet, great big boulders of Millstone Grit. Further down at Brimham Rocks they have been eroded into all sorts of fantastic shapes. I asked Tom if they would be shooting any grouse this year and he said the cold weather in June had got rid of all the chicks and they would maybe only shoot one day. From his conversation it seemed that he spent his life shooting, fishing or looking after the land. He stalked in Scotland, fished, shot pheasant and grouse, and seemed to have a whole variety of guns. His mother had died five years ago and he seemed a rather lonely person and not quite of this time. It was hard to guess his age but I think he must have been in his early 40s. He had a missing front tooth so wasn't particularly vain.

All the paintwork in the charming hamlet of Wath is a subtle pale pink. Not a feminine pink but a pink just slightly pinker than cream; it's extremely exotic and I'd noticed it for years. As we dropped down into the village I asked Tom where the colour had come from. Apparently his mother hated white or cream and she had come up with it and all the houses on the estate had been painted that colour ever since. So that was a mystery solved.

We went into his kitchen for a cup of coffee. There was no sign of feminine life here although there was a sweet little tin bowl of peas by the back door that one of the local ladies had picked for him in his garden. She lived in one of the cottages down the road rent-free and in return his garden was an anally retentive temple of perfection mowed in criss-cross fashion with neat beds of vegetables and a wonderful herbaceous border.

Then we made a short detour down the road to the pub. I've been going to the Sportsman's Arms for as long as I can remember and today was owner Ray Carter's 50th birthday. He lives in a converted station house opposite. We drank a bottle of champagne in the garden and already I could feel the day's schedule was going to pot.

I took the high road out of the village past the green, a small triangle surrounded by tall stone walls. In the car park of the Sportsman's a marquee was being erected for a wedding the following Saturday and Radio 1 blared from a car. Nothing was happening on the village green, where a few sheep munched away. I noticed a tiny chapel about the size of a small living-room stuck on the end of one of the houses. I turned left and took the road climbing steeply up with fine views of the Gouthwaite Reservoir behind me and in front of me Pateley Bridge, which has hardly changed since the 1920s. The only thing that was a blot on the horizon was the Heathfield caravan site tucked away up to the west by Foster Beck. I passed a few cottages and then a clump of trees, and at the cross-roads the road started to descend steeply.

I entered Pateley Bridge past a church which had been converted into flats and turned right into the Nidderdale Museum. Founded in 1975, this is housed in what used to be the workhouse (built in 1863) which then became the council offices. It's run by former teacher Eileen Burgess and her friends. There are about 80 unpaid volunteers and it won a National Heritage Award for 'Small Museum of the Year'. It's stuffed with objects of every description. They have far too much stuff to display and are permanently bringing things out of the basement and trying to cram them in. Eileen told me that the agricultural room was due for a massive refurbishment to incorporate even more pieces. Now when people die in Nidderdale instead of leaving their possessions to the jumble sale or their relatives they bequeath them to the museum, so there are fine displays of obscure farm implements from turnip cutters to butter moulds. There's a full chemist's shop and a cobbler's, as well as cases of stuffed fish, doilies, costumes – you name it, it's here. My favourite amongst the 15,000 exhibits is the display concerning butter sculpture. Just after World War I Nidderdale was the centre of an extraordinary achievement: the Misses Mudd (there were six Miss Mudds in all) were highly skilled in the now lost art of making chrysanthemums and flowers from butter, and they went to the Royal Smithfield Show in London where their work was displayed and they won all sorts of gold medals, returning home to much acclaim. They won many prizes in the north but it was for one brief moment that Nidderdale shone throughout the entire country and the agricultural world, and it was for butter sculpture. There's a photograph in the museum of two of the Miss Mudds standing on either side of a glass case down which is streaming iced water and inside is a floral display of exotic flowers – dahlias and chrysanthemums – made entirely of butter. I recommend a visit; it just takes your breath away. I suggested to Eileen that they should perhaps recreate the sculpture and she was nonplussed. Then I asked if there was any possibility of it being issued as a postcard and I understand that it's under consideration at the moment.

I left the museum having purchased a postcard of an engraving of the former Nidderdale Brewery, which was on special offer for only 30p. I made my way down the High Street I know intimately. Junk shops and antique shops may come and go, and occasionally a brave soul may open an Indian takeaway or a pizza parlour, and of course there are the trendy fleece shops, but Pateley Bridge basically has a very short summer season and so the High Street remains more or less as it was in 1925. My favourite coffee shop has a pot hanging outside the window and faces the cash machine, which was the source of a great deal of excitement when it was installed a few years ago. Having campaigned for ten years to get their own cash dispenser outside the bank, the locals formed a queue when it was unveiled. Two old ladies were at the front and were photographed next to it even though the machine wasn't yet operational. The café I like has plastic tablecloths and ten different kinds of breakfast and I usually spend Saturday mornings in there with a cup of frothy coffee reading the local newspaper, the *Pateley Bridge and Nidderdale Advertiser*, which is only fractionally different from the *Harrogate Advertiser*. The parking problems of Pateley have been front-page news for decades.

I went down the street, past the newsagent and the post office (the same place), the chemist (also the beauty shop) and Weatherhead's the butcher, where I bought a home-made pork pie for my lunch. A few months before for an article in *The Times* I had chosen Weatherhead's (established 1876) as my favourite shop and was photographed (rather unattractively I thought) holding a pork pie in one hand and a piece of black pudding in the other to accompany the article. Far from putting people off, Ian Weatherhead reported gleefully that as soon as the article appeared people were on the phone trying to order black puddings and pork pies by post from places as far away as Suffolk.

Then I crossed over the River Nidd and turned left into the green expanse of the showground. The big event every year here in Pateley is the annual agricultural show. It started over a hundred years ago and now takes place on a large 48-acre luxuriant field bought by the Agricultural Society in 1927. Occasionally during the year there's the odd car-boot sale on the showground, there's a cricket ground within it and sometimes they even allow caravans to park on it for some kind of rally or other, but generally it just sits there waiting for that exciting moment in mid-September when it will be jam-packed with displays of every kind, from sheep to poultry tents to rabbits, everything in fact you'd expect in one of the best agricultural shows in the north of England. Joe Stoney, one of the show's organizers, walked through the ground with me and explained how the number of local farmers in the area has reduced from over 50 just after World War II to now only ten. He farms 1,000 acres with his son Trevor and can barely make a living, the BSE crisis having devastated their business.

Joe's sense of humour is dry. I asked why the show is so late in the year. Why didn't they have it in the summer while all the tourists are here? The fact is it often rains on Pateley Show day, and the summer was over by then. Joe's answer was somewhat oblique to say the least: 'All the other shows are then, and by the time it comes to the Nidderdale Show, the stock is all, you know, like in prime condition, the sheep look good by then.' I had to agree on that. The sheep did look better by September, because they look pretty sad and sorry in July.

Joe told me the Agricultural Society was founded in 1895. A group of farmers got together and they put the first show on, costing the grand sum of £75, raising the money by subscription. After that, every year the show got a little bigger. I asked Joe if he regretted the end of the kind of farming that had existed in the 1920s in the dale, when the Society could afford to buy all this land. 'Times have to change, no doubt, but I think we've gone to the extreme. Those 50 small farms in those days were making a living, they wouldn't make much profit but they were making a living, and most of the farmers would employ a man as well. Today they put two or three farms together. Even the sons are having to go out to work as they can't afford to stay on the farm. They need another income coming from some other source. So I don't think any farmer would really encourage his son now to go into farming. I can see the day coming when, of the 10 or 12 farms around here, there could only be 2 if it goes on like this.'

It's a sobering thought. Even the show itself has stopped being a purely agricultural event, as Joe explained, 'Now, we'll have 60-plus trade stands, and we've tried to keep it as agricultural as we can – but you still have to have these motor firms, the tractors, the sweets, the grocers.' My favourite part was still the chickens – I'd never seen such weird feathered things in my life. Some looked more like powder puffs than anything that would lay an egg.

I said goodbye to Joe, and at the end of the showground I went through a stile and walked a short way down a very nettly path, emerging in someone's driveway and then out on to the road that leads up the cliff on the south side of Nidderdale towards Guise Cliff. I crossed some fields and went through a farmyard where obviously the owner hadn't taken advantage of any grants to tidy up his property as it seemed like a tip with rotting black bin liners and discarded machinery every way you looked.

Further up a track I entered a wood, Yorke's Folly high above me on my right. This is a ruin but it was built as one in 1809. The local landowner, Squire Yorke, decided to bring employment to the locals by constructing an exciting classical folly on top of the cliff. The locals were paid the minimum wage and the result was three classical columns with two arches. Sadly one of the columns fell down in a storm in 1893 and all that remains are two of the stoops. It's still a very distinguished landmark.

I climbed up through the woods where large boulders lay dropped as if part of some secret arrangement. Ferns and bilberries sprouted all around them. It was a pretty steep climb and I emerged by a large outcrop of rocks in front of a radio transmitter. I rested, enjoying fine views in every direction, east down the valley in the direction of Harrogate and up it towards my home and Great Whernside beyond.

I took the long-distance Nidderdale Way track as two very keen hikers came in the opposite direction with full kit, loads of maps in plastic folders and so on, and walked down the road a way to find a spot out of the rather chilly wind. After I'd eaten my pork pie by a little brook I walked down to the old hamlet of Heyshaw, now a grouping of farms and expensive homes. I walked round the back of one of the farmyards and cut across some fields to a road. This is all very exposed countryside and there was a very chilly wind blowing. It was hard to believe it wasn't later in the year. I kept a woolly hat on to stop myself getting a headache.

Eventually I took the road down to Thornthwaite, chickening out of crossing a field where a sign said 'Bulls'. I couldn't work out which of the exotic foreign cattle were bulls at a distance but I decided not to risk it as there were calves in the field and I'd read in the paper only a few days before about a rambler being trampled very badly by a nutty cow. As I dropped down towards Thornthwaite I left the wind behind and I got hotter and hotter. Thornthwaite is an interesting unspoilt hamlet, very spread out. When I first came to live in Yorkshire it still had some of the original inhabitants, but now almost every single house and old building has been done up by people commuting to Leeds. White paint and carriage lamps have sprouted absolutely everywhere. Ponies are in stables and children's bicycles are in driveways. Thornthwaite was one of the last outposts of the Baptists in Nidderdale and they still use one of the chapels there. There's a charming medieval packhorse bridge over the little burn and I took a detour to go over it. An elderly lady and her husband were sitting in folding chairs and she was painting a water-colour.

I climbed up the hill opposite, past the church with its wonderful graveyard and took a footpath where the new residents had decided not to trim the nettles, obviously to deter people like me as the footpath ended up in their driveway. I got completely stung, put on my waterproof trousers to prevent any further damage and emerged in an extremely bad mood into a posh paved drive. Dogs immediately came rushing up to me barking hysterically and a small boy appeared. 'Get your bloody dogs off me, this is a public footpath,' I yelled. I rejoined the little road through Thornthwaite. What had been the village school was now another gentrified house.

I climbed up another hill and realized I had made a fatal mistake with the route today as there was far too much down and up for one day. I passed the Royal Naval Signals Station at Blubberhouses and behind the chainlink fence lay housing and what might have been a sports centre. The road was absolutely dead straight heading east towards Menwith Hill and the Golfballs. As I started to walk along it desperate for a cup of tea some military defence police drove up in a Land Rover. After they'd recognized me and made sure that I wasn't a peace campaigner about to attack their installation they left me alone. I met up with the film crew, drank about five cups of tea and then walked on to the Menwith Hill Station that's run by the American National Security Agency, and is the biggest spy station in the world. Under its many geodesic randomes, known locally as the Golfballs, were satellites that tune in to all the electronic communications in Europe. I was planning to meet a member of the local peace camp who was going to explain to me why she was so opposed to the station, but first I walked on a footpath through the edge of the site which the Ramblers Association had gone to great lengths to keep open. It was very pretty, full of butterflies, flowers and a large selection of wild grasses.

I emerged on to the road on the western side of the station. Immediately a *Yorkshire Post* reporter got out of a car, 'What are you doing here?' I said. 'I just heard you were here,' he replied. Obviously someone had tipped him off. I didn't want my photograph taken because I had to spend the next two days walking through Leeds with Vic Reeves and we certainly didn't want to attract any crowds. I pleaded with the man not to take my photograph now but leave it till I finished walking in Leeds on the Friday afternoon. He refused. So I got in the crew's Land Rover and drove off for an hour until he'd lost interest, and then I returned and got someone to tell the peace woman that I wouldn't be interviewing her as there was simply no point.

I walked past the Golfballs. They looked fantastic in the setting sun. When I first came to live in Yorkshire in the late 1970s, there were only about six of them. Now they present a spooky mass, like giant puffballs but with a more sinister purpose.

Soon I reached the spot marked on the map as Dangerous Corner, and where Harrogate Council had recently covered the road in red and green paintwork in an attempt to stop the death toll. This is the junction of the B6541 and the A59 on the corner of the Golfballs. Locals were queuing up to cross the road, as it's a short cut back from Leeds to Pateley Bridge and the dale. I decided to call it a day. I'd walked a long way and my legs were aching and I was pretty pissed off that I'd wasted an hour avoiding a reporter.

I went home and had a bath, and then I went and had dinner with Vic Reeves. He was in fine form, apart from the fact that I didn't recognize him as he'd shaved off all his hair and was wearing metal-rimmed glasses. When I entered the bar I walked straight past him and he had to shout out, 'Hey, its me!' which I thought was hilarious. He was really looking forward to our walk the next day and I eventually rolled home at quarter to twelve rather the worse for wear.

DAY 21

DANGEROUS CORNER TO THE SUBURBS OF LEEDS (ADEL)
We ford a deep river

I headed south along the B6451 in the direction of Farnley. Cars belted past and the sooner I could get off this nasty bit of road the better. I turned left along Pennypot Lane, a famous shortcut into Harrogate. I don't know if it's a Roman road but this lane with no road markings goes in a completely straight line along the top of the ridge that runs from west to east for miles. It's a fine shortcut if you don't get caught behind an old lady or a learner driver. A short time before my walk I was taking someone to the station in Harrogate early one Bank Holiday Monday and I noticed a bizarre occurrence. There seemed to be crowds of people gathered for no reason. At the side of the road were two ponies and traps. When I dropped my friend off and returned, an illegal race had taken place complete with betting, spectators, and start and finish lines. Two horses with small carriages had pounded along this road trying to break all speed records and the whole thing seemed to be over by 9.45 am. Today there were no horses and no spectators, just more cars dashing past.

After about a mile I turned south along an old drovers' lane that took me due south and skirted round the hidden valley I used to walk when I lived in Darley. The landscape around here looks deceptively flat and uneventful but hidden in it is the Haverah Park area, with a couple of reservoirs. This hidden place full of herons, ducks, loads of mushrooms, reeds and grass, is absolutely beautiful and visited by surprisingly few people. I skirted the western end of the reservoir and made my way up to the remains of the lodge of the Haverah Park estate. This fine set of stone buildings is now in disrepair. I followed a track south-east, rising back up on to the bleak flat top of the moors. I walked through a large field of cows and saw an enormous rust-coloured bull staring at me very fixedly. Creeping along the edge of the wall I climbed over it, skirted round the Scargill Reservoir and then had an unpleasant mile across extremely deep, reedy scratchy grass until coming out on Broad Dubb Road. I left the road by a slight bend.

Heading south through the plantation I walked over Stainburn Moor. I could see Harrogate away to the east, and of course the only really visible building you could see at this distance was that disgusting piece of architecture, the Conference Centre.

Away to the west, tucked down in lush wooded valleys, were the reservoirs of Fewston, Timble and Norwood. I left the forest behind and was on Lindley Moor, which is scrubby, awful land. There seemed to be no end of earth-moving equipment left to rust up here. A field on my left had been dug up for no apparent reason and two farmers seemed to be busily hacking it up even further. It was full of rubbish and rubble. The path I was walking on was suddenly blocked by giant piles of what looked like derelict houses, bricks, bits of metal and plaster, house tiles; there were huge pyramids of them. It seemed as if I was walking through a builder's tip. The whole place had a dismal air as if there was a secret plan to build a new *Brookside* estate up here. Then I followed an old road that had fallen into disrepair, an easy walk down over Napes Hill. I hit the corner of the Beckwithshaw Road near Hilltop Farm, and after about a mile of dodging cars using it as a short cut to Leeds, I could stand it no further and decided to take a footpath off to the right heading across to the River Washburn at Stainburn Bank.

There were thick nettles around the entrance to the stile so my legs got stung, then I skirted round a field of lively cattle desperately searching for a way out. As I approached the wall the cattle started getting more than skittish and came racing towards me. I don't like the stand-off of wills it takes to make cattle stop. What you are supposed to do, according to experts, is just stand still and they stop, so the whole progress towards the edge of the field consisted of me standing still and them halting for about two seconds, and then them regrouping ready to attack me, and me trying desperately not to run. By the time I reached the dilapidated stone wall around the edge of the field I was a sweaty mess.

I climbed over it into a field of corn getting even more stung as I went. I ploughed through the corn until I found the path through it, and now my legs were getting scratched as well as stung.

Luckily then I found delightful Pilwhite Lane, which I followed south down towards the river, by a sweet cottage with a wonderful garden in front of it. I followed the River Washburn south and skirted around Leathley Mill. The owners of Leathley Mill are like all people who buy expensive houses in the commuter belt between Harrogate and Leeds – they loathe walkers. They had managed to erect a wooden fence leaving approximately six inches between nettles and their driveway so I skirted around it. On the other side of it was an expensive looking cat, an expensive looking car, a lot of carriage lamps, white gateposts and immaculate gravel. I emerged on to the main road and streams of commuter traffic.

I walked down a road by the phone box, past a very grand house that seemed to be part of the Farnley Hall Estate. It was certainly built at the same time, an imposing mansion, the stonework of which had blackened with time. It had a swanky lake out the back and looked very expensive to maintain. At a footpath sign I turned right and crossed a field.

Vic Reeves had already set up his easel and had promised me that he would execute a water-colour in the style of Turner, as this is where Turner visited between 1808 and 1824, visiting Farnley Hall and the Fawkes family, producing many water-colours and drawings of the scenes in Lower Wharfedale. What I saw instead was a demented cow. Vic had painted an animal that seemed to have left the earth on all fours with one giant red udder and a startled expression. It looked more like Chagall on acid than Turner, and Vic was quite pleased when I pointed that out.

We left the water-colour and crossed over the field. Wharfedale and Leeds lay in front of us. This part of the dale hasn't really changed that much since Turner was here, although there are more houses, and Pool Bank still rose up in front of us just as it was when he painted it over 150 years ago.

We crossed over one field and another, ignoring where the footpath went but striking out in a straight line. Bulls didn't seem to be too much of a problem here. Vic had decided to dress for the walk in a pair of trainers, cream corduroy shorts, a rather trendy white Helmut Lang jacket that didn't look the slightest bit waterproof and a Comme des Garcons shirt. He'd put on his black Vic Reeves sunglasses and so was instantly identifiable even with a shaven head. He looked as if he'd stepped out of the menswear department of Harvey Nichols ready for a stroll along the front at Puerto Banus in Spain.

I'd met Vic Reeves (Jim Moir) a couple of years ago, and soon discovered that he is a rather shy and highly intelligent man. A lot of work goes into being Vic Reeves. He's passionate about any project he gets obsessed by – from collecting cars to painting (he really is a talented artist) to walking. The idea for my walking in a straight line had initially been his, and our plan now was to visit his birthplace, Leeds, and the suburb where he grew up, Adel. I soon realized that like everything else he does, he'd entered into this walk 150 per cent prepared. He'd spent weeks speed-walking round the Romney Marshes near his home with a personal trainer, had lost about a stone in weight, and was super fit. He must be one of the most recognizable people in Britain (by anyone under 55) as I was to find out over the next two days.

Eventually we reached the main road by Pool Bridge. The easy option here would have been simply to cross the River Wharfe by the bridge but Vic, having had the idea in the first place of crossing England and Scotland in a straight line, wasn't going to be deterred from his original dream. When we looked on the map the straight line, as the crow flies, went about a hundred yards to the east of the bridge. 'That's it,' he said, 'we'll have to ford the river.' The crew looked appalled. He retraced his steps from the centre of the bridge back to the northern bank, climbed down on to it and we walked along through the field about 50 yards, then he removed his shoes and socks (I'd already given him a rather worn rucksack to keep the plastic rainhat in which I'd bought in Bonnyrigg all those weeks ago, and a towel as I suspected that fording the river might be an option). I'd found the towel at the bottom of my airing cupboard, it was dusty with time and had a large map of Florida printed on it with the slogan 'Florida, sun and fun'.

Lower Wharfedale looked nothing like Miami. It promised rain any minute. I took my shoes and socks off and was glad I had my walking stick. I clambered down into the water. It wasn't nearly as cold as the stream that I'd forded out by Selkirk a few weeks before. In fact this was positively warm in comparison.

Vic strode across the river, and there was a point when I thought the water might reach his shorts but he rolled them up a bit. I had slightly more of a problem as mine were longer and baggier plus I had quite a heavy rucksack on my back and a walking stick. Luckily the stick stopped me toppling over. I yanked my shorts up even higher, hung my boots around my neck, and made it to the far bank, getting my bare feet slightly ensnared with fishing line before I attained the far bank. Vic whipped a camera out of his pocket and he and I photographed each other. The crew waded straight in behind us halfway and decided to press on even though their feet were soaking wet. Carl, the director, got in the water, got slightly wet and then chickened out and ran back over the bridge to the other side. He didn't go up in my estimation for doing that.

We dried our feet sitting on some rocks on the other side, climbed up and were met immediately by a man whose glasses seemed extraordinary. They were thicker than the thickest milk bottle bottoms I had ever seen. He declared himself to be the water bailiff for the stretch of water we were on and then explained that he had cataracts in both eyes which were going to be removed the week after next, and that's why he had the glasses.

He'd been on the National Health waiting list and his name had finally come up. It seemed to me that with the glasses he was wearing he couldn't possibly see any poachers and he certainly wasn't of an age or physique where he could rush along and catch them, but I decided not to mention that. Our opening exchange was a foretaste of the bizarre world you inhabit when you're with Vic. For some reason he attracts nutters and even sane people start behaving oddly when they meet him.

VIC TO WATER BAILIFF: *'How do you do?'*

MAN: *'I'm all right, how are you.'*

VIC: *'Not so bad.'*

MAN: *'Yes, I am at the moment because I've been dead in the last two years.'*

VIC: *'That's not good is it?'*

MAN: *'Oh it is, because I'm breathing now.'*

VIC: *'Well, I suppose in that respect it is.'*

MAN: *'I've had two heart attacks, angina, a stroke and gall stones in the last three years. I was dead on arrival when I got to hospital.'*

VIC: *'So we're actually looking at a miracle.'*

We crossed a field that doubled as a football pitch, climbed over a gate and walked up through a housing estate where we met a woman who was laying crazy paving in her front garden. She gave us the directions to climb up Pool Bank. We walked down a street of semi-detached red-brick houses and rejoined the main road where traffic was thundering into Leeds. In a hollow completely overshadowed by the massive bank was a gloomy stone house that builders were in the process of renovating. They assured me that this was a public bridleway but it seemed the owners had cleverly removed any signs telling you that that was the case. Vic and I climbed up the hill relatively slowly, although for him, Mr Super-Fit, it presented no problem. I, of course, am not so fast early in the morning and I toiled up slowly. When we'd almost got to the top the crew appeared. 'Why didn't you bloody well film us climbing up the hill,' I screamed. By now we were on the flat bit. Time and time again they never seemed to understand how quick it would be for us to climb hills compared to them and we were constantly getting to the top of them or down them before they arrived on the scene.

I asked Vic when he'd started walking. 'I used to think when I was a child, why are my parents so keen on walking, there is no point to it, then all of a sudden you start doing what they were doing,' he said.

We crossed the main A660 into Leeds and took a turning up to Bramhope village. This was the heart of the Leeds commuter belt. White paint and dolled-up houses were everywhere you looked. Hanging baskets proliferated. In the centre of the village we turned left, heading east towards Leeds. Now Vic decided to break away from the suggested route and once again try and walk in a straight line. I agreed with him as there are few things as boring as constantly sticking to some easy to follow route chosen by our researcher that seemed to involve lots of footpaths and suburban roads. We walked through a gate and into a rugby ground. Using the compass we plotted our route south-easterly and pretty soon walked past the clubhouse. Outside two men were tending a barbecue. Instead of the normal kind of barbecue you'd expect rugby players to have (giant pork sausages, steaks and hamburgers) this was a bit of a designer barbecue, with rows and rows of red, green and yellow peppers roasting over the charcoal, smelling delicious. The two blokes didn't look like rugby players either. When we walked up they laughed and offered us some peppers that we ate greedily. I asked if it was a rugby club reunion. No, they said, but didn't elaborate. Out of the clubhouse a man emerged wearing a shower hat on his head. Over the shower hat was a wreath of weeds, pink flowers and white daisies, dandelions, and knotted into it were huge bunches of dried grass. It seemed to be some bizarre harvest festival celebration. I thought it was a typical Vic Reeves surreal stunt that he had secretly organized, but for once Vic was as astonished as me! The man was wearing a T-shirt and shorts and looked a bit embarrassed. Behind him stood about half a dozen people in their 20s. 'What on earth's going on?' I said. 'Is this some kind of weird rugby club initiation ritual?' It emerged that they were all employed by the same company and this was an awayday where they were learning to bond with each other and develop team spirit. I was speechless. I couldn't see how wearing a shower hat and a crown of dandelions made you bond with anything. We pressed them on what company had decided that this was the best way of improving the workforce's morale. They wouldn't say, perhaps terrified of losing their jobs.

Vic and I waved goodbye and struck out in a south-easterly direction across the rugby pitch, passing an empty stand until we came to the edge of a field where we climbed over a gate and passed through a succession of fields heading towards Leeds. We'd left far behind the village of Bramhope. When you travel in a car Leeds seems to have joined up with Bradford, spreading its urban tentacles for miles over the surrounding hills. On our walk we discovered that Leeds had many green arteries and was a very pleasant city with the countryside reaching almost to the centre. The housing estates of course cling to the road.

Vic and I walked for a couple of miles through fields, avoiding bulls. We crossed Marsh Beck which Vic did rather stylishly using a leaping technique inspired by Evil Knievel. He went off in a reverie, 'A lovely old bridge from where farms used to be farms and the farmer would have crossed on there with his ox and cart piled high with wheat and Constables.' Vic is potty, no two ways about it, constantly muttering asides as we walked.

At one point we walked through a boggy section, and then suddenly came to a beautiful but completely deserted farm. It seemed extraordinary that no commuters had seized on this real estate opportunity. It was marked as Rushes Farm on the map. Huge barns lay derelict with their doors bricked up. I had to dissuade Vic from shinning up a ten-foot stone wall to keep to our line. He had cow shit on his jacket where he'd fallen over painting the water-colour. Now he'd walked through a cow pat and his trainers looked disgusting. I was planning to take him to tea at the bungalow where he grew up. Would the current occupiers let this poo-covered madman through the door?

Vic forgot his hangover and started bleating about his lunch. I'd stupidly mentioned how great fish and chips were at Bryan's in Headingley. He started moaning about were we going to make a detour to it, and I rapidly had to change the subject as we were nowhere near it.

Carrying on, we reached a plantation in the centre of which was a fishpond. Vic was being irritatingly pedantic about our straight-line route.

VIC: *'There's a footpath but we need to go across that pond.'*

JANET: *'We're not doing it, let's just follow the footpath round.'*

VIC (POINTING TO A FISHING PLATFORM): *'Look, there's an entrance.'*

JANET: *'Don't even think about it.'*

VIC: *'And that's where we get out, over there. Do you think it's filthy?'*

JANET: *'Yeah, I do, I'm not swimming, look at the weather. It could harbour all sorts of germs. Please, let's just walk around the edge.'*

VIC: *'Straight across.'*

JANET: *'You're not going straight across, please'.*

VIC: *'Shall I?'*

JANET: *'You don't have to, look, it's not a loss of face.'*

VIC: *'I haven't got my underpants on.'*

That decided me. I firmly marched Vic round the pond to the footpath. He looked enough like a tramp covered in muck without getting wet as well. I implored him to wash his legs down before we got to his old house in Adel, as the lady was really looking forward to seeing him.

Three anglers were silently watching the water, resolutely ignoring us. Now we got ourselves in a bit of a mess because if we carried on in straight line we had to plough our way through a field planted with corn, so we climbed over a gate and found a footpath right on the other side of it and so needn't have gone through any nettles and scratchy weeds. Next we circumnavigated a golf course taking care not to cross a green. We met a woman who was having trouble with her shot and I asked her what was the problem. 'It's dreadful. I've really got to picture it now but I'm not very good at picturing, that's my problem,' she replied. I asked if Vic could help out, as he claimed to be an expert. He hit the ball straight into the bunker. 'I could have done it better myself,' she protested as all her companions fell about laughing. 'You've humiliated that woman, she's doing badly enough already, you could at least have aimed for the green,' I hissed at Vic as we made our excuses and left.

Then we met a couple of guys who were replanting a green and asked us to stamp in the turf for them, which we happily did. We climbed over a gate and emerged on to Holt Lane. We were now getting closer to Vic's childhood home in Adel. We decided to take a lunch break and sat on the pavement by a bit of green. No one batted an eyelid. Occasionally a telephone engineer's van or a post office van would go past but we passed 20 minutes in complete peace munching on our smoked salmon sandwiches before resuming our tramp through suburban Leeds.

We walked down a couple of roads and then on to one called The Drive, very original I thought. These houses were extremely grand and all had leaded windows, hanging baskets, gravel driveways; it looked completely cosy and comfortable and middle-class. I was beginning to accuse Vic of lying about his roots when we turned right into his street, New Adel Gardens. These were semi-detached bungalows much further down the income bracket than the lavish commuter homes we'd just passed. These looked as if they were still lived in by their original inhabitants. They were built in the late 1940s and early 1950s. At number 20 we walked up the driveway. The present owners were thrilled to see us and issued Vic and I with fluffy bedroom slippers so their carpet didn't get dirty. A big tea was laid out in the kitchen. The lady had made a carrot cake, a fruit cake and a Madeira cake, and had set out a bowl full of crisps and another one full of chocolate bars.

The lady of the house, a straight-backed prim and proper woman with grey hair, took us on a tour of the place. The room that Vic had slept in faced the street. We walked around the garden that now had had a lot of time and effort spent on it. Then it was back to the front room for more tea. The lady had asked all the neighbours what they remembered of Vic and one astonishing fact emerged – apparently quite a few of the people who had lived there when he grew up were still local residents and the one thing they remembered about him was that he used to go and pee in everybody's gardens. He looked dumbfounded. 'I'm sorry,' she said, 'that's the only thing they remember about you.' It was the first time all day I'd seen Vic lost for words. He'd been burbling on about the leopardskin carpet the living room had had in his day. Now he was strangely silent. To make him feel a bit better I told him I remembered growing up in Fulham in west London, and I used to go to everybody else's birthday parties whether I was invited or not, eat all the food, attempt to win at all the games, and then try and open their presents. My mother would be asked to collect me and I would be sick on the way home, often in somebody's garden. 'Great team we could have made,' Vic said, reassured he wasn't the only one with unpleasant childhood habits. Then I remembered being sick on my new shoes and my mother hitting me around the head all the way home. The lady of the house was starting to look a bit queasy and I thought we might be overstaying our welcome. So, full of carrot cake,

Madeira cake and a couple of Wispas, we put our muddy shoes back on by her front door, said our goodbyes, and left. Vic saw the wooden number 20 sign by the front door that had been made by his dad. He was starting to get a bit sentimental, so I dragged him back on to our route.

It had been a bit of a detour to New Adel Gardens and I wanted to return to my line so we headed east along Adel Lane and then dropped all the way down a hill heading south. Then we crossed the ring road and once more were in the countryside. We decided to follow the Meanwood Trail as far as we could towards the city centre as it very closely followed our line. From suburbia now we were back in the countryside. People were horseriding and walking and enjoying this urban trail. It contoured along a ridge and then down through a valley heading south-east towards Leeds city centre, completely secluded and rural. It was now about 2.30 pm. We'd started walking at 10.30 am and only had a 20-minute stop for lunch. We both felt very tired. I think it was all the scrambling over gates and the endless meeting of people. Vic was desperate to do some shopping in Harvey Nichols and kept mentioning it over and over again like a religious mantra.

The trail went round the back of some houses and we could see a large building site over to our left. Eventually we emerged on to Monks Bridge Road by a tattoo studio and decided to call it a day.

We got a lift into Leeds city centre. At Harvey Nichols, I looked at Vic and his outfit was truly disgraceful. One foot had gone in a large cow pat. He had cow poo all over his foot, all over his sock, up his leg and then there was the cow muck on his white designer jacket. It didn't seem to bother him. The doorman at Harvey Nichols let us in without batting an eyelid. We must have been the only two shoppers with rucksacks and I had a walking stick. We looked like crusties come to invade the store. Vic headed straight for the menswear department where he bought an expensive pair of Gucci jeans and an equally pricey sweater. He perked up. 'What about changing your socks,' I said. 'No, I'll have to wear these tomorrow for continuity,' he said, smirking. We had a cup of tea in the café in Harvey Nichols. Around us were the middle-class gentry of Leeds, shopping, snacking and checking out what each other was wearing. The main colour theme in the store seemed to be grey as per the latest issue of *Vogue*. To me the whole store seemed to be four floors of grey clothes and then a ground floor with a lot of expensive make-up. Vic and I headed for the facepack section. His skin had gone bright red from exposure to the elements and so had mine so we invested in a couple of costly tubes of face cream for calming down sensitive skin. Clutching our purchases we drove back to Pateley Bridge. It was 6.30 pm and I was shattered.

I dropped Vic off, went home, had a very quick bath and then picked him up and drove over to McCoys restaurant near Northallerton for dinner. Eugene McCoy and his brothers Peter and Tom are old friends and Vic had been desperate to go and see them. It was 11 pm when we finally left the restaurant. I was shattered. Luckily someone else drove us back. Vic lay on the back seat and snored and farted all the way. When we got to the Sportsman's Arms I tried to get him out of the car. He was incoherent. I got him on his feet, opened the door of the hotel, pointed him in the direction of the stairs and gave him a small push. I'd hoped he would find his way to bed. I got home brain dead. The next day I had to walk into the centre of Leeds and my head was exploding. I took three headache pills and passed out. It was a dreamless sleep.

TO LEEDS CITY CENTRE

I picked Vic up at the hotel. He seemed none the worse for wear after last night. We drove to Monks Bridge Road in Headingley. We turned off by the tattoo studio and continued along the Meanwood Trail. It was a narrow pathway between the houses that eventually re-entered trees and a valley. It was thoroughly enjoyable. I couldn't believe how close we were to the centre of Leeds. On our right we could see the backs of some grand Headingley houses. We seemed to be miles from anywhere and yet we were so close to a busy city.

Vic regaled me with the story of the time Alan Yentob, then the boss of BBC1, had invited him to a meeting at Television Centre at the end of the day, and on the spur of the moment cajoled Vic into accompanying him to a dinner at the Tate Gallery, claiming that David Bowie would be sitting at their table and Vic would get to meet Princess Diana. Neither were sitting anywhere near Vic but undeterred, he went up to Diana and said, 'I see you're looking at me, I've noticed you winking at me all night. Sorry, I'm not available.' She said, 'No, I was just looking at your striped jumper,' so he said, 'Well, you're not having it then!' Vic added, 'God, I got completely wrecked that night.' I imagined Alan Yentob dying of embarrassment!

We emerged on to Grove Lane, crossed over it and continued on the trail heading south-east. The tracks eventually joined up with Cumberland Road, a grand road of posh mansions that are now part of the university. We headed south along it to Headingley Lane, the A660. Crossing the road we decided to make a small detour into Headingley (a little bit off the route) to take a look at an extraordinary cinema, one that Vic had assured me was one of the oldest in England and was still lit by gas. He's a great walking companion, a mine of useless information. Heading along Victoria Road we were now in the part of Headingley with back-to-back houses, and many of them had steel bars and grills over the windows and looked like fortresses. Occasionally a car would go past with music booming from its sound system. I'd been told that when the police try to raid these houses it's so hard to get in that the people inside have longer to get rid of the drugs. These houses form an interesting pattern of streets and it seems a shame that the area has degenerated like this. It's also where a lot of the students live but as it was the holidays there wasn't much sign of life. Vic was waxing lyrical about the brickwork, when he suddenly grilled me about how often I dyed my hair red. He claimed to do his own roots once a month.

On the corner of Brudenell Road and Queens Road stood the cinema. It too had metal gates locked and padlocked firmly. I was cross we hadn't rung the owner in advance to look inside it. It was charming but all around it the streets looked derelict and the houses poverty-stricken and run down. As I approached the cinema a small black boy of about 12 with a shaven head was selling drugs to a girl of about ten. He got them out of his sock and gave her some folded up bits of paper. We got right up close to him before he noticed he was being filmed. He looked a right little scallywag with a gold chain and the face of a much older man. It was thoroughly depressing. One of their mates hung around for a bit but then, realizing that his face might be on camera, he scarpered. I don't know why the government spends all its time and effort moaning about drugs and teenagers when it's people of this age they should be dealing with. There's nothing sadder than seeing 10- and 12-year-olds smoking dope and buying whatever they were buying; I just hoped it wasn't heroin but there's a huge problem in Leeds and this is one of the places where it all goes on. The cinema must have been really tiny but as we couldn't get inside we tried to work out how many rows it had. The posters indicated it showed Asian films but more than that we couldn't find out. I asked a small boy what the cinema was like inside. 'Shit,' he replied, so we were none the wiser.

We headed east along Brudenell Road to Hyde Park where we crossed over the park and found an old stone milepost by the road that said it was 187 miles to London. The way that I planned to go, trying to keep to my straight line and not always succeeding, means that it probably won't be 187 miles but many more by the time I get there. The park was deserted. Vic told me that his granddad once went for a drink at the Skyrack pub down the road and went home afterwards forgetting he'd left Vic's dad in the pram outside.

We walked along the main road until we came to an imposing statue of Queen Victoria surrounded by a prim flowerbed. This marked the beginning, not only of the centre of Leeds, but also of the university campus. We headed down Clarendon Road and entered the university along University Road. There was a wide variety of architectural styles here and surprisingly quite a lot of people. It throbbed with activity in spite of being the summer holidays. I guess these were all the retake victims. I have always liked the fact that Leeds University has a fine engineering department housed in the grand buildings that you see from the A660. They look like something that you'd expect to find in Russia or St Petersburg rather than in central Leeds. Now our route took us through a jumble of various styles until we entered a wonderful section which had been used for the filming of *Blake's Seven*. You don't get more 1960s than this. Tubular raised walkways had strange shapes punched out of them. Nothing was a square as all corners had been rounded off to look terribly modern and space-age, and concrete was everywhere you looked. Some of it had been rather softened by the introduction of Japanese-style gardens but then there were concrete piazzas with large expanses of water. It just seemed so perfectly typical of an era where going to university was meant to be exciting and avant-garde.

University campuses from the 1960s are in a league of their own when it comes to architectural statement. Think of East Anglia, Sussex and now Leeds. Here octagonal concrete planters were filled with no plants but only gravel. They were probably full of students' fag-ends during the term. Vic declared, 'This, my friends, is the future,' flapping his arms about in true oratorical style, to a non-existent audience. 'Yes,' I replied, 'the whole world will look like a shopping precinct.'

We emerged in the city centre and paused in front of the stupendous City Hall, another massive classical building, and went down the hill to emerge by the Town Hall with its classical columns and imposing façade, designed by Cuthbert Broderick. This is a building I remember so well from my childhood when my father (then an electrician) sent my mother, sister and I a postcard of the Town Hall from Leeds. It is still the same blackened majestic building today. Thankfully it hasn't been cleaned yet. The scale of it really impressed me as a ten-year-old. Maybe it's one of the reasons I studied architecture, who knows? Leeds has many fine buildings but the other thing you notice about the town is the huge number of clocks. Every civic building has a clock. Loads of shops have large clocks. Clocks loom at you from every corner.

We headed east along the Headrow. City workers were on their lunch break and started to recognize Vic in rather alarming numbers. We reached Briggate, now a pedestrian shopping precinct and the home of Harvey Nichols. This was where Vic and I were going to part. He had planned to spend the rest of the afternoon doing even more shopping for his holiday and I was going to head on out of town. We walked down Briggate, the arcades on either side were full of trendy shops. I said goodbye to Vic outside Harvey Nichols. A doorman in a posh uniform opened the glass door for him and he happily entered wearing the same outfit that he'd had on yesterday, still with cow muck on his socks, shoes and white jacket. He seemed totally unfazed by his appearance.

I walked down Briggate past Dysons, established as a pawn brokers and jewellers in 1835 but now a trendy restaurant with surely the grandest clock in Leeds on its front. At the bottom of Briggate I went under the railway bridge, headed down the hill along Bridge End and over the river, where massive gentrification and restoration is taking place. The problem with Leeds is that the city centre is spectacular but going anywhere in a car around Leeds is ghastly. It has ring-roads, through roads, inner-city ring-roads and God knows what heading in every direction, and you have to be thoroughly vigilant not to end up in Ilkley or Harrogate. After I left the River Aire I walked through the ghastliness of a massive road intersection. I headed along Meadow Lane, crossed Great Wilson Street and was in a huge one-way system. I walked along Dewsbury Road on the A653 passing the gas works on my right. There was very little human habitation here. I went past the old Tetley's brewery. This is the home of giant superstores, and large signs overhead marked the start of the M1 to London. I'd have to work out how to start my journey to London from Leeds without walking along the sliproad on to the M1.

I decided to leave that problem for another day. It started to rain. Lorries passing me on their way to the M1 hooted and waved. I got my black plastic raincoat out and thought, that's it, I've done Leeds, what's the next big town? I didn't think I was going to go through another before London.

SOUTH OF LEEDS TO RYHILL
Executive sex and the nondescript

I arrived in Leeds the night before my next walk after a disastrous train journey from London. All was going well until just before Wakefield where we stopped and were told that a train had broken down in front of us, blocking the line. Irritatingly it was called a unit in the new consumer-orientated world of GNER. Eventually we got into Wakefield to be told that it had broken down again in front of us. Then we reversed out of Wakefield, and went back into Wakefield, and then we had to get off the train and on to a dirty diesel train, finally arriving in Leeds an hour late. Then the taxi driver didn't know where the hotel was and worryingly took me down a street that turned out to be dead end by the canal which was a bit frightening. Finally I arrived at the hotel to be shown to a very nice room with a high vaulted ceiling and black-and-white striped walls. By then it was 9 pm and what should have been a simple journey had left me feeling exhausted. Without having a bath I just stuck on a different sweater and went down for dinner.

In the middle of the night I was woken up by a woman screaming her head off as she enjoyed executive sex. I stuck a pillow over my head and went back to sleep. In reception the next morning there were a load of women in those dreary blue suits so beloved of secretaries who've clawed their way up to the lower ranks of the marketing force. I tried to work out which one was the screamer from the night before.

I started by the junction of the A653 and the M1, Spaghetti Junction, hoping that I was on the right road. It was totally confusing, with endless walkways over the roads, not exactly pedestrian friendly. I had washed my hair that morning but I don't know why I bothered as I was covered in grime from the cars racing past. I stopped in a motorway service station to go to the loo.

A tailor's in a red-brick building stuck out incongruously amongst all the car breakers and second-hand car yards. Then two elegant white columns with 1858 emblazoned upon them announced Boyne Engine Works; now it was a low-level industrial park. I walked past a gospel hall (1932) with a big 'For Sale' sign in front of it, and then got lost by Hunslett Parish Church. Even the Leeds city map seemed to be out of date. Street signs were few and far between round here and there were loads of new roundabouts. This part of the city is a temple to the car. Whole communities have been removed to create motorways, feeder roads, one-way systems and roundabouts. I left the traffic and walked south along Belle Isle Road. Old terraced houses, new terraced houses, dual carriageways with grass down the middle, roses planted by the Council, rubbish everywhere, litter strewn on the sidewalk. I passed under the M1 as traffic thundered overhead.

Belle Isle was full of identical semi-detached brick houses. I walked across a large green roundabout sprouting a wooden sign that said welcome to Belle Isle North. It had no distinguishing features of any kind, except I was now in spick and span suburbia. Tidy, no vandalism, and a completely featureless suburb of Leeds. The new houses looked exactly like houses built in the 1930s except for the red wrought-iron gates and those horrible new fake-Georgian front doors. But I'm not knocking Belle Isle, because I've seen loads of worse suburbs than this.

Two women aged about 28 were screaming at their kids, pausing only to light fags and puff on them. I've never spent a day walking before where I've seen so many people smoking. Is it something about south Yorkshire? They drive round with fags hanging out of their mouths or hanging out of the car window, they pick their kids up from school with fags in one hand, and clearly fags play a big part of their lives in a way that you just wouldn't see in London.

I walked up a long straight road climbing all the time, past the Belle Isle working men's club, a grim-looking brick building. Sharp Lane had new little boxes, detached houses complete with ruched blinds, woodwork at the back, conservatories and barbecues in the gardens. In the background there was the distant roar of the M1. The grass verge full of rubbish, brambles, then – hoorah! – the bridge over the M1, which would take me out of Leeds and towards Wakefield.

In the rest of the country it was a sweltering hot day but here between Leeds and Wakefield the sky was uniformly grey and there was a strange smell in the air that never left my walk that day. I was beginning to get obsessed that I had trodden in something until I realized that the whole place just had a strange smell about it. If it wasn't one kind of farming smell, it was another kind of dubious industrial type smell.

As I crossed over the streams of traffic below I decided that I was probably halfway on my journey from Edinburgh to London. Now I was going to walk through south Yorkshire, a very different environment to the bleak moors of the north Pennines and the heathery perfection of the dales. I would be seeing a part of the country that had seen enormous change over the past few years. The old heavy industries like coal and steel had virtually died out, but what had replaced them? I looked forward to finding out.

I walked down a main road, cut along a lane running parallel to the M1 where there was a surprisingly pretty row of cottages only a couple of hundred yards from Britain's most loathsome motorway. Bizarrely, in the gardens of two of the houses were large boats that looked as if they had been there for decades, nettles and weeds growing right around them. In another lay an abandoned caravan.

The suburbs between Leeds and Wakefield are a curious mixture of stone cottages, luxury bungalows, middle-class semi-detached houses and occasionally real architectural gems from the last century that are now surrounded by housing estates. There is a love of leaded windows and a surprisingly large amount of middle-class homes in an area where unemployment is high and much change has happened over the last two decades. It's an area split by roads, the M62, the M1 and now the new relief road from the A1 to the M1. I hadn't escaped these roads yet, as I was to discover during the next few hours.

I walked to an area called Robin Hood, vaguely following the A61, then through a housing estate and then across my first golf course of the day at somewhere called Lofthouse Hill. This golf course was still being built. The drab red-brick clubhouse was already finished and a portacabin had a sign on it grandly announcing 'Academy of Golf'. It's a long way from the Royal Academy in Piccadilly to a prefab on an old slagheap outside Wakefield, but I suppose they are both temples of learning, in their way.

Some golfers were out playing on a couple of holes even though the course wasn't finished. Avoiding them, I continued through suburbia. I crossed a second golf course, followed a main road round and was right outside Pinderfields Hospital on the edge of Wakefield. All the public land that I'd crossed so far seemed very scrubby and dried out when we were supposed to have had one of the wettest summers on record. I turned down a narrow footpath at the back of the housing estate.

Ahead of me lay the River Calder and the Aire and Calder Navigation Canal, in a large area of farmland and wasteland that has been reclaimed. Old quarries, tips, weirs and locks – it sounds much more romantic than it really was.

North of Leeds I'd been tramping on peat but now I was walking over coal. So much money could be made from it in the 18th century that the mine owners were willing to invest heavily in the latest transport systems to carry it out. And that meant canals.

The River Aire became navigable to Leeds in 1700. It rapidly became a commercial success, transporting coal from Yorkshire's coalfields and bringing in raw wool, corn and agricultural products. Within ten years it was the premier navigation route in

England, linking the port of Goole to Leeds. The network was extended when the Leeds and Liverpool Canal was completed in 1816. To compete with the railways, the waterway was adapted to allow steam haulage, with bigger locks and higher bridges. The canal has never stopped being used as a commercial waterway. From the 1960s it was used to supply over 1 million tonnes of coal a year to the new Ferrybridge Power Station. Today, more than two and a half million tonnes of coal are transported each year on it, but with the regeneration of the surrounding area and the creation of new nature reserves, its leisure activities have also increased.

Down in the valley by Ramsdens Bridge I could see the umbrellas of fishermen set up for the day. I crossed a field where the hay had been cut, scratchy and hard beneath my feet. A lady was out walking with her child who was wearing one roller-skate and whinging. I came to the bridge over the canal. Next to it was a large pale-blue metal bridge for crossing the river. Then I passed under my first railway of the day. Apart from being intersected by canals and motorways the area is also criss-crossed with railways. This was a fine viaduct. Underneath it lay a disused railway embankment. I climbed up on to it and followed a footpath to a main road, turning right and eventually arriving in the pretty village of Heath.

Set around a village green this 18th-century village is full of fine buildings, including Heath Hall, for sale at the ridiculously low price of £225,000 (ridiculously low, that is, in terms of London prices). Built in 1707, it was altered and extended by John Carr between 1754 and 1780, and used as a military hospital in World War I. Between the wars it was unoccupied, then it became a World War II army base. Between 1962 and the early 1980s it was extensively restored.

Perched high above Wakefield this is a good example of one of the expensive pockets of living that exists side by side with prefabs and bungalows in this mixed-up part of Britain. Originally Heath had three big houses around its large common: James Paine's

Heath House, John Carr's Heath Hall, and Heath Old Hall, demolished in 1961 following mining subsidence. The development of the village was largely due to the Smyth family, successful West Riding wool staplers who invested much of their surplus capital in landed estate and by exchanging properties; they began to build up their estate on the meadows above the Calder, starting with the buildings around Heath Hall. It seemed a debate raged now between residents of Heath on the conservation of the village, some residents believing that further building should be allowed for progress to continue.

At the end of the village green I crossed Heath Common, picking up a B road in the direction of Walton. I went under another railway arch, this one even bigger than the last and more magnificent, although covered with huge graffiti. One slogan just said 'grim'. They could say that again, I thought, as I picked my way through rubbish, nettles, Tizer bottles and black plastic bags.

I crossed some disused mineworkings that had been turned into a nature reserve. Waterways had been made out of the disused Barnsley Canal and two fishermen were sitting on the banks waiting for nibbles. A large sign read, 'No fires, no swimming, no litter, no shooting (a bit of a worry, that one), no live baiting, no spinning, no keep nets, barbless hooks only, no night fishing and no fish to be removed from the water'. How many 'no's' could there be on one sign?

I could get no sense out of one of the fishermen; perhaps years of handling maggots had affected his brain. Here's how the conversation went:

JANET: *'What have you caught?'*

MAN: *'A few perch.'*

JANET: *'Do you eat them or chuck 'em back?'*

MAN: *'Oh no, I don't eat them.'*

JANET: *'Why, do they taste horrible?'*

MAN: *'The thing is, German people and French people will eat any fish as you may know. The British are very funny about their fish.'*

JANET: *'Have you ever eaten perch?'*

MAN: *'It's not cod or haddock, is it? I've eaten roach, certainly.'*

JANET: *'What does it taste like?'*

MAN: *'Quite reasonable. But not in this country. Well, it's a British tradition, apart from trout and salmon, people don't eat the fish they catch.'*

JANET: *'I thought you were going to say it's a British tradition to have a lot of rules about any bit of open space.'*

MAN: *'And of course even sea fish, if it's not plaice, haddock or cod, the British won't really touch it. I love it. I love all sorts of fish, but the average British person won't touch them.'*

I said goodbye, walked across the nature reserve, pondering his logic. Here there were swans, seagulls and ducks. It seemed an idyllic spot and people were out walking their dogs and enjoying the afternoon that was gradually turning to sunshine. Following one of the active railway lines I crossed under it at a point called Nine Arches. Then after a short spell along the main road I turned south-east on the edge of the village of Walton and crossed a field where you could obviously see a wealthy hand had been at work 100 years ago planting magnificent trees. At the end of the field was a high wall. This marked the end of the estate of Charles Waterton who had lived at Walton Hall nearby until his death in 1865.

Below, on an island, in the centre of a lake, was Waterton's House, now a hotel. From this distance it looked an idyllic setting. I was looking forward to staying there later.

I followed this extremely high wall, climbing over several stiles, until we emerged on to yet another golf course. Was Waterton's dream reduced to this? I talked to two golfers. One turned out to be a retired policeman from East Anglia who had

had his own crime-solving programme on local television. He seemed well informed about Charles Waterton, but thought a golf course a wonderful improvement to the landscape, pointing out that the arable land opposite had once been open-cast workings, and that a golf course provided employment. I still thought that golf courses were a pretty sadistic way of improving on nature.

Charles Waterton, born in Wakefield in 1782, was known as the father of taxidermy. He was a keen naturalist and roamed the world collecting wild animals, which he used to allow to wander freely in the grounds of his estate, making the world's first nature reserve. Apparently he called it 'this little rural theatre', and he wandered the grounds barefoot, reading Latin poetry.

I left the golf course and headed over the brow of a hill, around some woods and entered farmland on the edge of another nature reserve. Skirting a large area of water, I came to Hawpark Lane. On the other side of the road there was the sailing club of Wintersett Reservoir, itself built to supply the Barnsley Canal. By now I was feeling pretty tired and when Jonathan from the sailing club offered to take me across the reservoir in his dinghy it was an offer I couldn't refuse. He obviously fancied himself as a hunk in trunks because even though the danger of falling in was pretty minimal, he was wearing a completely skin-tight wetsuit with Bermuda shorts and a sleeveless jerkin. I refused to wear the life vest as I can swim two miles and doubted that I would come to my death by drowning in a completely calm reservoir. He fired up the outboard and off we started. Jonathan told me that every weekend there were highly competitive sailing races on the reservoir. I wondered how boring it was to go round and round the same stretch of water but he seemed to have been doing it for over ten years. The sun came out and although there was a chilly breeze it was a pleasant way to end the afternoon. He took me to the southern edge of the reservoir and found a spot where I could gingerly get ashore. I climbed through some undergrowth until I found a path. Unfortunately it was covered in brambles.

I headed in the direction he had vaguely pointed towards Ryhill but I got lost and ended up walking in completely the opposite direction until someone came and found me. I suppose when you walk mile upon mile and you forget to put your compass on that's the kind of thing that happens at the end of the day.

I got a lift to Wakefield Art Gallery, to take a look at their Charles Waterton memorabilia. It was pretty impressive. An oil painting by Captain E. Jones in 1824 showed the great man capturing a cayman (a kind of crocodile) by sitting on its back, while a line-up of natives pulled man and beast along by a rope! In a case of taxidermy, there were several of his 'creations', weird one-offs he made by putting odd pieces together. The 'Nondescript' looks like a man with a beard, but was made from a monkey's backside. A leaflet told me more bizarre facts about Waterton. He always slept on the floor, wrapped in a blanket, with an oak block for a pillow. I hoped that things had moved on at Waterton Hall since then.

Back at the hotel some golfers were in full swing and the bar was jammed with corporate hospitality and people on conferences. The menu was pretentious and nothing was simple. Avocado had to be baked, asparagus to have ham wrapped round it, steak to have slimy sauces and salmon to come *en croute*. I managed to sort out the first course by asking for a plain avocado with plain asparagus, but the main course was a problem. I had the salmon but the pastry was grey, having been prepared in some factory miles away, and the vegetables were either undercooked or overcooked, microwaved in any case. The wine was good though. On the next table there were ten people on a conference. They sounded as if they were in marketing, all very pleased with the sound of their own voices – south Yorkshire's answer to the spin-doctors of the South. The noise level was incredible and they kept using marketing jargon I can't cope with, like 'interface' and 'feedback'. After an hour or so I was completely fatigued as looking at maps until 11 pm really does your head in. I went back to my room and fell asleep making lists of things I'd have to do tomorrow.

DAY 24

RYHILL TO DARFIELD
Pigeon fanciers on the Internet

The television news said it was sunny with above average temperatures everywhere in Britain – except here in south Yorkshire where a uniform grey pall had settled over the entire sky. It was quite cold as I walked down a bridleway out of Ryhill round the back of some new little brick boxes that were just being completed. The path was full of people taking their dogs out for an early-morning poo on the path. Some of the new homes had got hopeful barbecue sets in the garden, brand new teak garden furniture and laundry trees festooned with wet washing that would surely never dry in this weather. Back on the fields the farmers were starting to plough them up. These fields weren't as enormous as I've encountered round here, being still almost human-sized. There was a story on the breakfast news this morning about the Australian government's plans to extract oil from underneath the Great Barrier Reef. Will the result be an environmental disaster along the scale of what I'm walking through in south Yorkshire?

Last night at dinner we discussed whether it would be worthwhile getting an environmentalist in the film to talk about what's happened to this landscape, and whether replacing a lot of coal tips with endless pools of water for fishermen is in fact a long-term solution. Wouldn't we be better off creating jobs for people and places that teenagers could enjoy? On the evidence of what I've seen all these nature reserves are just like sticking a postage stamp on a great big sore, and nothing has been created for young people like bike tracks or skateboard parks. In the middle of Britain's industrial heartland we've probably got the largest number of nature reserves in the country, like a kind of mini-wetlands. There's no evidence that the people who live around here either want this or want to use it.

I crossed a field of stubble that was parched, dry, cracked and hard underfoot. The church at Felkirk appeared through the mist. For one brief moment I could have been in southern England, until I saw the network of pylons in the background. I crossed a huge ploughed field, all the hedgerows gone, to the church. I trudged another field wearily and saw enclosed within double barbed wire an old disused railway line. I joined that for easier walking down the hill. It was a riot of berries and rosehips so autumn had well and truly arrived.

I passed two other walkers, the first I'd seen for days. They were two men in their 60s who looked like ex-miners. One was wearing rather unexpected camouflage kit but they both had rucksacks and sticks, and bid me a cheery good morning as I went under the inevitable pylons, two sets criss-crossing each other. As I climbed up to Shepton the smell was back. This time it could be horse manure. It was very strong.

The clicking of the pylons was punctuated by the cheeping of thousands of starlings surrounding them, swooping in and out of the wires. I went past some intensively worked allotments, where one had no vegetables but thousands of chrysanthemums all flowering in a profusion of colours. A garage door was open, and inside stacks of Chinese lanterns stared at me, grinning insanely with Halloween faces on them. Outside a van was parked, 'Wholesale party and greeting cards' written on its side. Then it was immaculate bungalows with perfect gardens, nets washed to within an inch of their life. Across the A628 I headed towards Grimethorpe. People in cheap cars were driving them like Ferraris. Women in Adidas sweatpants were coming out of the village shop carrying the paper and a packet of fags. There's not much evidence that people round here do any walking at all except to exercise the dog or go to the village shop. I passed the working men's club and was back in open countryside. Attached to the lampposts were protest signs saying 'Ban open-cast mining'. Huge lorries crashed along the road carrying earth, covering me in dust. Every now and then a wally in a white Bedford van recognized me and hooted.

I approached the Grimethorpe link road, phase 1, stage 1, partly funded by Barnsley Capital Challenge Programme and partly assisted by the European Regional Development Fund, in other words a giant new road linking Grimethorpe with the outside world. This part of the road was finished and workmen were digging and drilling furiously to landscape it. It went about a quarter of a mile and culminated in a roundabout bypassing Grimethorpe itself.

I decided to go and investigate. Grimethorpe was a profoundly depressing place. Derelict houses, row upon row of terraced houses, and semi-detached miner's houses. There was a drab uniformity about the entire place. A village built around pits that were closed for good in 1993, cut off from main roads, with poor public transport. How could they hope to attract new business and new employers? Unemployment ran at 33 per cent, compared to 12 per cent in neighbouring Barnsley, and almost 40 per cent of the locals had to find work outside the area. People here live on an average annual income of just £8,000 a household, compared to the national average of £20,000. And yet Grimethorpe has a unique spirit. The Colliery Band, started in 1917, is still going strong, now sponsored by RJB Mining. The band starred in the hit film *Brassed Off*, about closures in the mining industry, and play concerts all over the place. I walked up to a group of buildings that used to be the headquarters of the National Coal Board. Upstairs a band rehearsal for a concert in Switzerland was in full swing. Downstairs were the offices of Grimethorpe Electronic Village Hall, funded by Lottery and European money, which provides computer facilities and training on the Internet, giving locals the opportunity to become computer literate. It had been set up by Archie Kearford and John Fraser, two local men previously employed by British Coal until the mine closed.

Archie was large, jolly and had a fine line in self-deprecation and lots of jokes about Grimey (Grimethorpe). John had got a job as the IT adviser to Sheffield Wednesday football club. It seemed their centre was a huge success and people of all ages were dropping in to use it, from kids to the local pigeon club – there's not much to do in Grimethorpe.

John and Archie spoke movingly of the mining spirit that prevails in the village, because although the mines have closed this spirit carries on. In the old days people used to go on holiday together. They used to marry each other. On the way home from work they used to go and visit people who were ill. The pit brought everyone together. John and Archie are trying to bring back that spirit through the computer centre, but I couldn't imagine a more depressing place to grow up in if you are young. It seemed to me (and Archie and John agreed) that all the nature reserves were airy fairy ideas and what was needed were qualifications and jobs, and building a pond wasn't really going to help. Grimethorpe still didn't have a swimming pool although there was talk now of building a leisure centre, but an architect had drawn up new plans for the town centre which Archie and John regarded as laughable as it featured yet another pool called a water feature. What Grimethorpe seemed to need was a swimming pool, not a 'feature' which would be full of rubbish in about two minutes.

Archie told me that the Metro centre in Barnsley had a swimming pool but it cost £3 to use and was eight miles away. What use was that in a town where the young people had no prospect of a job? When Archie was at the local school it was never visited by a careers officer as it was just assumed as sure as day follows night that you would work for the National Coal Board. Grimethorpe couldn't be more in contrast to nearby Barnsley, which has an air of affluence, not to mention an incredibly complicated one-way system with endless roundabouts. There are brand new multi-storey car parks, shopping malls and the Metro centre with its big swimming pool.

According to Archie, their own project, having won Lottery funding, was now attracting the attention of people far and wide as a model of how to help the unemployed: 'We get visitors from all over the world, we've had the governments of Poland and Hungary come and have a look at what we're doing. As for Barnsley, we might as well be the little house on the prairie – they're not interested. I think the only two businesses left here that are fairly major employers are the brickworks and the double-glazing factory, employing about 80 people each.'

I asked John if he thought computers might replace the working men's club? After all, the pigeon club was here, putting their pigeons on the Internet. Once they might have been discussing their birds over a pint, but now they are tapping all the information in and communicating electronically. 'Computers can be sociable,' said John. 'The Internet allows you to come into contact with people who you wouldn't normally meet. As an unemployed person from the village you wouldn't come into contact with an airline pilot or even politicians, but the Internet and the communications technology that we have available to us now actually allows that and breaks down a lot of the social and political barriers. It's quite easy for people from Grimethorpe to talk to people in Russia.' Perhaps in a way that working men's clubs can't do? 'You can't get as drunk,' said Archie. 'Not in a virtual pub.' And we all laughed.

I walked back to the roundabout on the new road, the sound of the brass band wafting down the street. There used to be a joke that went, 'The only good thing about Grimethorpe is that it had two roads out of it!' Now there was a third, with the new one cut through the ruins of the old colliery. But rather than encouraging people to visit the village, might it just enable them to get past it quicker?

Past the roundabout it was like World War III. On either side were old open-cast mine workings and down the middle the brand new road was being finished. Men were going backwards and forwards on earth movers. Ahead were slagheaps grassed over but still incredibly ugly. Who would ever walk along this eight-foot-wide pavement? Who would use these giant roundabouts? What traffic would it generate and, more importantly, where would it be going to?

After a while the asphalt surface of the unfinished motorway petered out and then I walked for half a mile along a nastier surface, a railway track with great big chunks of stone. My hips were killing me and my legs felt like lead weights. I bathed all the grit out of my eyes with a bottle of mineral water, but they still felt sore and scratchy. I drank another bottle of water to try and remove the taste of dust from my throat. I could take the railway line no longer. It was a bit like a scene from the Japanese war movie *The Long March*, so I dropped down on to what looked like a ploughed field. In fact it was an old slagheap where the grass had been cut and it was like iron beneath my feet, unforgiving furrows that were just as bad as the railway track. I rejoined the railway, crossed a bridge and the river and finally made my painstaking way across a freshly ploughed field. Two herons rose up in front of me. I crossed over the stream and then followed a track up into the hamlet of Edderthorp. The noise of the road building was tremendous and at the end of it was an open-cast quarry just to add to the general visual aura of gloom and despondency.

I crossed another large ploughed field, the footpath totally eradicated. Finally I climbed a cobbled path with an old high stone wall alongside it, the Dearne Way, into Darfield.

DARFIELD TO POCKET HANDKERCHIEF LANE

So William Hague wasn't the school swot?

I walked up School Street, past stone cottages, the Conservative Club, and Darfield Cricket Club where a groundsman was busy attending to the pitch. Coronation Street was on my left. Darfield seemed to have lots of clubs and judging by the size and state of the ground I could tell I was now in a part of the country where cricket is important. The stone cottages had all been renovated with wisteria and ivy growing up them and pleasant gardens. They weren't big houses but they looked well cared for.

It was another grey day. Again on the television this morning I had seen it was sunny in the south of England but here south Yorkshire had grey cloud cover of a uniform thick nature. Leaves were rustling underfoot as I passed the cricket ground. It was well and truly autumn. There wasn't much sign of life here in suburban Darfield. Earlier, on the way here, I had passed a large industrial plant that looked like a chemical factory. It turned out to be a bread factory. At the hotel last night I had asked for fresh fruit for breakfast. 'We only serve tinned,' came the inevitable reply.

Darfield Village Club was a fine stone building built in 1911 with a pediment. Darfield Museum was two bow-fronted old stone cottages in a state of utter disrepair, but as there was a long list of sponsors nailed over the door, perhaps rejuvenation was beginning. School Street led into Vicar Road. The old houses had been prettied up with hanging baskets, shutters, fake stained-glass in the front doors, ruined only by the odd TV satellite dish. Some of the new houses opposite them had been tricked up to look like old houses, with fake stone, hanging baskets, leaded windows and fake stained glass. It's all a bit like trying to recreate a Hovis ad, a cosy view of post-industrial Britain that never really existed. Let's forget about the TB, poverty, clogs and early death.

As the road dropped steeply down ahead of me I could see more of the inevitable wasteland that passes for green. Further down the hill was posher Darfield, detached bungalows, ruthlessly manicured lawns, conifers sprouting and firmly kept in check, bow-windows (leaded of course) and the predictable line of wheelie-bins on the pavement blocking my path.

Three men in the space of ten minutes said hello, each out walking overweight black labradors. On the news this morning President Mandela had given his support to President Clinton over his sex scandal. I was getting thoroughly nauseated about the fact that everyone had now decided to say let's leave President Clinton alone. If he had been a woman she wouldn't be getting a second chance – she'd be down the dumper, hauled over the coals and out of office – but in this new age of morality everybody is so frightened about the alternative that they've decided to forgive and forget. Somehow it leaves me feeling thoroughly uncomfortable.

I joined a wide grassy footpath, the Dearne Way, alongside the River Dearne. On my right was a huge area of scrubby wasteland with water, geese and ducks, and pylons in every direction. There was a grey pall over the area, the sound of building work and construction resounding. Am I being snobby in so hating the landscape of south Yorkshire, finding it so unattractive? Is it because I've lived in north Yorkshire for 20 years where the green is luxuriant, the moors exhilarating and the vistas splendid? Here the green spaces are just what is left between the towns and they have been subjected to the ravages of heavy industry, intensive farming and speculative building. Now they have been taken over by nature parks, golf courses and even more house building, so although you may come across pretty pockets the sum total is unplanned and ultimately depressing, and if you lived here you would be wondering where to go for some real countryside. Even the horses that grazed in the meadow by the river didn't exactly look like pedigree animals, with long tails and piebald coats. Ten of these sad creatures were standing together huddled for warmth, as I passed, with their heads bowed and their tails flicking. Where is there to ride in this area criss-crossed by roads and railways? Do they just ride round and round in the same scrubby patch of land to the sound of earth movers and cement mixers?

In north Yorkshire the geography is clearly visible as generally the valleys run from west to east or north-west to south-east, delineated by drystone walls and B roads. Here the land only gently undulated, intersected by giant pylons, the river meandering along its course, with no one caring about the land on either side of it. It was surrounded by hawthorn run riot, scrubby nettles and weeds. The river itself was full of weeds and rubbish. The field on my left was being ploughed up.

I crossed another new road, the A61, and walked through a nature reserve, created this time from a former war-time airfield. The Old Moor Wetland Centre, as it has been renamed, was a tip where coal was stock-piled for the Wath Manvers Colliery until recently. A huge lake had been constructed, surrounded by a very wide sandy path, and shrubs were tidily planted. There was an interesting beach area with pebbles and strange shapes that resembled sunbeds made of rock stuck in the water. A boat ramp. I was sure it was well intentioned but the result was about as much to do with the real countryside as Disneyland. Behind me was a nature reserve where deep holes had been filled with water and there were swans and reeds, and the bulldozers were still in action finishing it off. As it had been open for only about four weeks, perhaps that is why it looked so unreal.

Now I was at yet another new road outside Wath upon Dearne. This was Tony Blair's Britain all right. Words like 'experience' and 'regeneration' were used in massive amounts round here. What does regeneration really mean? When it comes to the roundabout I was at, it seemed to mean putting a pile of rocks in the middle with one pointing up like a kind of fake druid stone. The pavements were especially irritating, divided into red stripes with bicycles painted on them and arrows and next to them ordinary asphalt with people painted on them as if you didn't understand it was a pavement. I looked across at the lake and saw a bleak landscape tidied up with loads of grants, but what had it really created? Was it anywhere the local people would really want to go? Already the telltale signs of hankies, tins, bits of plastic and rubbish were gathering in the shrubs round the edge. Would anyone ever actually sit on those blue metal benches so architecturally designed facing on to the bleak stretch of water? Wouldn't kids have preferred a cycle ramp, somewhere to get dirty in, somewhere a bit more jungly and exciting? Wasn't this just too tidy for words? Won't it just be another place for all the pot-bellied coarse fishermen I've seen so many of to sit, smoke endless fags with a tin of maggots by their side and wait for the perch to nibble at their bait, only to pluck it out of the water and throw it back again.

I entered Wath upon Dearne via a shoppers' car park, walked up the street, crossed by the bus station and then headed up out of town first by the primary school and then to the comprehensive where I was met by the headmaster, Mr Godber, who taught politics to William Hague. He said he had 1,700 pupils and 26 school buildings. They are dotted all around the campus, prefabs and temporary buildings, while the main Victorian school building was woefully inadequate. In spite of that he said they had done well when they'd been inspected by the authorities. I talked to him about having William Hague as a pupil and he was amazingly tactful.

This area was once called the Socialist Republic of South Yorkshire: it's the last home of the hard left – Arthur Scargill, Dennis Skinner and Tony Benn. It's strange then, that the most famous son of Wath upon Dearne is the leader of the Conservative Party. William Hague had been 16 years old, the same age as the people I'd seen lounging about in the playground with their Sporty Spice platform trainers and their

Adidas kitbags, when he addressed the 1977 Tory Party Conference and caused a sensation. It's hard to believe.

As we walked down the main corridor, I asked Mr Godber if the young William wasn't a bit of a weirdo? Mr Godber, white-haired, bespectacled and trim, was diplomacy itself: 'It was unusual but he actually found some kind of succour from that. I think it made him more determined.' Didn't he stand out at school? Was he one of those sneaky kids that everybody rather laughs at, a school swot? Mr Godber disagreed. 'Not in the least. He was very sociable with lots of friends and lots of normal activities,' he said. 'Lots more hair,' I couldn't resist adding rather sarkily.

Had anyone else from the school followed William Hague into politics? 'One or two people have gone from our sixth form into universities to read politics, and some of them are in local government. Quite a number are active in politics. And I'd like some more on the green benches. Not necessarily on the Conservative side, I have to say, in fact I'd very much like to get some balance.'

We walked past a display the students had put up to coincide with the school's European Awareness Week. But did he agree with William Hague about a single European currency? Mr Godber, diplomatic to the end, replied, 'I'm waiting for him to persuade me one way or the other.' Very worthy of a headmaster.

At this point the lunch bell went off and pandemonium reigned. Pupils wearing an amazing variety of sportswear (how it passes for school uniform I'll never know) and clumpy shoes pelted round the corner. I left the school noting that an ice cream van was parked in the playground doing astounding business. I wouldn't have permitted that if I were Mr Godber.

I walked up the busy main road at the side of the school heading south, past the Roman Catholic secondary school, which was surrounded by the kind of steel railings that would deter a riot. These pupils were wearing a stricter version of school uniform than that at William Hague's old school. Mr Godber told me that he had just introduced trousers for girls. The average skirt length seemed to be about one foot long, complete with Marks & Spencer's opaque tights and thick high-heeled black Doc Martens. Not much has changed since I was at school.

This was the middle-class part of Wath upon Dearne. Detached houses faced on to green open spaces, leaded windows much in evidence. Hanging baskets, of course, and a lot of Land Rover Discoveries in Wath Wood Road. A roundabout planted with red geraniums and a few starter homes marked the end of Wath upon Dearne and the beginning of Swinton. Under a charming canopy built in the 1940s and donated by a councillor I entered Creighton Woods and headed east along a well-used footpath. I passed two women pushing their kids and said hello to them as they recognized me. Two people came out of the woods in front of me, looked around very, very furtively and went back in again doing a lot of coughing. They were either smoking or taking drugs.

I crossed a field diagonally to a main road. The sun had at last come out and it was going to be a pleasant afternoon. In the middle of the stubble a pair of men's grey trousers lay discarded. I had to leave my line and walk around the edge of Swinton on the B6090, a circuitous route because I wasn't allowed to cross the railway line by the steel works at Thrybergh. I slapped some factor-20 on my face, took my sweater off, tied it round my waist and the sun went in. That was my 15 minutes of bronzing for the day. It had now reverted to the normal grey gloom.

South of the hill I was walking down lay a bleak industrial landscape, bisected by pylons and the steel works. I passed over the railway line, and the community centre in Kilnhurst was now renamed the Community Resource Centre, much more Tony Blair's Britain. On my right was the Kilnhurst working men's club. I crossed a canal and then the River Don with a railway running alongside it. You can tell the health of an area by the price of the used cars and the most expensive one in the lot on the road was £3,400. The pub had a 'For Sale' outside and the Jet petrol station was completely empty. Lorries went past continuously, interspersed with the odd tractor.

A sign announced environmental improvements for Kilnhurst, and not before time I'd say. Just after Rotherham United's training ground, Lodge Farm, I walked out of a pub car park and skirted a ploughed field. I had a fine view of the training ground and what a superb piece of green it was, with three or four pitches laid out on it. The best grass round here for miles.

I couldn't find a way out of my field and crawled through a bit of wood in the corner, over an old rubbish dump by a ruined house, then along an old track towards a car park full of cars. Yes, it was yet another golf course again, Thrybergh Park, that had a castellated Victorian building complete with two round turrets and square ones on the corners. I couldn't believe how many cars were parked there, it was jam packed. People had panama hats on. Caddies were sitting enjoying tea with their golf trolleys at their sides. What gentility after what I'd just walked through. The best thing about this walk was that at the points I felt low, my hips ached and my knee was really sore, I would see something as fantastic as this Victorian Gothic building with the ladies in their golf gear sipping tea, and it would lift my spirits. It was just so incongruous.

I walked out through an avenue of plane trees about 100 years old. A ladies' competition was in progress, and they seemed to be having a lot of trouble. Balls kept hitting trees, mingling with falling leaves and bouncing on the ground very definitely in the wrong place. At the entrance a sign boldly announced Rotherham Golf Club in dark green, looking very expensive.

In Thrybergh I went past some posh houses along the Doncaster Road, a fine Georgian manor house by the church and some very swanky new homes with high ornate wrought-iron gates and manicured lawns. Then it was through the poor part of Thrybergh over the hill to Dalton, past the terraced houses and the worker's cottages, when I emerged at Hollings Lane. I turned left by the working men's club and the post office, where sulky-looking mothers waiting for their kids by the infant school were pushing even more babies in prams. Then down some steps by a playing field and across a valley. There was going to be more walking uphill, and I almost felt that I couldn't bear it.

Dalton Library was a sad and sorry sight – a prefab covered in graffiti with a tin roof. It looked underused to say the least. Then I got the shock of my life as I went over a footbridge. Ten yards away on my right two young men in their 20s were cocking a gun and firing it at something in a ditch. 'Put that away,' I said. 'You're on a public footpath, you're not allowed to do that.' 'Who says we're on a public footpath?' 'You're standing by the sign, fuckwit,' I said. They cocked it again, again at the ditch. 'For God's sake, put that gun away, children are playing round the corner,' I said. Reluctantly they did so. One of them had three whippets on leads. Feeling a bit shaky I walked up round the edge of the field rather than go down to the road. I wanted to stay well clear of them. At least it felt soft under my feet after the miles of asphalt I'd just walked on. Higher up, the farmer was ploughing and dust was swirling in the air. I rejoined the road and slowly made my way up the hill to Dalton Magna and a cup of tea. I was shattered. This felt like more than eight miles.

I resumed my walk along the road. A farmer with shoulder-length grey hair and a sweatband, looking like a refugee from Woodstock, drove a flatbed trailer past me, scattering bits of hay in all directions. More and more lorries seemed to pin me to the hedge. I was still climbing up the bloody hill without a pavement. It was a dangerous twisting road. The next thing that spooked me was an alsatian leaping off its chain at a gate on my left. Now I felt thoroughly rattled and, just to cap it all, a large dead rat lay in the road under my feet. It was the size of a small dog and had a thick unattractive long tail and little feet.

I thought that all these posh houses with wrought-iron around them looked exactly like middle-class homes in Jamaica and wondered if the fortifications were for the same reason, to deter burglars. They didn't look the slightest bit elegant, more like prisons.

I entered Wickersley and nearly got mown down by an old lady driving a Land Rover. Kids were coming out of school. There were quite a few men picking up the kids, which shows what unemployment is like in this outpost of Rotherham.

I headed south of Wickersley after a large roundabout, past some stone buildings, two bow-fronted houses, the working men's club and then an extraordinary edifice with a large pointed tower that had just been turned into six luxury apartments. Next to it the old cemetery had been turned into a bowling green with a little pavilion with steel shutters and a clock on the top and a fine wrought-iron weather-vane which showed one man bowling and another standing. I carried on through suburbia, 1950s detached bungalows, big new houses with two cars in the garage, monkey puzzle trees, the odd man doing a bit of mowing, one practising golf in the front garden, then it was open fields and more pylons and my road curved towards the M18.

Just before the M18 a bungalow faced the motorway. In front of it a floral sunlounger hung, motionless, expectantly waiting for sun. The roar of the traffic was deafening. Over the motorway bridge I turned right at the Consort Crown Hotel with its little gold crown, and next to it a restaurant, an incongruous place to have an entertainment centre.

I headed south through Brampton-en-le-Morthen parallel with the M18, then followed Long Road (as dreary as it sounds) to Pocket Handkerchief Lane. That was quite enough road and lorries for one day.

PART FIVE

Darfield

to Uppingham

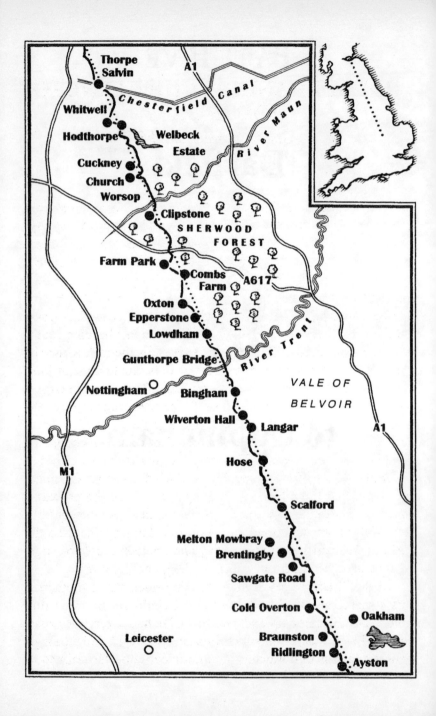

DAY 26

POCKET HANDKERCHIEF LANE TO HODTHORPE
Golden plovers, surely?

What a wonderful station St Pancras is. On the way up from London there was thick fog and that magical blue sky that you get afterwards, intensely bright until 20 miles from Sheffield, where uniformly grey cloud reappeared. Pocket Handkerchief Lane was a romantic sounding name for a horrid little B road used as a shortcut by plenty of cars. At the end of it I crossed the B6463, narrowly missing a large lorry carrying an abnormal load, as it said on the side. Then I crossed some fields of stubble heading south-east in the direction of Burne Farm, aiming for the A57. A river by the farm had several tributaries and was to be my first major foul-up of the day. I reached the brook and couldn't see a way to cross it so I went up and down as I could see the crew waiting for me by the main road. I eventually found a place where a dead tree had fallen across the river. Inching my way across it I held on to its branches. They snapped one by one depositing me into about 18 inches of water that went halfway up my shins and filled my boots. Cursing, I clambered out the other side twisting my wrist in the process. I forlornly trudged across a newly ploughed field, encrusting both water-filled boots with mud on the outside. Looking like Edna the inebriate woman I crossed the road and another couple of large, recently ploughed fields, all hedgerows long since removed.

In the distance I saw a man standing stock still. I thought it was a scarecrow until he turned and I could see he was using binoculars. He came up and said hello. He had a very nice rust-coloured tweed jacket on which I instantly coveted. Sadly though he was a serious bird watcher, a humour-free zone. He claimed to only watch golden plovers that aren't really that rare so it all seemed a bit odd. He very kindly located some golden plovers for me and handed over his binoculars but I couldn't see anything, they were indistinguishable from the stubble. Plover man then warmed up a bit and told me that ahead lay a rookery I would find very interesting. Somehow I thought not, but I politely thanked him and carried on with my walk. That very day the *Daily Telegraph* carried a story saying that crowds of bird watchers had flocked to Scotland to see a rare bird, causing huge traffic jams. A large flock of birds swooped up from the hill in front of me. Golden plovers, surely?

I skirted round a small fishery where half a dozen or so fishermen had their rods out hoping for perch. Then I crossed between two magnificent quarries, one of which was still being worked, and emerged on to the main road at Kiverton Park by the level crossing. The men lounging around outside an engineering works told me that the stone from these quarries was used to build the Houses of Parliament. By the Chesterfield Canal I met Christine Richardson, a canal enthusiast, who assured me that the stone had come from somewhere else locally. It had been chosen because it was such a beautiful honey colour and had withstood the pollution well in London. We walked along the edge of the canal that's going to take another four years to fully restore. It's over 46 miles long and was built in six years, a remarkable achievement in the late 18th century. I love canal walking as it gives you a unique view of the landscape.

Next was Thorpe Salvin where a lot of old buildings had been reduced to rubble and new ones were being built. An ugly bungalow with two garages rose up in front of the elegant remains of the 18th-century hall. Beds of petunias surrounded the village pub and there were floral displays all around the churchyard and a fine gold-painted clock on the end of the church. Some posh houses had two Range Rovers in the drive, and there were 'Britain in Bloom' signs everywhere. A sad sight was the Coronation Garden, completely bereft of flowers, even the empty planter supplied by the local gun club. A man drove past me with a trailer full of plants; maybe he was going to restock the Britain in Bloom garden. Everybody in the village had lavished a lot of care and attention on their gardens. It seemed a million miles away from Grimethorpe, only a few miles up the road. Half beer barrels had been turned into planters with yuccas and conifers in them by the side of the road. The final house in the village, Little Orchard, had a large sign declaring 'No public access'. It was a riot of leaded windows, with a room in a tower, high fake Elizabethan chimneys, the height of pretentiousness.

The large fields round here provided forlorn sights like the old stone gateposts sitting marooned where hedges once used to be. I was on the quietest bit of road I'd walked along for days.

Behind me was an aerodrome full of small private planes. This was a much more middle-class landscape than that nearer to Sheffield. I was on the very edge of south Yorkshire, Nottinghamshire and Derbyshire. It was still relatively flat but it felt rural, whereas the land around Barnsley and Grimethorpe felt tired, over-used and unloved, where all the regeneration work in the world mightn't be able to put the soul back into the area. I walked down Whitwell Road that became a track over Firbeck Common. Then it was an enclosed footpath, Firbeck Lane, and as I headed due south on it I had to battle with flies in the humidity of the afternoon.

As I approached Whitwell and the A619 my path was completely blocked by a burnt-out wreck of a car, with the bonnet touching one hedge and the boot the other. It had arrived relatively recently and set on fire, singeing the hedges on both sides, an ominous sight more suited to *Pulp Fiction* than rural Derbyshire.

Nothing marked the boundary between Yorkshire, Britain's largest county, and Derbyshire. I thought how many days it had taken to cross Yorkshire. I'd encountered every climatic change and every kind of scenery: lush grass, bleak bog, pink heather, open-cast mining. I'd forded rivers, crossed Leeds with Vic

Reeves, visited Harvey Nichols and Grimethorpe and the depressing industrial wasteland around Barnsley. Now I was heading for Nottinghamshire.

I walked through a council estate in Whitwell, a world away from the floral perfection of Thorpe Salvin. This was poorer, with terraces of immaculate bungalows and very neat gardens. I went over an enormous ploughed field, down a hill and over a railway line, where miners' wives were collecting their children from school and the rush-hour seemed to have begun even though it was 3.30 pm. It had turned into a fine afternoon. Men were also collecting their children from primary school or were painting their fences and fiddling with their cars, these weekday occupations a sure sign of unemployment. A bungalow on the edge of the village had a small outdoor swimming pool with water running through it. The mine was on the horizon to the south, a tower on top of a slagheap. In the middle of a field was a warehouse full of building materials with a chainlink fence around it and a sign saying 'Guard dogs loose'. A dozen dark-brown hens emerged from under a hedge, startling me.

I stopped by the cottages at Penny Green. Driving back towards Rotherham I saw men with huge model aeroplanes preparing to fly them. They weren't old enough to be retired so it is likely they were unemployed and had built the planes themselves.

DAY 27

HODTHORPE TO FARM PARK
Underground mysteries

It was my last night in Sheffield, and to get away from the horror of constantly thinking about the walk, writing about it and reading maps, I went to the cinema. I had an early supper and went to see *Lock, Stock and Two Smoking Barrels* at the Odeon. It was one of the funniest films I'd seen for a long time. The two leading actors overacted like mad but Vinny Jones stole the show. At the bar in the Odeon there was no red wine, as I suppose nobody ever drinks it round here, only sweet white wine and slimline tonic. Two drinks cost half the price they would be anywhere in London. My favourite bar, Vic Naylor's in Clerkenwell, was used as a location in the film. I'll have to tell the barman what drinks cost in Sheffield.

I turned on the breakfast news today and saw that there was a seven-car fatal pile-up on the M1 and it was closed near Sheffield with an 18-mile tailback. So it took an hour to drive to where I was to start walking. It had been raining torrentially for hours and the weather forecast said worse was to come.

I left the last few houses of Hodthorpe behind me, and walked through the disused tip of the old Whitwell Colliery, a lunar landscape with terracotta-coloured pieces of clay and grey slurry all around, water gushing through it in a series of bubbling brooks, sometimes in pipes, sometimes flowing freely. At the top of the slagheap there was a good view of the countryside around, the weather was so bad that visibility was poor and the light almost yellowy-grey. There was a stile at the end and I emerged on to the road, crossed it and then followed another wide green track to a main road where I entered the Welbeck Estate.

I was now in Nottinghamshire. It was hard to believe the contrast in the two landscapes. I had gone from terraced bungalows and council estates in Hodthorpe with handkerchief-size gardens to the surreal world of the 16,000-acre Welbeck Estate. The home of the Bentinck family is like a county within a county. The narrow estate roads wind for miles and the public can only walk through its huge expanse on footpaths. The big house, the Abbey, is now run by the Ministry of Defence as a private college for young people who are training for Sandhurst. The family live in Welbeck Woodhouse, another large house on the estate.

The estate was full of weird and wonderful buildings, follies, orangeries, lodges and gatehouses, and the largest indoor riding school in the country. I wasn't allowed by the reluctant trustees to see any of this. The pottiest things at Welbeck are all underground, and were built by the 5th Duke of Portland, an eccentric recluse. He used local people who'd lost their jobs in the weaving industry to build a whole palace below the park. There was a tunnel under the lake, two miles long, to enter the Abbey, lit by artificial light. An underground picture gallery and ballroom was the largest room in Europe without pillars. The Duke was obviously England's answer to Bavaria's mad King Ludwig.

Try as I did, I couldn't get permission to see any of underground Welbeck. All the trustees wanted to talk about was the charitable trust they'd set up to help craftspeople, who were provided with workshops on the estate. Their work was exhibited in the Harley Gallery there.

Lady Anne Bentinck, daughter of the last Duke of Portland, and head of the family, was in her 80s and in Scotland. Instead I was to talk to Neil Elliot, who'd been the estate manager for 35 years and had now retired. I was gutted I couldn't get to see one of the best architectural curiosities in England, but there was no budging the Bentincks.

At the entrance I walked down a long avenue of newly planted conifer trees, rather ugly and tasteless I thought, through a field, past buildings with corrugated metal roofs and then down a grander driveway, emerging by a huge neo-classical building which turned out to be the indoor riding arena, another building I couldn't see inside. I was told it was used as book storage. Neil turned out to be the actor Denholm Elliott's brother and he definitely had a twinkle in his eye. I once sat next to Denholm at a tedious British Academy Awards dinner and noticed he was smoking a huge joint all evening.

The rain was torrential. Neil put on a wide-brimmed hat, inserted his hearing aid and we chattered under the shelter of an archway, watched by Derek who runs the craft workshop. The explanation of how the Welbeck family inherited the estate was so complex I got lost halfway through. It involved lots of different bloodlines, Bess of Hardwick and culminated with no male heirs for the title, and now the estate is to be inherited by a half-Italian prince. This could all be wrong but it was very hard to follow. I do know that Welbeck is one of the five Dukeries created in the area in the 18th century – each of the Dukes was given land to build an estate – and four still exist: Welbeck, Worksop, Clumber and Thoresby.

What a shame Welbeck Estate wasn't really open to the public, except on footpaths. Neil explained that one of the previous dukes had kindly let the sailing club and another boys' club use the lakes, and that they didn't have open days because the Ministry of Defence were very nervous about who saw where they train people. We all know that's total hogwash because it is only a sixth-form college, for goodness sake.

The courtiers who were given the Dukeries have created some of the largest estates in Britain that are now run like businesses with farms, forestry plantations and workshops. It's all a far cry from when Neil started work on the Welbeck Estate not too long after the last war.

I said goodbye to Neil, having drunk a cup of coffee in the stables closely watched by Ministry of Defence police. My route out of the estate passed high greenhouses on each side of the road, with neo-classical urns adorning the tops of walls. It was all on a massive scale.

In the pouring rain I went down a broad avenue and through the deer park with its avenues of horse-chestnut trees hundreds of years old, with a stout fence keeping the deer in the park on my left and farmland on the right. The deer were white, extraordinary looking creatures, and there were several stags with large antlers. The result of centuries of inbreeding, they looked ghostly in the dim light.

There were a couple of beautiful estate houses, Victorian Gothic follies with all the ornate woodwork painted a tasteful shade of magnolia rather than common white. I turned right through a pretty wrought-iron kissing gate and followed a footpath south over a series of fields to Cuckney where there was a moat in front of the church. In the village the friendly landlord of the Greendale Oak offered me a room with a hairdryer and a couple of towels to try and dry off, but I was wet through to the skin and my boots were sodden. I put on my other pair of boots but they were lightweight ones and immediately started leaking when I went back in the rain.

The pub was packed even though it was in the middle of nowhere. There seemed to be a club lunch going on. Twelve middle-aged men were eating together. I was shaking from the exhaustion of walking for two and a half hours in teeming rain, I couldn't really focus and my hands were trembling a bit with tiredness. A man came up and aggressively shoved a bit of paper in my face. 'Why don't you join the real walkers,' he said, 'and do a walk like us.' I suppose he meant it as a joke but it didn't seem very funny to me. I looked at him: 'I am a real walker.' He said, 'We're the real walkers.' I said, 'I've walked 500 bloody miles this year, I'm a real walker,' and he said something about losing my sense of humour. But I couldn't imagine going up to someone in a pub who was wet through and doing that to them. It's a very masculine society around here where wives tend to follow what the men do and I suppose he just thought, well, that's how you behave. On the way out they started up again about real walkers. I said to the publican, 'Do these men think this is funny, do they actually realize how far I've been walking since August? I've walked over 300 miles continuously and I might be losing my sense of humour a bit, but I hope not. I've got a sense of pride in what I'm doing and what I don't need are sneery jokes.' And the publican said, 'Oh, don't upset them, they're the local Rotarians, we need their business.' So that put me in my place.

I walked out of Cuckney along an old drovers' road called Sandy Lane, with a high embankment on either side. Because of the weather it was a pretty wet experience. I emerged on to the A60 as the sun came out and saw a big sign that said, 'Welcome to the District of Mansfield'. Hopefully it would be a nice steamy afternoon so I could dry off. As I came over the brow of a hill I saw Warsop below to the south, a cluster of red roofs in the feeble afternoon sun. On my left were two huge slagheaps, rounded mountains of grey with a chainlink fence all the way around and 'Danger, Keep Out' signs. A part of Warsop is called Mount Pleasant, so presumably it doesn't look at these slagheaps.

At Church Warsop I walked through the cemetery, a sad and basic place compared to the splendours of Highgate Cemetery, which I had been through recently. The graves were weedy and many looked completely uncared for. No one could afford large monuments or urns like I'd seen at Welbeck here, although there were fresh flowers on quite a few of the graves, but on closer inspection everything except the chrysanths were plastic. It wasn't a graveyard for the people who live on the Welbeck Estate, but a graveyard of a town where everybody is employed in more or less the same kind of job with more or less the same kind of income, not poor, but just at the bottom of the middle-class.

I walked through a housing estate on the outskirts of Church Warsop, crossed a bridge over a river when suddenly hundreds of school children were coming in the opposite direction. A few recognized me and started chanting 'Aren't you the lady off the telly?' even though I looked like a bedraggled rat with mud-spattered waterproof trousers, hair dripping wet, carrying a damp hat, dictating into my tape recorder like a nutter. The sun went in, needless to say. My legs felt like lead weights, which always happens after you stop for lunch. I was hoping that secret reserves of energy were going to materialize but somehow I didn't think they would.

Next it was under the disused mineral railway, through fields with high hedges that had lots of sloe bushes in them but no berries unfortunately. Now I came to a fingerpost that announced Centenary Route Five. This was the first time I'd seen a footpath sign as lavish as this for many miles. I went along another wide bridleway, then a private road and through a wood with beautiful broad-leaved oaks and well-made paths, obviously privately owned and used for pheasant shooting. I crossed some newly planted fields and headed uphill to the disused windmill at Bradmer Hill. Here was a world of waste, of discarded new motorway lighting lying on its side, scoops for earthmovers, machinery and general pipework. A man was throwing a lot more rubbish down. I hoped he wouldn't notice me. I crept through and emerged into a huge parking lot full of container lorries.

At the crossroads there was no sign of the disused windmill. The lorries and cars were belting along the A60 and I followed a B road marked to the Sherwood Forest Farm Park. After 25 yards a car went past, nearly hitting me and hooting frantically, scaring the wits out of me. When I looked back all the people were waving hello, but do they have any idea how frightening they are if you're walking alone? In a lay-by four German tourists were reading a map.

I thought I'd leave the rare breeds and the pigs for tomorrow, so we drove back to Sheffield passing estate after estate of miners' houses. Heavy rain had resumed. I'd just finished in the nick of time. My legs were starting to feel really heavy and aching. I almost passed out in the car with tiredness so we stopped. I ate a sandwich, drank a bottle of water and felt a lot better. On the way into Sheffield it was the rush hour. It was like night yet it was only 6.30 pm. I guess it wouldn't be long before the clocks were turned back.

FARM PARK TO COMBS FARM
Happy pigs, a colliery and Sherwood Forest

I turned into the entrance of the Sherwood Forest Farm Park with its rare breeds collection. It was awash with 'No Parking' signs sticking up one after another, four in all, and another sign saying 'Caution Low Bridge, Double Deckers Park Before It'. I was beginning to feel a theme park coming on. Then there was another sign, 'Thousands of animals and birds in a lovely natural setting'. I'd just walked through endless fields of cows and we were in the countryside, so what exactly did that mean?

On the railway line in front of me a train roared past pulling dozens of trailers of coal. This railway line is very much in use. Now I could smell pigs. By yet another sign for 'Slow', I looked into a field and hundreds of pigs came running towards me thinking it was feeding time. Pink pigs all living outdoors, each pig-pen with a little house. Happy pigs. Now another sign, 'Caution, speed ramp'. Finally there was a giant chart with a three-pronged trident that said Farm one arrow, Houses and Office second arrow, Fishing third arrow, and one off to the right for Farm Park Entrance Car and Coach Parking. Finally a gate announced, 'Sorry the Farm Park is closed, we are open at weekends only during October', and in a field behind a flock of jacob sheep munched contentedly on the grass.

On my left was a final sign under some trees saying 'Iron Age Pigs' and in a little tin shelter some gorgeous dark-brown hairy pigs surrounded by an electric fence. One more map, the Sherwood Forest Farm Park Fishery Plan, contained colour photos of people holding giant fish, maps of stockponds and little marked-up fishing positions for coarse fishing.

In the field of free-range pigs I met Simon and Felicity Shaw-Brown, the owners. They, unlike the pigs, were extremely unhappy. It seemed they got £30 a pig less than it costs to rear them, so they were thinking of having all the ones that we filmed slaughtered over the next couple of months as it was uneconomic to keep them any longer. Imports of Danish bacon were undercutting British bacon and as we produce our pork in a more humane way, we can't compete with the cheaper imported meat. While I felt sorry for Simon and Felicity I couldn't help thinking that the problem with a lot of British farming is that we simply make too much of everything. They admitted we over-produce pork and I suppose their rare breeds theme-park farm was one solution, but it doesn't really present a realistic picture of what farming is all about in Britain. People have to decide whether they want to pay more for food that's decently produced and tastes better, and until that day comes, farmers are going to be in the quandary they are in now.

Simon told me that 10,000 farmers had marched to the Labour Party conference to protest, but Tony Blair didn't understand their problems. They presented me with a frozen pack of sausages that I promised I would eat. I assured them that I only ate organic meat anyway, and was a big fan of British meat. I was partly on their side but not entirely.

Even Sainsbury's admitted that its Swedish pork could come from pigs given feed banned in Britain because of BSE. But I can't see why Sainsbury's, like other supermarkets, doesn't do more to promote and buy British products.

I said goodbye, clutching my sausages, and crossed a bridge over the River Maun, full of thick brown mud after all the recent rain, an idyllic spot with a fishing lake next to it. Ahead in the woods I could hear the pop-pop of pheasant shooting. Down the road was Clipstone Colliery, another example of the juxtaposition of heavy industry and lush farm estates here in Nottinghamshire. Emerging from Cavendish Wood on to a broad track I could see huge areas of forest around me. I wondered where

Sherwood Forest actually started. I was intrigued. I'd already walked through the Kielder Forest; would this be different? This wood was tall pine trees about 30 or 40 years old, and it was silent and still. I wasn't quite sure how to get to Clipstone. The odd squirrel crossed my path. After a couple of hundred yards I saw a woman coming in the opposite direction walking her dog. He shook his head and slobber flew through the air and landed on me. She apologized. I asked her the way to the council estate and she told me the direction to the cemetery instead. So rather than be rude, I thanked her, walked a couple of hundred yards and then turned in the vague direction I was aiming for. Luckily I could hear Jane our driver shouting my name about 50 yards away and I emerged on to a narrow footpath and there she was.

The entrance to this bit of forest was full of rubbish and very unattractive. There were places where people had vandalized it, set rubbish on fire, torn down branches off trees and just burnt them for the sheer hell of it – how depressing. I emerged into an estate of semi-detached houses, obviously all miners' houses because the Clipstone Colliery was opposite. I walked down it and turned the corner, and I was on the main road facing the colliery entrance dominated by the twin winding towers (64 metres high), landmarks to an era when coal dominated this part of Britain.

I walked through the gates and met with Chris Daniels, the colliery manager, who was extremely cheerful and positive, which was surprising really as there is only five years' worth of coal left in the seam, and the two lift towers which once used to be the tallest in Europe may be relegated to a museum. The noise was deafening. Coal was being spewed from conveyor belts into giant heaps. We were watched by a couple of men by the tower. Chris motioned at them to get back to work, and they just ignored him. He told me that the average miner in this colliery earned £25,000 a year. He had all the bonhomie and confidence that one might expect from a manager earning well over £30,000, but the fact of the matter is that when the colliery closes it will be one more nail in the coffin of this region. As I had seen continually in my walk, economically it was at a turning point, as so many collieries have closed in the last 20 years and not enough new jobs have come in to replace them. Having organic farms you can visit for an away-day and creating nature reserves isn't really the long-term solution.

Clipstone, at its height in the late 1930s, was owned by the Bolsover Colliery Company, who had four pits in Nottinghamshire and two in Derbyshire. The colliery's land covered 51 square miles, and it owned 3,000 houses, employing 10,000 miners. British Coal took over the mine in 1947 and closed it in 1993, to be reopened under the private ownership of RJB Mining. Once employing 1,500 people, now Clipstone only needed 200. What job security did those people really have? It was all very well for Chris to talk about meeting targets, but once the current seam was finished, what would happen to the workforce? Chris said he wouldn't like to see the place end up as a theme park, with the winding towers in a museum.

We walked out of the back of the colliery and over some land that they still owned on the edge of a spoil tip, and Chris pointed me in the right direction through Sherwood Forest (I'd finally arrived at the real thing!) and we said goodbye.

I walked under a disused railway, itself a symbol of the change in the area. The Mineral Railway was once a busy line and now I'd crossed and recrossed it several times in the last couple of days, and it was silent with weeds growing over the tracks. I entered the Sherwood Forest where a ranger gave me a map of how to find my way out again. I walked round the edge of the forest, heading south around the broad-leaf section on a wide pathway. The grey sky and threatening rain of earlier had lifted somewhat. It was still grey but there was the occasional blue patch although the air was distinctly chilly and you could tell it was autumn. Leaves were beginning to fall from the trees. It was an extremely pleasant walk, slightly downhill. On my left were acres and acres of the tallest, most elegant thin pines you could imagine with the light showing through them. It wasn't at all like the claustrophobic man-made Kielder Forest. I walked through an avenue of horsechestnuts, the leaves falling to the ground, feeling sorry that I would soon be leaving Nottinghamshire.

Even Sherwood Forest was undergoing dramatic change. Once it stretched over 20 miles from Nottingham to Worksop, eight miles wide. Created by William the Conqueror, it was a favourite hunting ground. Over-grazing gradually reduced the forest, as did the expansion of Nottingham, Mansfield and Worksop. The development of coal and farming further split up the mass of trees. As the coal mines have closed, so the forest has been replanted and reclaimed as a nature reserve and leisure park. You could Adopt an Oak for £10 and receive a certificate when your tree was planted in the world's most famous forest, once home to Robin Hood and his merry men.

I can't describe the sheer luxury of walking through a forest as beautiful as this one in the middle of the week with no one else about. My path was over a carpet of chestnut leaves with conkers strewn everywhere. Squirrels darted about and continuous bird song delighted my ears. What could be more perfect? Then it was over a patch of open heathland where the heather was still pink and new fir trees about three foot high were poking up through the grass. There was an endless succession of huge wild mushrooms, ceps that would be delicious if they weren't all full of slugs attracted by the recent rain. I picked a few slug-free specimens, taking my sandwiches out of their foil and folding it very carefully round them, hoping that I would be able to take them back to London and dry them.

The calm of the forest was soon shattered when I left it. I followed a track at the side of a field south to the A617 by Rufford Forest Farm. I turned east along the busy A617, and it was sheer hell. Lorry after lorry buffeted me. The quarter of a mile I walked could have been four miles, it was so horrible, with an icy wind blowing. After a bend in the road I saw a gap in the hedge and climbed over the fence heading due south across huge fields. This is intensive farming country. A huge field of carrots was followed by one of spinach and then finally over the giant soft furrows of a potato crop that had just been picked. Walking up and down it was worse even than walking through newly planted forestry. I had to wade through some brambles to emerge on to a side road. The heavy drone of the traffic on the A614 heading north and south had replaced the forest birdsong.

A cindery track took me past a field of beetroot, all the leaves rusty red in the afternoon sun. I'd left Sherwood Forest well and truly behind. Intensive farming with sheds like warehouses sat on the top of the hill, full of cattle or chickens, with feeding tanks above them. I walked between them, huge extractor fans for the air conditioning, an inhuman environment if I ever saw one. A sign said 'Security Cameras in Operation'. It was all very threatening, like something out of a Stanley Kubrick film or Lindsay Anderson's *O Lucky Man!* At the end of the sheds was a portacabin with a sign, 'Security Cameras in Operation, Video Surveillance'. I climbed up into a ploughed field where a farmer was working nearby and I didn't want to risk interrogation. The ground was extremely soft so after a couple of hundred yards I got through a hole in the hedge and walked down a private driveway out to the main road. I crossed over into yet another field of giant furrows where potatoes had grown. Finally I climbed over an electric fence and emerged on to the A614 underneath a giant roundabout sign. Crossing the road took a lot of nerve but I emerged by the Combs Farm shop and then I walked up the lane to a hilly area ahead.

My next big landmark would be the River Trent, marking the start of the South of England.

COMBS FARM TO THE RIVER TRENT
Nottingham's rich commuter belt

A freezing cold wind, grey sky and rain all night. The beginning of October and winter seems to be here. I had a sleepless night, probably brought about by eating a large portion of duck at 9.30 pm. I woke up every two hours reviewing career, life etc., and finally got knee cramps at 3 am.

I walked up a hilly ridge behind Combs Farm on a red track accompanied by my friend Janet who was already whinging that the countryside was dreary. Well, she didn't have to trudge across endless potato fields like I had done, so she had no idea of what boring countryside is really like. We crossed a lane and a sign announced the Robin Hood Way going over the top of a series of little hills with views right out over Nottinghamshire for miles and the noisy A6097 a long way below us. It was good to be on a footpath but crossing the ploughed fields was difficult because they were so wet. We just slithered about.

At last the landscape had more of a domestic scale than I'd encountered over the last couple of weeks.

A wooden bench under a tree had the footpath sign nailed to the seat just to confuse us. We slid down the muddy hill in a straight line for Oxton. A narrow groove approximately nine inches wide had been left unploughed for you to put your feet in. As Janet pointed out, it was ideal training for tightrope walking, especially when combined with a downward slope and the wind behind you.

A wide old stony track took us into Oxton, the sides banked steeply about ten foot high, and pheasants scurried in and out of the hedgerows. There was a little wooden bench and Janet took my photo sitting on it. I hoped it wouldn't look as grey and dismal as it really was. A sign on the first house said 'NO salesmen, thank you'. They had a caravan in the drive and a herbaceous border of the ugliest flowers you can imagine: salvias and marigolds. Another house had two gnomes either side of the front door which were Hells Angels on motorbikes made of terracotta. Main Street Oxton had a pretty village green and there were lot of very beautiful red-brick houses presumably owned by wealthy people commuting into Nottingham. In Sandy Lane we crossed an idyllic ford over the river with a trout lake and ducks scurrying away from us, rather ruined by a man with a very noisy piece of machinery cutting a giant hole in the road. There were lots of pretty little cottages restored with old glass and mugs in the window, all very *bijou*. The driveway down to Park Farm although a public footpath, looked forbidding. A large sign on the first telegraph post showed a ferocious looking dog and said 'Warning, guard dogs, private road, no access without permission', and a woman drove by us in a Range Rover looking suspiciously at us. But we were on a right of way, madam!

The footpath through the wood at the end of the drive was completely blocked so we carried on up the drive, up the hill and into the wind. It started to rain. Signs said 'Please use the OS original footpath route for health and safety'. What illness would I contract if I departed from it?

The gate through the wood had barbed wire looped all over the top of it and we ramblers were confined to a narrow path with a fence on one side and a hedge on the other. Park Farm sat isolated in the valley below. We dropped down to the track at the bottom of the valley with two huge fields on either side. I was surprised how under-populated this area was as it was so close to Nottingham. The farms were a long way apart and very large. To get to Epperstone we walked across a wet field but it cleaned our boots and we entered the village along a quiet road. Another middle-class village enclave with brick houses and well-tended gardens. Janet waxed lyrical over the cottage gardens, remarking on how abundant the flowers were even though it was the beginning of October. The trouble with walking with her was that as a keen gardener she needed to look in everyone's front gardens. Now she was wittering on about wild cyclamen while I strode on trying to get away from the sound of strimmers.

Along the main street past the post office, two horseriders came towards us. We were after all in hunting country, the Vale of Belvoir the other side of the Trent. The Cross Keys pub had a blackboard outside advertising 'Senior citizens' lunch, Tuesday to Friday'. We wondered if we should drop in.

This was a village of most impressive houses. Outside a Victorian Gothic pointy one a woman was Hoovering out her car with the sounds of heavy metal at full volume, a somewhat discordant note in the rural tranquillity of Epperstone. The village hall was a brand new red-brick establishment and just about as swanky as everything else in the village, with a kind of landscaped pebbled parking area round it. Two exciting signs jolted us out of this middle-class cocoon: 'Danger area, red flags flying, firing in progress' and 'No unauthorized persons allowed'. It was a disused Army firing range. A car whooshed past with the number-plate DI 888 and two ladies on horseback cheerily said hello to us. Down a muddy public bridleway, past manicured fields with expensive looking horses in them, a mill pond with lilies growing on it and a posh house with a tennis court and a three-car garage.

We carried on walking quickly into Lowdham, trying to stay off the A6097. It wasn't as posh as Epperstone, and had new bungalows and much smaller houses, terraced cottages. A shop window full of interesting looking old plates and teapots but luckily the sign said 'We are open Monday to Friday 4.30-6.00'. Not very convenient! Their odd hours saved me at least £7 because I saw two Wedgwood plates I wanted. A wonderful clock hung on the gable end of the old school and a sign below said 'The above clock was erected by public subscription to commemorate the Coronation of King George and Queen Mary, June 22nd, 1911'. It was the only thing of any style and distinction in Lowdham.

We ate our smoked salmon sandwiches sitting in the car park of the Old Ship pub in the High Street. The stench coming out of the kitchen window was indescribable. Chicken Kiev, garlic butter and fried onions all in one pungent aroma. A refrigeration lorry drew up and from its back disgorged a lot of ready-made frozen food. I drank a glass of tonic water as per Janet's instructions to stop my leg cramps. Immediately I got stomach cramps and felt bloated.

We passed another shop with very bizarre opening times (the Bookcase): Monday closed all day, Tuesday 9.00-1.00 and 2.00-5.30, Wednesday morning – Oh God, I couldn't cope with it! A huge sign by the Magna Carta pub announced Christmas bookings now being taken. We both felt profound depression.

On Station Road the level-crossing gates were down, giving us a chance to inspect the station house – a pretty Victorian Gothic building with green and white tiles inside the front door. Now we had to rejoin the main road, a dual carriageway, luckily with a pavement. Even on a busy main road home-owners have delusions of grandeur. A bungalow had a high brick wall, brick columns with ornate wrought-iron gates and a pineapple on top of each column by the entrance, and leaded windows, of course. The village of Gunthorpe was off to our left as we pounded along the A6097 between Leicester and Doncaster.

On the other side of a field on our left was a cream-painted square folly, castellated with two little turrets, which turned out to be a huge place selling hideous caravans. Now we went over Gunthorpe Bridge over the River Trent, the widest river I'd crossed so far, which was full because of the rains of the last few days. It was a peaceful vista in every direction if only there hadn't been huge lorries pounding past. To the east there was a motorway-type sign at least ten foot square for river users, announcing a lock.

Even beautiful rivers are now just major highways – as if we haven't got enough of those.

THE TRENT TO HOSE
Bloodshed and burials

The River Trent was a symbolic moment in my journey. It flows right across England from Staffordshire in a great loop of 170 miles to the Humber Estuary and the North Sea. It marks where the North ends and the Midlands begin. This part of middle England has been a battleground for far longer than the last General Election. The English Civil War over 300 years ago turned village against village in a far more bloody conflict.

The day started with me crossing and re-crossing the River Trent several times for the benefit of the camera. The director, John, was obviously intent on building up a sequence to rival the movie *The Bridge on the River Kwai.*

Now thankfully I left the main road and walked along a lane in the direction of East Bridgford. On the other side of the river were loads of pubs and bars; if only it were summer!

My path skirted a sewage works firmly protected by a thick metal fence with triple barbed wire along the top. I went through some woods and emerged on to a small road and eventually rejoined the main road, crossing it directly opposite a sign saying 'To RAF Newton', and went down towards Glebe Farm. An orange windsock waved feebly in the breeze ahead. I was high up on a flat ridge. Away to the south-east lay the town of Bingham and the River Trent lay beneath us to the north.

The blue sky of earlier had completely disappeared and been replaced by the now familiar grey sky, clouds firmly locked together, and the icy wind of the past few days had resumed blowing. The red telephone box in Newton was definitely in need of a lick of paint. Perhaps the locals could lavish some of the attention on it that they give to their gardens. As I passed Newtree Farm a piece of white paper was stuck in the window with large red crayon letters written on it 'Yes'. How intriguing. The last couple of houses in the village were pretty grand affairs with high brick walls. Soon the brick gave way to chainlink fencing and I was walking round the airforce base, RAF Newton.

No longer operating as a 'real' base, it's used as a flying school for cadets and student officers. At the end of a road to my right I could see the red-and-white striped barrier of the air base. A muddy track took me south skirting the edge of a housing development. I walked around the edge of a potato field where there were absolutely masses of potatoes left behind. What was wrong with them? Why hadn't the machine picked them up? It was a mystery. I was in a quagmire. No one in their right mind would choose to walk down this footpath, it was like wading through treacle, and I kept tripping on the odd spud.

Soon the new housing estate gave way to the more functional looking housing of RAF Newton. Apparently there were very few families still living on the base and the houses were for sale. We had tried to ask the Ministry of Defence if we could film there but it had taken so many phonecalls and we had got passed from person to person that we had abandoned the idea.

To my right was a huge sign saying, 'This is a prohibited place within the meaning of the Official Secrets Act, unauthorized persons entering the area may be arrested and prosecuted. RAF police dogs on patrol'. To me it looked just like another potato field.

Now surveillance cameras were aimed at me crossing a field of stubble. Considering the RAF were trying to sell these houses off to civilians it wasn't exactly a salubrious or welcoming environment, more like a basic housing estate from the 1950s. The base looked deserted. Apparently there are only four families left living there. I passed a white barrier that announced 'Crashgate, keep clear'. The Ministry of Defence was anxious to sell properties like this and yet literally a hundred yards down the road from it new homes were being built virtually identical in size, using more or less the same coloured brick, and which would probably be snapped up immediately. If only the Ministry of Defence would employ people to go around and take down all the barriers, the surveillance cameras and the nasty signs of military oppression, and just do a tiny bit of landscaping, these houses could be made to look just as attractive as their new counterparts. But then the last thing the Ministry of Defence probably thinks about is marketing.

At the other side of the A46, I crossed a newly planted field over a deep ditch via a footbridge and then across another ploughed field. It makes me laugh when farmers say they will reinstate the footpaths after they have ploughed the crops and planted. The only way they get reinstated is by people walking on them. I entered Bingham along the side of a scrapyard and a railway line, turned on to the main road and a train thundered past on the level crossing. I walked past some council flats and Victorian cottages. It was hard to see many signs of the Civil War here in Bingham.

One of the houses I passed had a man standing on crutches in the front garden directing his wife on how to do the weeding. They had constructed some ornate trellis forming two huge wire spiders' webs, with a wrought-iron spider sitting in the middle of it and along the top some gaily coloured plastic butterflies. This was now a posh suburb with pampas grass, detached houses and the inevitable wrought-iron gates. A sign outside announced a public meeting with Kenneth Clarke MP at the local comprehensive school.

It was a long slow climb up the hill, one my tired legs didn't want to make. Crossing the A52 that runs between Grantham and Nottingham at a staggered junction, I then headed down to Langar. I could see for miles although it was misty and grey. Rutland lay ahead, probably more hilly, and I hoped my legs could cope. Now there was a nasty section along the road to Langar which was far too busy, with loads of lorries going far too close to me. I stopped off at Wiverton Hall to find out some more local history. It was fortified as a Cavalier garrison for King Charles in 1643, and burnt to the ground by the Roundheads in 1645.

The present Wiverton Hall is a fine early-Victorian castellated Gothic mansion built around the ruins of the garrison. Vicky Martin was in the middle of moving in. She was an attractive woman with blonde hair – it was hard to tell her age, late 30s I'd guess – with an equally attractive husband. They had three children and were moving from a village nearby. They were going to do the place up gradually. So far they had completed re-rendering the outside and had started the enormous task of decorating the inside. There weren't that many rooms but the proportions were baronial. The Gothic windows were high and attractive and the place had a wonderful light and airy feel to it. The staircase was elegant with Victorian Gothic wrought-iron banisters. I wished Vicky luck, remembering that I too had once tried to restore a Victorian Gothic house; sadly it had all ended in divorce as neither my ex-husband nor I could afford to complete the job.

I said goodbye and walked through a wrought-iron gate at the front of the house and in a straight line across a field I found a rickety old wooden bridge over a stream, and then I cut across a newly ploughed field back on to the road to Langar. Although the storm clouds were gathering it hadn't rained yet.

Across the fields to my right was the Georgian outline of Langar House. As I approached Langar I could see the church poking through the trees in Langar Park. Sadly between me and the park was one enormous ploughed field. Its size was grotesque, totally at odds with the scale of any of the old houses in the area.

Langar Hall, a fine Georgian mansion dating from 1797, had had some grim mementoes of the Civil War unearthed in its gardens. The Hall (now a hotel) was the most beautiful colour, kind of mustardy mixed with terracotta, a graceful building with a lovely park. Owner Imogen Skirving had tea with me and told how one day when the builders were digging the drains they came across a whole lot of human remains in the gardens and, after some investigation, it turned out that there had been a massacre at Langar during the Civil War. Apparently the local landowner (a Cavalier) had a private army of locals, maybe half a dozen or so. On a Sunday morning they were standing on guard when Roundheads from Colston Basset sneaked up and killed them all. From skeletons and skulls and it was estimated that they were 16 to 19 years old. Imogen put them all in coffins and gave them a proper burial; she kept a skull on her desk for a while but in the end added that to the grave with the others.

In those long ago days an ambush would have been much easier to do because the fields wouldn't have been the giant prairie-like empty spaces they are now waiting for potatoes to go in them; in those days it was strip farming. The hills were contoured into a series of ridges and there were hedgerows to hide behind; the crops were rotated and people only grew what they could eat. The landscape of Leicestershire has been changed irrevocably by modern farming methods.

The house backed on to the churchyard and the church tower was only feet from the back part of the kitchens. I walked out of Imogen's gardens, through the churchyard and its sad set graves, and found myself back in the village.

Some school children were kicking a ball on a piece of green outside the school. I walked down the sleepy street past the post office and the phone box, crossed the main road and took a footpath at the side of someone's house. It was soon a track but then degenerated into pasture. I went over a couple of stiles that seemed very broken down and then I was in a field of piebald ponies, an unusual sight. There were two or three foals and they scuttled about, nervously kicking up their hind legs. I meandered through the meadow trying to find a way out. I put on my waterproof trousers because the clouds had got even more threatening and rain seemed imminent. I looked back and all the ponies had resumed munching away at the luxuriant grass.

As I crossed a series of ditches on old plank bridges completely obscured by nettles, wood pigeons flew out of the trees flapping noisily. Around Farlow Lodge someone had cunningly removed the footpath sign at the main road. I walked down a driveway and picked up some yellow arrows further along. I crossed another ploughed field and now had about three pounds of earth attached to the bottom of each foot pulling me down. At last I could see the church at Hose on the horizon, my destination.

What a charming little village Hose was, completely dormant at 4.30 on a weekday afternoon. A huge black-and-white cat sat on a car bonnet. There was a jumbled collection of brick cottages, some painted white, and streets with names like Back Road, Middle Road and so on. Its church was a beautiful honey colour.

Then it was back to stay at Langar Hall, and a fine dinner and a comfortable bed. And hopefully no dreams about massacres in the garden.

Heath village, near Wakefield

A lot of rules to fish on the disused Barnsley canal

Right: Sign on the old station house, Lowdham, near the River Trent

Below: Happy Old Spot piglets near Cold Overton

SHUT THE GATE

THE PENALTY IS FORTY SHILLINGS FOR LEAVING THIS GATE UNLOCKED

Above: A dead fox beside the sign for Rutland

Left: Dovecote at Brook

Right: Putting my feet up in the Bede House grounds, Lyddington

Below: Sign on a tree in woods near Corby warning of snakes

Facing page:

Above right: At Chelveston air base

Right: The giant Cardington Barns, home to airships

Right: My military escort at Chicksands

Below: Sign on a wall in Old Welwyn

Above: With Elton John near the M25

Right: Tower Hamlets cemetery, ruined and overgrown

At the Millennium Dome, Greenwich, with architect of the Mind Zone, Zaha Hadid

What a relief! Celebrating the end of the walk at the Trafalgar pub in Greenwich

HOSE TO SAWGATE ROAD
Weird cheeses

It's Monday. Yesterday I had to go to hospital to have my knees X-rayed. On Saturday night I had drunk quite a bit and, wearing high heels, I walked down the stairs at my friend's birthday party and my knees locked out. There was a sharp pain in my right knee and I felt as if I had torn something. I panicked. I hobbled home at 4.00 am; luckily alcohol dulled the pain. I rang the doctor on Sunday and was sent to hospital to have Britain's number two knee expert brought in to look at them. The noise in my knees was terrible, such clicking and grinding. The expert said there was wear and tear but that I hadn't ripped anything and my right knee was severely inflamed from all the walking. He gave me some anti-inflammatory drugs and told me to come back for a scan.

This morning I got up feeling dreadful. Maybe it's the pills. I crawled to St Pancras station at 6.45 am to discover there was to be no food on the train because the boiler wouldn't work. I stood in a queue of 15 people to purchase a cappuccino. I got on the train and sat in a carriage marked 1. Then a man came up and said as I didn't have a premier-class ticket I couldn't sit in the carriage. When I pointed out that the windows said 1 and my ticket said 1 he gave in but pointed out that I should pay more because this was premier class but they had forgotten to put the stickers on the windows. Premier class meant you got free food. When I pointed out to him that there was no food anyway he relented. I asked if I could have some fruit salad in a paper cup. The buffet girl said she couldn't give it to me because it might involve washing up and I won't like it anyway as it was tinned. What answer is there to that!

Yesterday Richard Branson was on the radio with Andrew Neill and when asked about the Virgin trains fiasco on the eve of the Labour Party conference in Blackpool, he replied, 'Yeah, we certainly fucked up', and then at the end of the programme had to apologize for his language. He was actually in the Caribbean at the time of the great fuck up, not travelling on one of his trains. I had complained to Virgin trains only a few weeks previously when my mother was seriously ill in hospital and dying. I travelled on Virgin trains four times to Llandudno to see her. Every time the train was late and finally the train was extremely late on her birthday and I missed an hour of my precious visiting time. When I asked the ticket inspector why, he said, 'We're always late, it's Railtrack's fault.' When I wrote to Virgin and told them all this and said that now she'd died I would no longer have to use that appalling service to Llandudno Junction I simply got a letter back with a £20 voucher which I could only use on Virgin trains. That's tantamount to saying you can run in the next race but shoot your foot off first. Then two days later I got another letter from Virgin from their customer relations department asking me to fill in a form saying how I felt they dealt with my complaint. When I return it I shall employ Richard Branson's own language and say, 'You certainly fucked up.'

I was now in Hose, a village halfway between Nottingham and Leicester. The countryside is flat and it was pouring with rain. I crossed a field outside the village by a largely redundant footpath that followed the road and involved climbing three stiles, which was agony as my knee didn't want to bend. I walked along a deserted road en route to meet a Stilton cheese maker.

Hose is right in the middle of the Vale of Belvoir, horse country, and they were out even in this weather. Every house had stables and there was no shortage of money round here. The Tories were starting their conference that day and William Hague already seemed to have put his foot in it by saying that the person that he wants to identify with most is Rotherham Man. He is referring of course to the place where he grew up, Wath upon Dearne, outside Rotherham, where I walked and interviewed his headmaster. But the newspapers have had a field day talking to the locals who returned maverick left-winger Dennis Skinner in the last election with a majority of over 21,000; you'd be hard pushed to find anyone who would admit to voting Tory. Apparently there's only one Tory on the local council. So although William Hague wants to appeal to the hard-working values that he associates with the area, perhaps using Rotherham as an example wasn't such a good idea.

Although the weather had taken on a decidedly autumnal air with temperatures at night much lower than they had been in previous weeks, the summer still seemed to be lingering on. There were sweet peas pushing through the wall of someone's cottage by the church in Hose and in the hedgerows I saw pink clover amongst the rosehips. Gardens were full of flowers, late roses still blooming although they were looking a bit sodden.

It was absolutely pelting down as I walked along the lane and by Brockhill Hall Farm I met Roy Egglestone who produces milk for Stilton cheese and is chairman of the Long Clawson Dairy. I was in the middle of dairy country; as well as being a hunting area, this part of Leicester contained five of the eight dairies which made Britain's most famous cheese. I'd been told that marketing men were trying to persuade us to buy Stilton all year round – most of it is sold just before Christmas. And new cheeses are being developed too, in a bid to get us to eat more of it. Roy was determined I should sample these latest exotic members of the Stilton stable. He'd laid out a whole display in the back of his car and of course the Stilton was delicious, but then I tasted something quite revolting called Orange Bliss which had bits of orange in it, and White Stilton which had incorporated lemon rind. The best of the new cheeses was something called Innkeeper's Choice, which was softer and creamier than Stilton and had chives in it. Stilton dates from the early 1700s, so why mess about with something that's perfect?

At least Roy didn't produce the two other cheeses I read about in the Clawson publicity handout, Mature Cheddar with fruit cake, or Cheddar and pickled onion! The dairy made over 3,000 tons of Stilton a year, but also sold 1,000 tons of all those weird cheeses, so somebody obviously liked them. According to Roy cheeses were like cars. After a few years everyone wants a new model and they all move on to something new. Fashions in cheese, can you believe it? Roy chopped me off a big lump of Melton Mowbray pork pie and a piece of stilton, wrapped it in paper and gave it to me for lunch. I turned down the offer of a bottle of port to go with it, and walked on in the rain.

I climbed a field up to a line of pylons that went down to the village of Scalford. The brambles at the start and finish of the paths around here showed how little they were used. Content cows looked out over almost every hedge. At Wolds Farm a group of farm workers were incredulous that I was walking down the footpath as they had never seen anyone use it in years. They told me that only town people rode here as the farmers couldn't afford to, and thought riders were a snobby bunch looking down on everybody else.

Just before Scalford, when I couldn't find the footpath, a lady came out of a house and showed me that it went right through her front garden. I emerged in Scalford by the pub. Finding my way out was just as difficult. I walked down South Lane and then couldn't find a footpath. I'd seen a Jubilee Way sign and ended up on top of a railway line with a lady walking underneath. Here's the conversation:

LADY: *'How did you get up there? You should have come across the field behind you. You're in the middle of the two rights of way.'*

JANET: *'Oh. I'll get on your one anyway.'*

LADY: *'Can you get down there?'*

JANET: *'There's so many cows in this field.'*

LADY: *'They'll not hurt you.'*

JANET: '*Wanna bet? They're really frisky today, there must be some madness in the air.*'

LADY: '*I'll tell you something. Don't go down into that field with those two Shetland ponies, because they are a bit mad.*'

JANET: '*The Shetland ponies are vicious?*'

LADY: '*Yes, exactly.*'

JANET: '*OK. The cows are looking very frisky though.*'

LADY: '*Only because you're different!*'

JANET: '*I'm not that different...*'

After a few miles of slithering and sliding along the Jubilee Way I cut back up to the road by a farm that had closed. It was locked up with the curtains drawn. I could now see the outskirts of Melton Mowbray. I headed towards it although I soon turned off on yet another footpath, by a sign saying 'Tumbledown Farm. Open seven days a week, 10.00-5.00'. The footpath had double barbed wire and brambles, and it was obvious that no one walked down it. I walked into Thorpe Arnold crossing over electric fences. I struggled over one lot of barbed wire and a field of stubble and then through a mire of mud round the back of a farm. Finally I was on an asphalt road, thank goodness, as my legs felt like lead-weights, plus I was getting a cold sore. I was going to have to sleep for a good ten hours and have a late start tomorrow.

The farm at Brentingby was a beautiful old house on three storeys, dating probably from the 16th century. Opposite it the old church with a tower had been converted into a large house. I met Julia who came to live in the area about eight years ago from Worcester. She lived in Hose and felt passionately about the problems facing people in the countryside. She was going to marry the farmer's son here at Brentingby. She and her husband planned to build a new house for his dad on the other side of the lane. She was a witty girl with a peaked tweed hat pulled well down over her lively eyes, a good laugh. We walked over a railway line and due south along a succession of tracks talking about problems faced by the small villages of Britain with shops closing, lack of public transport, high petrol prices and lack of affordable housing. She was extremely articulate. I didn't want to touch on the subject of hunting, which I know she felt passionately about, because I just couldn't endure all the correspondence that would result when it was aired on television. It's the one subject, like bull-fighting, that people in Britain get driven to extremes by, a bit like the wind farms I mentioned last year in Wales which resulted in a 24-page letter from opponents of it. The sun came out briefly and the sky, although a wintry blue, was nevertheless blue for about 15 minutes. Then the sun sank behind another grey cloud and it was just a rather dreary autumn evening, getting chilly at that.

We drove back to the hotel through Melton Mowbray, not as pretty as its pies. I'd soon made a complete mess in my bathroom, I feel ashamed to say, and it's such a pretty hotel, Langar Hall. My bathroom looked like a Neanderthal man had occupied it. I had a bath, then I washed out my waterproof trousers in the bath, and my shoe laces, then I tried to scrape as much mud off my boots as I could with tissues and bits of paper and finally I washed out my boots in the bath and then the bath was full of stones and mud and grass and I attempted to clear up. I dried my waterproof trousers on a towel, which left mud all over it. Then I washed my hair and left red hair dye stains all over another towel. So when I came down for breakfast the next day I apologized in advance, before the cleaners arrived.

DAY 32

MELTON MOWBRAY TO UPPINGHAM
Passports for Rutland!

Guess what? Another completely grey sky, with no break in the cloud, but at least it wasn't raining. It was very cold and I was walking along wearing a woolly hat. I turned south from Sawgate Road on a footpath between two ploughed fields, the kind of fields I now dreaded. I woke up three times in the night with my inflamed knee even though I had taken a couple of painkillers before I went to sleep. Although I had apologized to the hotel for the state of my bathroom this morning and asked if all my washing could be done, I don't think I'm the kind of guest they'll be too keen to have back. Businessmen are so much less trouble, aren't they? They arrive with a suit, have a conference and leave, probably having run up great big bar bills. I couldn't stop yawning this morning and I thought my jaw was going to dislocate at one point.

An ominous loud roaring noise came from just over the hill, from an air base. I crossed the middle of a massive ploughed field with no footpath, and a jet flew overhead. The earth added about another pound in weight to each foot. Finally, I scrambled over a couple of ditches on my hands and knees and climbed up a field of stubble to a B road by Jericho Farm. I turned left at a T-junction and headed east towards Oakham, leaving Leicestershire. A little way after the sign announcing that I'd entered Rutland I passed an extraordinary pink house. It was painted knicker pink and over the letterbox was a cut-out iron witch on horseback with a broomstick.

The road took me up a long hill, the hedgerows bursting with blackberries. I was dying to stop and pick a few, but I had to walk over 12 miles today and every time I crossed a ploughed field it cut my speed down by half.

I left the road and crossed a field heading south-east over to the A606 and turned into a gated road to Cold Overton. By Northfield Farm four Old Spot pigs, all brown and furry with a litter of piglets, were a touching sight. A sign announced 'Naturally reared meats'. A mile or so down the road I saw a very dirty old sign that said 'Grange Bungalow, Ian Frazer, Taxidermist' outside a little Virginia-creeper-covered bungalow with a caravan. Grange Farm had a hunter on a horse on its sign, and then a man rode up the edge of a ploughed field, a rare sight round here where all the riders have been on the road. Already the landscape had changed and was much more hilly.

I entered Cold Overton past some very grand parkland on the left, and a small wrought-iron gate with stone columns with a shield on them on either side. Stonehouse Farm had Gothic windows with a Victorian gothic stone porch, triple leaded arched windows, all very pretty. The farm cottages had the same Victorian Gothic doorway with 'Est 1845' on the stone crest over the front door. The village was full of fine honey-coloured stone cottages and farms. The church was sensational, an absolutely beautiful mustard colour with yew trees around it. I walked past the gravestone of Wren Evans who died in 1871. The hall was flying a flag and was, I'd guess, late Jacobean, a fine three-story house with circular columns and gateposts with a grand point on the top.

I followed its high wall along to a T-junction at the end of the village where I turned left in front of the nurseries heading down the hill towards Oakham and Langham. There was a fine rain but it was relatively bright, although the wind was freezing and, as it whipped up, acorns pelted down on to the road from the trees on my left. I was aiming for a radio mast I could see over on my horizon. I took a long footpath across a field of stubble, which was well marked, and I could see that someone had ridden it earlier this morning as there were fresh horseshoe marks. Sadly the ground was completely waterlogged. I climbed up a hill towards the radio mast.

Rutland was already grander, hillier and much more lush than Leicestershire. It's funny how you notice the geographical changes so precisely just a couple of miles into a county. Rutland immediately meant luxurious parkland and rich farmland, and looked monied and middle-class. The hedges were well cared for, dense and recently cut, trimmed precisely along their tops and sides. I walked down a bridleway that was asphalted at first, past the BT radio mast sitting on top of the hill, with a fine view over the whole county. Unfortunately it wasn't sunny. I passed a bunker with grassy sides, a TV aerial on top of it and double wooden doors that were locked. Was this a regional seat of government? Somewhere the prime minister fled to in the event of a nuclear attack? It was all very mysterious. The wide path ended and I went through a small gate into a field heading due south for Braunston in Rutland.

Far away to my left I could see Rutland Water, grey in the afternoon light. But then suddenly it started to brighten up and handkerchief-size pieces of blue started to appear all over the sky. The horizon still looked threatening but above me and to the south things were definitely cheering up. Then I entered a lovely green enclosed lane heading down towards Braunston with high hedges of hawthorn and brambles on either side. Thank goodness the grass wasn't too muddy and I was protected from the wind. At that moment the sun came out briefly and it was a glorious moment. I passed a scrapyard and emerged into the village, turning left to the Old Plough just as two lots of toffs drove past in new Range Rovers with personalized number plates. Andrew, the landlord of the Old Plough (built in the 1780s), mixed me a Rutland independent cocktail he'd created for the party they had had on the night Rutland celebrated regaining its independence and being separated from Leicestershire, 1 May 1997. The drink seemed to involve lots of spirits, orange juice and mint oil, and it tasted absolutely delicious, although any alcohol does after you've walked ten miles. Andrew was a really engaging chap and made me laugh a lot.

I met Eddy Martin, who taught business studies at a local independent school and was one of the main leaders of the campaign for Rutland's independence. He had me in fits of laughter with all the reasons why Rutland deserved to be independent: it was created in Roman times, it had a definite identity, more people wanted it to be independent than anywhere else in Britain, and so on. The local government shake-up of the 1970s meant that Rutland was swallowed up by Leicestershire in 1972, and for 25 years local people campaigned vigorously to get Rutland back on the map.

According to Eddie, 'I certainly felt evangelical about it but then do did 30,000 of the 34,000 people that live in Rutland.' Eddie was soon fired up and ranting. 'But you've seen how beautiful Rutland is as you've come through. Why shouldn't we govern ourselves. What are the arguments against? Small is beautiful and we're showing it already. On the Continent, in Switzerland and Sweden, they've been having small councils like ours for years. Successive market research showed that 84 per cent of the people of Rutland wanted to govern themselves. That was the message that we, as the elected representatives of the people, got, and that's what we fought for. So David took on Goliath and after a long battle we won. Democracy is dead in Britain as long as it's governed from Whitehall. Return government democracy back to local people, then we'll have a democratic nation.'

But wouldn't we end up with a Britain where there are thousands of mini-empires? To me the bottom line is that we are all British. Surely the next step would be UDI and the issuing of Rutland passports? It was a publicity stunt Eddie had already used! 'When we had our magnificent campaign we did indeed have a passport to Rutland, and BBC1 featured it and so did lots of other people around the world,' he explained.

With Eddie's passionate plea for democracy ringing in my ears, I left the pub and walked down to the church. The sun was shining and the cold wind didn't seem so bad – the cocktail had definitely perked me up. The village was full of pretty little honey-coloured cottages, some of which were being restored. Rutland very definitely had a character all of its own, I was forced to admit. Eddie might be right.

At the church was one of Rutland's enigmas, a statue of a fertility goddess. The church had a huge clock on the side of the square tower topped by a tiny spire. I walked through the graveyard with its pleasing arrangement of leaning stones, some dating from 1750, others with intricate carving. I passed the main entrance to the church and then round it to the west front where I found the extraordinary carving of the fertility goddess with a big smiling face or bared teeth (hard to tell which), and an enormous bust. I thought it was a rather optimistic symbol for the village of Braunston. Even the architectural historian Sir Nikolaus Pevsner had been baffled by the mystery woman. Where had she come from?

I retraced my steps through the village and headed towards Brooke, watched by a ginger cat in a window. A boy crossed the road in front of me, just out of school, operating a yo-yo with excellent dexterity. It was 6 pm and there was the best sunset for weeks, not a cloud in the sky, just the odd bit of pink fluff. As I walked along the B road to Brooke, past some council houses and boys kicking a ball around on a playing field, the pink brick houses were glowing in the horizontal light of the setting sun and the odd commuter car passed by. The hedgerows were laden with elderberries flopping over with their sheer weight. Two elegant young horses about a year old looked at me with curiosity as I passed their field. Yes, Rutland is stylish and charming, everything that Nottinghamshire isn't. It's slightly curvaceous, with little hills, small fields and a general air of self-satisfied well-being. It seems a good place to live with fine towns like Oakham and Uppingham and pretty villages.

I walked through several fields of exquisite racehorses. An owl flew out of a tree across the field and the evening was drawing in, it felt a bit chilly and I could tell it was autumn.

The road curved round over an ancient waterway with fine metal railings and an old stone bridge. Now I was being plagued by clouds of midges, a new departure as I thought we'd left them well behind in the last few weeks of freezing winds and driving rain.

Then it was past Brooke Priory with its three-car garage, an elegant two-storey building with leaded windows. An old dovecote stood in the garden, a hexagonal building with a pointed roof with a ball on the top, apparently all that remains of an old monastery. The ruins of a medieval village were near my route but all that remained was a series of lumpy pieces of land. Unfortunately these things never live up to their billing on the Ordnance Survey map. A pair of extremely fat pheasants squawked their way out of a hedge and into a ploughed field. The church at Brooke sat just below the road behind a triangle of green. The church was sensational, with a squat square Norman tower and a double nave. In the churchyard I noticed a gravestone: 'In loving memory of Thomas Jones and his dear wife Ada Virtue'. What a great name. It was Sir John Betjeman's favourite church, and I could see why.

I walked up a long hill out of Brooke in the gathering dusk and then down the other side towards the village of Ridlington, and over another stream with wood pigeons flying out of the trees and a background noise of a steady squawk of happy pheasants. Suddenly the road was very dark with high trees as I approached Ridlington. Also a lot of cars were suddenly belting up and down it and I was being eaten alive by midges. It was sod's law that I had thrown away the insect repellent yesterday.

When you're in the middle of a long walk like this one it's almost as if you're in a separate world from everyone driving a car. The sounds of traffic take on an intensity you can't imagine if you are within a vehicle. The sound of birds is soothing and relaxing. The green of the grass pleasant on your eye but the sight of litter is unimaginably offensive. Everything is heightened because you view everything at eye level and at the pace that you are walking at, I suppose three to four miles an hour. Viewed at that speed and at that height everything is probably ten times more intense than normal.

Now I crossed the A47 on the outskirts of Uppingham. Thank goodness a pavement had been provided to take me into town. One of the joys of walking is seeing the unexpected unfold in front of you, trying to read what lies ahead and not knowing whether you are going to see something of architectural merit. Signs, for example, take on hidden and wonderful meanings. I passed an ancient green wrought-iron bench, obviously placed at this rather unattractive traffic roundabout by a grateful member of Uppingham's population, although the view that it now provides is somewhat undistinguished – the National Farmers' Union headquarters and a large sign that said 'Put British pork on your fork'.

A teenager hurried past me wearing a white shirt, a black jacket and a black bow-tie. I thought this was a new version of Uppingham School uniform until I looked more closely and realized he was carrying a menu to the local hotel. The outskirts of Uppingham were like any other middle-class town in middle England, 1950s semi-detached houses and an ugly 1970s housing estate. There's an interesting convention that when you're walking on lanes or through villages you say hello to people, but if you're walking through towns or anything bigger than a village you don't. As I walked to the crossroads in the middle of town I passed one of the Victorian houses where the boys board and an unmistakable aroma of shepherd's pie wafted out across my path. That gruesome smell of school dinners. It doesn't matter if you're at a public school or state school, somehow they all smell the same.

That evening I went back to the hotel before going to have a massage. Then disaster struck. Driving on a tiny lane over the fields I had to navigate cattle grids and didn't see a high kerb, hitting it squarely on. My tyre blew out, I hit my head on the top of the car and it skidded to a halt. I managed to leave it in a driveway, went on and had a massage in a living-room surrounded by 18th- and 19th-century family portraits, wonderful china and tattered brocade curtains. The masseur,

David McLaren, had come to live here from the west coast of Scotland 20 years ago. He still went down to London once a fortnight for some of his patients. He was a good masseur, but I think a little intimidated by me. Nevertheless he got to work on my legs and said they were very knotted up.

PART SIX

Uppingham

to Welwyn Garden City

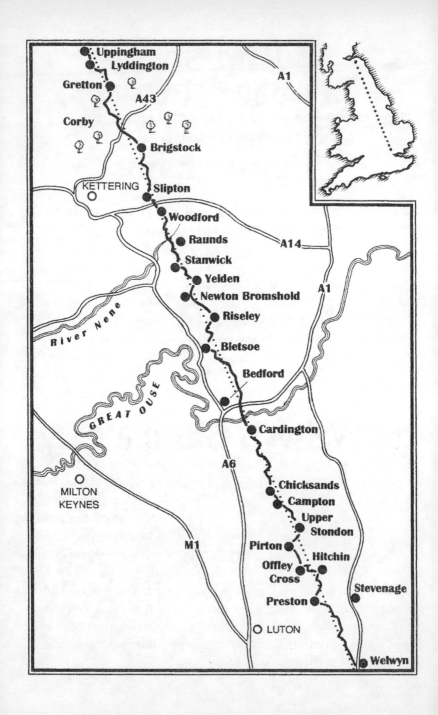

DAY 33

UPPINGHAM TO CORBY
Schoolboy pranks, a beautiful village and dangerous snakes

I awoke to the Central weather bulletin which seemed to be cautiously optimistic indicating sunny periods and showers, but when I looked out of the window the sky was grey and it was raining, even though I was probably only 20 miles from where the bulletin was coming from. I'd had my usual sleepless night that had become a bit too regular of late. I fell asleep at about midnight and woke at 4.00 am, went over everything in my mind and then couldn't get back to sleep again. I rubbed aromatherapy oil on my injured knee and even lay on my orange plastic massage balls on the floor to try and ease my stiff back. Then I got back into bed, made a few lists, read a couple of old newspapers and put the light out, but I couldn't go back to sleep with my leg throbbing like mad. Just as I'd fallen asleep the phone rang and it was my wake-up call. I drank some hot water with a slice of lemon – I've forgotten why I'm doing that, but after 20 years I daren't stop. The BBC's breakfast news was so unbelievably trivial and cosy it made me want to scream with rage. John Nicholson used to be a relatively serious presenter but now he's trying like mad to have body chemistry or something with his female co-presenter; it just makes me want to weep.

Today I was walking into Uppingham with Stephen Fry. It's where he went to school for two and a half years until he was expelled. Last night we had a jolly fine dinner and a good laugh. I've known him for quite a few years and he really is a larger than life character, both incredibly confident and insecure at the same time, a very appealing combination. Also, I like large people, and he's much taller than me.

The day was grey and cloudy as usual with a very cold wind. Stephen appeared in a black polo-neck, black jeans and a black jacket with brown shoes. He said he'd only been back to Uppingham a few times, although it turned out he had generously given quite a lot of money for the school to build a TV studio. Architect Piers Gough, who designed my house in London, had also designed a science and arts wing at the school called the Leonardo Building because he too was an old boy. Uppingham, it turns out, is a rather expensive school but it doesn't seem as academically rigorous as other public schools.

It was founded in 1584 by the Reverend Robert Johnson, a local cleric who was once tutor to the scholar Francis Bacon. Johnson's idea was to give a free classical education to locals, but over the years the merchant class began to dominate, because Johnson had endowed scholarships to Oxford and Cambridge. Over the next 250 years it gradually became a boarding school. Edward Thring, an inspirational educationalist, was headmaster from 1853 to 1887. He turned it into the first public school to have a gym and music lessons for all pupils. Everyone was taught according to their ability, and religion was the basis of everything. When the town had a typhoid scare in 1875, Thring moved the school to Borth in Wales until the town council fixed the drains. They returned triumphantly in 1877 by which time Uppingham's sewage system had been overhauled.

Nowadays the school has 650 pupils (and girls in the sixth form) living in 13 houses around the town. The school has 17 listed buildings, and famous old boys include Boris Karloff, chef Rick Stein, film director John Schlesinger and water-speed champion Donald Campbell.

I crossed North Street past a pretty Victorian house painted apricot, past the Methodist church and past a cottage with a fine gold sign over the door that's now an art dealer's. Now I was on High Street West, and turned right to the school.

I went in through the main gate and met Stephen in the quadrangle. I then re-enacted meeting him for the cameras under the watchful eye of Russell, the school's marketing manager. We live in a competitive age and Russell assured me that they needed to compete very vigorously to get boys and that was why his services were required, and that they had just taken an ad in *The Lady*. *Vogue*, Russell told me, was far too expensive to advertise in. There was also a promotional video to entice parents. We passed an impressive marble statue of Edward Thring – Stephen said he used to leap into his lap and try to snog him!

Then we went into the great hall, which in Stephen's day wasn't divided into two floors. One of his specialities (he must have been one of the naughtiest boys in the school, both clever and insufferably witty and patronising, ghastly teenage qualities that I also had in quite large quantities – they make you so loathed by teachers because you have an answer for everything) was to nip into the hall and reset all the organ stops when there was no one around so that when the organist sat down to play the hymn of the day at assembly, a completely contorted version of what they had expected came out. Another of Stephen's tricks was to go up on the roof and either pee on people or chuck things down on their heads.

Stephen told me about yet another of his pranks, 'There's the bell tower over there and if I'd snuck out of a lesson which was supposed to end at 12, at 11.50 I'd go up the bell tower and strike the bell 12 times to try and confuse them. It was absolutely pathetic. All the clocks in the form rooms were driven by a master clock, and I found it and used to fiddle around with that as well. So the headmaster would say, "Oh my goodness, we've only got three minutes left. Time flies when you're enjoying yourselves," and we'd say, "Yes, that's right." It was childish, but now I put it down to loneliness and the usual adolescent drivel.'

Stephen arrived at Uppingham when he was 13. According to him the school is famous for producing people that he defined as 'genial duffers', as it didn't compete then in academic league tables. Uppingham placed other values higher than just passing examinations. I asked Stephen if he'd been a regular user of the school's swimming pool. 'No, not really,' he said. 'If you want to swallow urine then just do it straight from the source. I see no point in wading in it!'

At that point I collapsed laughing and Russell the marketing man looked a bit stricken. We walked between the main school buildings on a cobbled path known as 'the magic carpet'. There was a break in lessons and all the boys and girls streamed past. They seemed a very pleasant bunch. Stephen spotted his nephew, who didn't seem too embarrassed at having Uncle Stephen say hello to him. Then we went into the buttery where the boys were all purchasing chocolates and coffee. Stephen took me to the music wing which consisted of lots of small practice rooms with double doors for sound-proofing. He told me that in his day he often used to pop in there for a wank or, even worse, go in the large room at the end where all the records were stored and cover the window with a coat, having nicked a baton from the music master's office, put on a record and conduct some very bombastic piece of music as if he was Georg Solti or Otto Klemperer.

Then Stephen and I went out into the town to Baines café, which was out of bounds unless you were a prefect. The sign outside read 'Baines Tea Shop for Gentry'. Stephen said the only time he had ever been into Baines was when his mum and dad came to see him.

He immediately ordered two poached eggs on toast and I had a black coffee as we were almost rigid with cold. He told me the story of how he was finally expelled. He was the youngest member of the Sherlock Holmes Society of London and the school agreed that he could go up to London one Saturday morning for a lecture. At these meetings detailed aspects of Sherlock Holmes' fictional life were discussed. Stephen got on a train to London, went to the lecture and then didn't return until the following Wednesday. He had discovered the delights of the cinema and, posing as an 18-year-old, went to see *Cabaret*, *A Clockwork Orange* and *The Godfather* back to back. When Stephen finally returned to school he was summoned to the headmaster's study and his parents were sent for. He was then thrown out. He went to a succession of other schools and even got arrested for shoplifting before going to Cambridge, but he still remembers his time at Uppingham with affection, even though it ended in such shame.

We left the tea room and strolled through the market square, past the bookshop where a large sign in the window announced that in the evening Stephen Fry was doing a reading from his book *Moab is my Washpot*, which is all about Uppingham. Stephen told me that because it had sold out the event had been transferred to the school hall, which he found amusing. He was planning to take his nephews out to lunch and stay the night, returning to London the next day.

At the end of the High Street we went past some pretty cottages until we came to an exquisite thatched building which was one of Uppingham's two cricket pavilions. This ground was for the first team, something that Stephen never reached. I probably made Stephen feel worse because I was in quite a few school teams, although that was only because I was the tallest girl at school, a psychological deterrent more than an accomplished athlete. I hadn't been to a cricket match since 1965, when my friends had a friendly game and I made the tea. I made 500 (or so it seemed) cucumber sandwiches. I cut off all the crusts, wheeled it out in front of the pavilion just like the one we were standing in front of. The men came off the pitch, ate all my sandwiches, drank my tea and didn't even say thank you. 'What did you expect, a little peck on the cheek?' said Stephen, as we went on to the pitch and he embarked on a long and incredibly detailed technical description of the many different types of spin bowling. He lobbed a few balls in my direction and eventually I hit one straight into the crotch of the cameraman who wasn't terribly pleased and tried to pretend it had really hit his knees. On that note I said goodbye and continued my walk. 'Farewell, my dear,' boomed Stephen.

I retraced my steps to the market square, walked down through the centre of town and after the church turned left on South View.

The churchyard opposite had an elaborate tower on the corner with slits for arrows, and the metal gates to the cemetery had fiercesome points curving towards me. In the graveyard the yew trees had their tops lopped off flat. At the end of the graveyard I followed a well-used path with a high hedge on either side south towards Lyddington. A lady saw me looking at my map and asked me if I needed help. Everybody seemed very friendly in Uppingham.

On my right were some allotments with a boarded gate leading to them. Somebody had scrawled the word 'wankers' on it, not a very Uppingham word I thought, perhaps it was some schoolboy protest at the art of vegetable growing. I was thankful to be away from the traffic thundering along the London road. I crossed a stream via a boarded bridge and the path went up a muddy hillside. This pleasant path undulated up and down through pastureland and under sycamore trees. There was quite a dusting of small white button mushrooms that had sprung up overnight, plus the occasional crisp bag, Bounty wrapper and Smarties container, showing that this was a popular local route. I crossed the lush thistle-free well-mown grounds of a rugby pitch and a football pitch, and a less architecturally pleasing complex of buildings than Uppingham School loomed on my right, probably a technical college or secondary school with a car park bursting with cars.

I crossed a road and went up into a field. The farmer had just ploughed and planted it. He was standing there. He expected me to walk around the edge but when I pointed out that the footpath went across it he reluctantly gave in. I then walked downhill across a few more fields with the pleasant village of Lyddington ahead. I passed an ornamental lake on my right, with an unpleasant Tyrolean-style little fishing hut and a platform. I was heading for the site of Lyddington's famous medieval fishponds, now reduced to just a series of mounds in the earth but in their day the last word in aquatic engineering.

I walked round the edge of a tortured landscape with conifers standing isolated, probably by the same landscape gardeners who had created the new lake. I spotted Lyddington church spire across a field, and some creamy-coloured cows with calves looked at me balefully, sheltering under a hawthorn bush. The stream that was dammed to form the ornamental lakes meandered along on my right. I turned up towards the red-tiled roof of a barn on the edge of the village, now converted into a posh home. I walked out through the yard of Stonebarn Farm and on to the main road. Opposite was the most beautiful wall. It was honey coloured, made with large pieces of ironstone, with pale-green lichen growing all over it, a topping of two rows of tiles and over it a tree bursting with red apples. Over a cottage lintel the word 'Annette' was carved. I didn't know if it was the owner of the house or the name of it.

Outside the Bede House a group of people were just completing a tour. A really sweet kid asked for my autograph and I signed his postcard. He asked me what I was doing and I told him I'd walked all the way from Edinburgh. 'Corr,' he said, his face suspended in disbelief, and I said, 'I'm afraid I'm in a bit of a cross mood today because my knee is really hurting and I'm taking it out on everyone,' whereupon he turned to John Bush, the director, and said, ''Ere mister, why don't you give her the day off?' and everybody cracked up laughing. I couldn't be in a bad mood after that.

The Bede House was originally a medieval Bishop's Palace, and then from 1600 was used as an almshouse for the local poor. Pensioners lived here until the 1930s. In the great hall there was a long wooden table and two benches. I lay on one of the benches and tried to practice a bit of yoga. The early-16th-century carved wooden cornice to the room was ornate and very beautiful. Here the pensioners had to assemble three times a day for prayers and other communal activities. Upstairs the huge vaulted roof timbers in the attic were magnificent.

I walked through the churchyard and turned down Church Lane. At the corner was a charming octagonal tower. Opposite was a cottage with a plaque dated 1626 in the wall and 'Priest

House' over the door. The village hall had an elaborate Gothic lettering at the top of the notice board.

Number 3, almost the last house, was Georgian with a Victorian addition. The steps were completely overgrown with pink flowers. Lyddington House itself was a grand three-storey affair with different coloured stones around the windows. I walked out of Lyddington feeling cheered by the harmonious environment, living proof that architecture can lift your spirits and restore your sense of well being. It was one of the most beautiful villages that I'd walked through on this journey.

A few hundred yards down the road the architectural delights of Lyddington soon vanished. The countryside became more open. On my left were several curious little rounded hills but ahead lay the inevitable huge fields of modern farming, with hedgerows long gone, and I walked past a handful of ugly modern bungalows. Now I was in Northamptonshire.

I wondered who lived in Lyddington and hoped it was a lively village and not one ossified by its perfection. Was it posh people who taught at Uppingham or steel workers from Corby? Somehow I suspect the former rather than the latter.

Suddenly a car pulled up with a trailer behind it. I must have looked depressed because the farmer got out and said, 'Have I chosen a bad day? I apologize.' It turned out that he farmed some of the fields I was going to be walking through and his daughter worked for the local newspaper, and he wondered if I could do a story for them. I said, 'I don't want to be churlish but I'd rather it all came out at the end when I've finished the walk and the TV series is going out on air.' He said he quite understood. He was a jovial fellow with a Keep Britain Farming sticker in his cab. 'That's fine,' he said. 'Cheer up'. I told him I'd try to.

I crossed a wide valley floor, past a sign that said 'Liable to flooding' and a waterworks which seemed to have been turned into a posh residence. A stylish woman galloped past me. Middle-aged with grey hair, a mauve riding hat and a blue blanket coat and great legs, on a tall, thin, elegant horse. It was a change from all the fatties on plump horses, I must say.

I went under a railway arch and up the hill into Gretton. By the sign to St James's church cemetery a black-and-white pony with a number rather vulgarly stamped on his rear looked over a gate. On a telegraph pole was a sign inviting me to a slimming class at the Uppingham School buttery, an unfortunate place to hold the class.

I cut up Clay Lane pursued by a barking dog, avoiding the centre of the village. All the old houses were of grey stone now, as opposed to the honey colour of Rutland. I took a picture of the pretty red-brick double-fronted Gretton Baptist chapel which was still in use with its graveyard neatly tended. I walked out past large farms with opulent farmhouses. I was going along the top of a ridge when suddenly the sun came out and blue patches began to appear in the sky and I thought that the afternoon looked as if it would be a distinct improvement on the morning. I was going to walk through a large plantation and then follow my line right through the middle of the Corby steelworks. On the horizon in front of me were two enormous chimneys signalling the start of a big industrial estate and Corby.

Soon I entered a wood where an extraordinary sign greeted me, 'Keep dogs on a lead and beware of snakes'. Next to it on the ground were the remains of a bonfire with sticks laid out in a strange fashion as if it had been a black magic ritual. On my long walk from Edinburgh I'd got used to swollen rivers and muddy fields, but dangerous snakes were a new phenomenon.

The plantation became a wide grassy ride. At a confusing junction of tracks I read my compass and sure enough there was a tiny footpath sign nailed to a chestnut tree. The trees were an interesting mixture of broad-leaves, oaks and plane trees alongside the inevitable spruces. I was pleased to see the leaves were turning orange; autumn was well and truly here. I emerged from the plantation by a deep gully. Ahead of me a red hawk flew up, an exciting moment.

The noise in the background was now a steady industrial hum and the two ventilation shafts that I'd seen earlier were right in front of me. I crossed a road and between a chainlink fence and a wire fence lay a narrow footpath. I was watched by security cameras. The smell was unmistakable – bacon sandwiches – but why would four huge grey circular tanks marked BLT4, BLT3 and so on have bacon inside them? Bacon, lettuce and tomato – tank 4. Surely not?

At the end of the tanks was an electricity substation complete with ugly pylons. I reached a wooden stile that looked as if a large angry dog had gnawed pieces out of the top of it. On the other side of the road also behind a chainlink fence was the British Steel plant. I was to be escorted through by the head of personnel, Gerry Garden, as my line ran right through the works. Now I was on busy Phoenix Road with pylons on my left and container lorries thundering past on my right. I passed the Corby MOT testing centre, then a tyre place and a salvage yard – I think that gives a general idea of the landscape. It was hard to believe that I had left genteel Uppingham this morning and here I was in the heart of industrial Corby. On the horizon way over in the west was a large Weetabix factory, painted battleship grey, a very high building with two elegant thin white funnels and the word 'Weetabix' emblazoned across it in giant letters. On a side road was a gypsy encampment with two caravans parked up, a couple of vans and a lot of belongings round a lamp post, including a large red plastic laundry basket and some stuff under tarpaulin. What a place to choose to live, although there were very wide grass verges which I supposed appealed to gypsies. Now I was on Steel Road. The gates to the works lay ahead.

Gerry was extremely genial with a black-and-white spotted tie and a broad Scottish accent. He had been born in Middlesbrough and worked in Corby most of his life but his parents were both Scottish. He explained to me how iron ore had been found in Corby even in Roman times and there had been steelworks here since the beginning of this century when a Scottish firm had set up a huge foundry and brought all the workers down from Scotland. That explained the strong Scottish tradition in Corby – even Scottish bread and pies are imported and there are football supporters' clubs for Celtic and Rangers. Two out of three people in the town have Scottish ancestors.

We walked along the assembly line through the factory, and I had to put a helmet on and ear protectors as the noise was deafening. Gerry explained how in its heyday it employed over 10,000 men, but now there was only 1,200 and just one woman, an apprentice. Steel wasn't made here any more. It arrived, was rolled flat and then formed into pipes. The noise and heat were extraordinary. The assembly line was about three-quarters of a mile long and was the biggest tube-making mill in Europe. I was interested to see that it had recently been refurbished and now had control rooms with television screens monitoring the progress on the line. People worked in teams and were rotated in different jobs so they didn't get bored. They were also wearing earplugs, something that wouldn't have happened in the old days. Gerry said that before many people lost their hearing working in the steel works. As we walked lengths of steel rolled past, being pulled and stretched into tubes.

British Steel was being badly affected by the strong pound and Gerry said he didn't know whether the factory would shrink any further but that it was inevitable as technology progressed that the workforce wouldn't be increased. I asked him how much people earned and he went uncharacteristically coy. When I quoted the miner's figure of over £21,000, he said, 'In that area,' and there were plans to pay salaries monthly, which would be good, I thought, for their self-esteem. Gerry was keen to point out how the works itself was being made environmentally more friendly. The large areas that were no longer used were being turned into parks in association with local schools and they had turned the horrible tarmac car park into one covered with gravel and planted grass across half of it. He said British Steel were worried about their environmental image and were spending a lot of money on educational projects, supplying videos and information to schools and working with the local schools, sponsoring gardens.

I said goodbye to Gerry and left the works by the main gate, turned left and then headed south along the revolting A43, a road with no pavement, just a grassy verge full of rubbish, with cars whipping past me. As I crossed a drainage ditch I looked to my left and saw a large heron fly up majestically, a surprising sight in the middle of Corby. Then a couple of moorhens appeared and a couple of ducks.

To follow my line was difficult. Between me and where I wanted to go was a large landfill site with a huge sign proclaiming a new 35-acre development for distribution industry and commerce, but unfortunately I couldn't cut across this undeveloped wasteland as it was surrounded by a high chainlink fence, the kind I'd already seen a lot of in Corby. Gerry had told me that British Steel was no longer the largest employer in the town – that was now a radio components factory. There was also a Golden Wonder crisps factory – perhaps that could explain the bacon smell that so baffled me earlier. They must be having a big run of smoky bacon crisps on the production line. Earlier I'd passed a huge Oxford University Press building, one of several in Corby, and apparently there was a book binding works as well. Gerry had said that when British Steel had laid off 10,000 unemployment was running at 33 per cent, but EC money and Government funding had poured in to try and rebuild the town and now it was down to the national average. Up to the 1960s it had been a one-industry town, but now it was very different, the distribution capital of the Midlands.

A large lorry labelled Corby Chill slowed down and waited for me, ominously. I stopped and crossed my arms in a threatening manner, I hoped. After a couple of minutes it continued on its way. I was buffeted by the wind coming off the back of one lorry after another. I turned down a B road and then straight into a field which was newly ploughed and dry, thank goodness. I crossed it, heading south-east. It was my biggest field of the day; I didn't know how many football pitches would fit on this; it was probably the size of Monte Carlo, an entire principality. I was heading for Cowsick Plantation and before anyone makes the joke, I'll say myself that I must have been a pretty sick cow to be still walking!

The sun was coming out as usual at the end of the day when filming had finished. It was going to be a very beautiful sunset as the storm clouds had all retreated to the east and the breeze had dropped. On the horizon a farmer was ploughing, surrounded by at least 200 seagulls swooping like a big cloud of white feathers tossed in the breeze over his head. I entered the stillness of the plantation on a track through beech trees. Soon it was mature plane trees and the odd Scottish pine, a welcome sight after the industrial nightmare of Corby. There was the gruesome sight of a dead squirrel hanging from a tree, tied up with a piece of string. I saw the prints left by deer and wondered where they were hiding. The roar of the traffic on the A43 kept up a steady hum in the background.

Under some fir trees in the woods I could see wire pens with baby pheasants in them running up and down. Now my track took me alongside the culvert of a disused railway line overgrown with brambles and rosehips. Leaves fluttered down across my path and I slithered over a muddy bank heading eastwards. The midges were gathering in huge numbers. Every now and then were bales of hay for fodder and barrels of water, so something was getting fed although I couldn't see any horses. Perhaps there were wild boar. A wall of grey loomed in front of me, it was the edge of a landfill site and I left the forest. Somewhat unnecessarily a large sign said 'Danger, keep out' – I wouldn't be rushing to walk up it anyway. It looked like a kind of grey porridge just poured there with no stability whatsoever. Eventually I turned south and headed out of the forest and away from the landfill site. A grey squirrel dashed across my path. I couldn't find the track to the road and took the wrong one, lost my temper, retraced my steps and finally found the road.

I was shattered. I ended my walk by Brickhill Cottages, halfway between Stanion and Brigstock. Once again my walk had thrown up extraordinary juxtapositions. The beauty of Bede House and the serenity of Lyddington just a few miles from the deafening racket of the steel assembly line at Corby, home of crisps, Weetabix and monster container lorries.

DAY 34

CORBY TO CHELVESTON
Bob Hope's concert spot

There was torrential rain and gales last night and flooding in Wales and Scotland. I started on the A6116 just outside Corby. As this was very near the Euro hub where every container lorry in Europe seems to gather, lorries were belting past regularly. I saw a huge double container lorry go twice round the roundabout because he couldn't work out where he was.

Last night I went to a dinner given by the art dealer Jay Jopling and met the artists Dinos and Jake Chapman, two brothers whose work has caused so much outrage. They are really intelligent and funny, very smart. They told me that they are working on an enormous piece about World War II, 45 feet square, in the shape of a reverse swastika made up of thousands of tiny German soldiers, featuring a concentration camp and gas chambers. When I said that I supposed the subject matter ruled out selling it to Germany, they told me far from it. They had great hopes of three potential buyers in Germany. I was astounded. The waffle of all the museum and gallery people present at the dinner and the hopeless preening of egos was something Jake couldn't cope with and I don't blame him.

I passed a kennels and cattery and then a dog training place. All I could hear was a man shouting 'Shut up', so I wondered what kind of training these poor dogs were getting, as they were barking incessantly. Every time I'd walked past a kennels on this journey I heard barking for hundreds of yards afterwards. It left an indelible imprint in my mind of animals in small horrible enclosures. If I had a dog I'd never send him to one of these places now I've heard the sounds emanating from them. Then I heard a rifle going off. I hoped it wasn't an animal being put out of its misery.

Three tufts of pampas grass in 100 yards were my first impression of Brigstock, but on the corner of Old Dry Lane and Back Lane stood a wonderful narrow building, four storeys high and a magnificent old factory. I guessed it was 150 years old with arched windows. The village was surprisingly homogeneous, the High Street a ribbon of creamy-grey cottages, the village shop open on Sundays until 6.00 pm, a sign of the times. An old man was shuffling about with a shopping bag and a walking stick, getting the day's supplies and hoping to say hello to somebody. There was a fine church built around a Saxon tower with an imposing spire. Over the river dozens of ducks quacked loudly. I passed some thatched cottages and a white one with three elderly women sitting in a conservatory talking at the tops of their voices. Then I went past a hedge clipped to look like a bird, not completely successfully, and the inevitable row of council houses and then the open road towards Grafton.

It was windy but muggy, and I got pretty hot and steamy. The road was undulating and I turned off heading east along a track for Snapes Wood. Two small blond boys ran out of the gamekeeper's cottage and crossed a field to meet me; it was the first day of their half-term holidays. The sky had turned completely blue and it was wonderful weather. Unfortunately the sound of a shot came from very close by. I'd been told that the wood ahead was owned by British Steel and that I had permission to walk through it, but the boys told me it was owned by the Spencers and no one had permission to walk through it, so feeling rather nervous I approached it across a green track in the middle of a ploughed field. In the wood at the first crossing of tracks I looked to my right and startled a baby deer that scampered off into the undergrowth. It was a broad-leaf wood of beech, ash and other trees. The track was a slow slog uphill, greasy with thick leaves underfoot but a pleasant walk in the sunlight. There were thick clumps of bluebell leaves and the wind rustled the tree leaves, sending even more down. I love walking through woods like this as it's like entering an idyllic secret world. This one was obviously run as a business as it had feeding bowls, pens for young chicks, wooden sheds for equipment and watchtowers for fire. The path became narrow and waterlogged, just a faint track between a thick carpet of bluebells and a wide clearing of trees. Then I found myself on a wide track with oak leaves underfoot and the only sound apart from the rustling of my boots were squirrels scampering up and down tree trunks.

In a green field between this wood and the next was a spectacular moat, and staring at me was a cream-coloured cow. Suddenly I had an enormous shock when a large grey military plane flew overhead, barely 200 feet up, just above the trees. The cows in the field didn't bat an eyelid.

I emerged from the wood and headed due south to Slipton. This was a beautiful landscape with not a house in sight. It was well managed and looked like part of a large estate. I was only a few miles east of Boughton House, home of the Dukes of Buccleugh since 1528, so this remnant of the once-great Rockingham Forest was probably part of the Boughton Estate. My only companions were pheasants scurrying into the hedges. Now another plane loomed overhead, grey and enormous, like a troop carrier. I entered Slipton and the huge Grange Farm looked deserted. I walked past two model cottages and an exquisite double-fronted Victorian cottage and then through the horror of a new development built in local stone with garages nearly as big as the houses.

Just out of Slipton I spent 20 minutes walking up and down the road looking for a way across a six-foot-deep culvert. Eventually I found a farm gate and crossed a field of rather lively cows, climbed over a lot of barbed wire, went through a wood and another field, and then on to a B road. On my right by a vegetable smallholding was a beautiful 1950s wrought-iron bench painted bright green. I crossed a little field where very fat sheep came running towards me hoping for food. Then, to my horror, the footpath didn't go under the A14 and I had to scoot across the busy dual carriageway. On the other side was a footpath sign pointing into a thicket. I walked up and down inside the brambles for 15 minutes and eventually found a very overgrown footbridge over another stream and went over a field of turnips with no sign of a footpath. Where I joined the road a car had gone into a ditch; both front windows were open and the inside had been vandalized. There was no one about and I wondered how long it had been there. The roar of the A14 was tremendous as I headed away towards the village of Woodford and the beautiful Nene Valley. The sun had come out and it was boiling hot. I took off my fleece and my waterproof trousers, feeling rather dizzy. I bit on a large juicy-looking crab apple from the hedgerow but it was so bitter it completely dried my tongue out. I walked along Mill Road into Woodford with its cream-painted 1950s semi-detached council houses. In the front garden of one was an exotic collection of plaster garden ornaments. Right next to a gnome sat a peaceful-looking Buddha. There were lots of caravans parked in the front gardens and women wheeling pushchairs. The High Street was workers' cottages, and Greg's fish and chip take-away was offering a Halloween special, 'house of horrors' – potatoes shaped as pumpkins, skulls and crossbones. At last the sound of the A14 had died away, replaced by the shrill squawking of starlings sitting on the roofs of houses opposite the old chapel. There was an interesting antique shop, closed of course, even though the hours of business were allegedly 'Tuesdays 10-5'. A green sticker said 'Say no to air freight at Alconbury, the Nene Valley Association'. Victorian cottages were replaced with old stone ones around the village green and the green-painted blacksmith's cottage had fine plasterwork around the windows. Apparently some of the people in the village still worked in the boot and shoe trade, traditional jobs in the area.

I talked to farmer Richard Burnham at Manorhouse Farm. He told me that quite a few people from the village still commuted to London. His house was magnificent. He was a very interesting man and we had an in-depth discussion about the story in that day's *Daily Telegraph* that claimed that over 20,000 farmers are going to go bust. He said it would take two to three years for farmers to go organic and how would the ground be kept fertile, how would we produce enough food and how would it all be economic? He was immaculate in his pale-green overalls with a pen neatly placed in his top pocket and cropped curly silver hair. I was going to pass through some of his meadows on my line down to the River Nene, the site of the original old village of Woodford.

On the banks of the River Nene were ancient willows and lots of barges moored in a lock. The minute I put my sunglasses on the sun disappeared. I took a well-trodden path, the Nene Way. Cars parked by the river suggested that anglers were out in force. For once I wasn't going to complain about a long-distance footpath – I'd been desperate to walk on one for days as I was sick of crossing ploughed fields. I crossed a disused railway line and then the river at Ringstead Mill.

Water mills like this one were really common between the Trent and the Severn, and around 5,000 were in use in the Middle Ages, providing cheap power to run industrial machinery. Some of the mills in the Nene Valley were used to make paper in the 1500s, using a process where linen and cotton rags were pounded into a fibrous texture. One of the two wheels here had been adapted to make paper, but the advent of wood pulp made the process redundant.

It was the first time that I'd walked in a T-shirt in sun for about two weeks, and it felt wonderful. The water was rushing over the sluice gates in Ringstead lock and bubbling on down the river and there was a series of ponds and lakes and locks, which all made for a very harmonious environment. I followed the road along a raised boardwalk supported by stone and concrete blocks. On my right swans were bobbing about on a lake made from a gravel pit and a pair of red tortoiseshell butterflies proved that summer wasn't completely over yet. I climbed upwards and ahead of me lay the wonderful valley of the River Nene and on the skyline the graceful spire of the church at Stanwick.

Top Lodge was a collection of stone barns, and a corrugated metal one disintegrating slowly. The sign on the gate read 'Walkers to be aware of bull and to keep dogs on lead and to keep to footpath', not much of a welcome. Ahead of me lay a bumper-to-bumper line of cars on the A6, glittering in the sunlight, an unwelcome shiny snake slithering through the landscape. I was approaching what was marked on the map as the site of the medieval village of Mallows Cotton. Sure enough there were some interesting green lumps of stunted ancient-looking hawthorn trees.

Unfortunately my path ran out before the A6, and I crossed a small stream on a plank, went over a stile and then the road loomed up above me. It involved climbing on my hands and knees down a ditch and up a steep embankment covered with thistles. I was cursing. I then had to dodge traffic belting along just before a dual carriageway section. On the other side I couldn't see the footpath sign at all so I walked along the verge nearly getting blown away by container lorries, and then went down a steep embankment and around an abandoned building, through thistles and nettles, until I joined a track heading towards the village of Raunds, with unattractive new housing looming over the top of the hill. I passed a brand new doctor's medical centre, then a building site, and turned right on the London road, passing the recently built fire station.

After a short section on the A45 I crossed over it and took the B road to Chelveston. This was the posher end of town with big detached houses and driveways. I passed the final terrace of Edwardian cottages and thought about how much more character these older houses had with their bay windows. People had put little antique model boats and vases in the windows, and everything seemed more personalized, as if the occupants valued things that were older, whereas in the new houses curtains had been yanked back or blinds pulled up to expose huge areas of glass where you could look into rooms that were devoid of any personality or visual style. It was as if the occupants weren't interested in belongings, didn't place any value on design and had no regard for the things of the past. What are their priorities? On this walk I'd passed through countless modern housing estates and looked at thousands of modern houses. I'd peered into dozens of living rooms and come to the conclusion that the world of modern design as featured in all the magazines, as sold by Terence Conran and IKEA, has barely filtered through to the mass of middle England. Visual style frightens them. They create huge areas of emptiness, put their furniture around the edge of the room, clinging to their three-piece suites upholstered in beiges and tasteful pastels. Their gardens are manicured to within an inch of their lives with no blade of grass allowed to sprout higher than the regulation length, flowerbeds are ruthlessly trimmed, flowers planted in contrasting shades. It's as if choosing something old or something a bit more unusual requires too great a commitment. In short, middle England is frightened of making a statement. Tidiness is valued above everything.

In the middle of nowhere sat a detached house with black and white leaded windows, the Kiriandra Pet Centre. There was a cattery, a boarding place for dogs and a grooming centre in two single-storey red-brick buildings, from which came the sound of hysterical barking. It was surrounded by a high chainlink fence, more in keeping with a war camp than a temporary home for a few dozen dogs. A quarter of a mile away and well on the way into Chelveston I could still hear the barking.

I headed along the road towards RAF Chelveston past the village hall and the parish church of St John the Baptist that reminded me that I was now in the diocese of Peterborough, firmly in the middle of Northamptonshire. There was a memorial to the American 305th bomber group of the 8th airforce. It was big farms, big cars, big houses and only a couple of cottages. I passed RAF Chelveston housing, all two-storey brick buildings, and then went down a bridle track that had a 'No Entry' sign. At the end I turned left on to a disused airfield. In front of me was an enormous rusting hangar, and between me and the hangar were dozens of cows all munching grass on the old runway. This was the aerodrome that had been used so much during World War II.

The US Air Force was based here then and at the height of the war Chelveston was home to 4,000 servicemen. Huge B17s – the Flying Fortresses – loaded up with bombs, roared along the runway where now I walked and cows grazed. What stars had performed for the troops in these rusting hangars! James Stewart, Jimmy Cagney, Marlene Dietrich and Bob Hope all appeared at morale boosting concerts. The King and Queen visited with their daughter, Princess Elizabeth, and Gregory Peck shot a movie here.

In the late afternoon sunlight the hangar had a golden glow about it, in keeping with its starry past. I walked past a Ministry of Defence sign that said 'Official Secrets Act, Keep Out, Private Property etc., etc.' It was hard to imagine what a hive of activity this must have been 50 years ago. I walked the length of the runway into the setting sun, humming Bing Crosby's 'What a Swell Party it is' to an audience of munching milk-machines.

DAY 35

CHELVESTON TO BEDFORD
John Bunyan and bathing problems

The hotel I stayed in last night, just outside Bedford, seemed inspired by Fawlty Towers. On the reception desk a woman had a name badge on and music was playing loudly. She gave me a key to a dingy room with a large cigarette burn in the middle of the bedspread. I went back to her and refused to stay in it, saying, 'I don't smoke and I refuse to sleep in a room with cigarette burns.' She said, 'I've got you down as a smoker.' I replied, 'That's not possible as I don't smoke.' The next room, number 48, proved to be cursed. The hotel was built along matchstick-box lines. The corridors of the entire upper floor were being repainted and the smell of gloss paint was overpowering. There were huge stickers everywhere saying 'Mind out wet paint'. Number 48 had at least been recently decorated.

I was shattered and very cold. I ordered a gin and tonic and asked for my bags to be brought here from the other room. I asked the porter to bring them but then I realized hotels like this don't have porters any more (in spite of having three stars), only school leavers with no training whatsoever. A young woman struggled up the stairs with my bags. Then she came back a second time with my third bag. I got into bed with all my clothes on and drank the gin and tonic. The room was freezing. I tried to turn the radiators on but nothing happened. I decided to take a hot bath, so put both taps on and then I couldn't turn the hot tap off. Panicking as it was starting to overflow, I rang reception and asked for someone to come and turn the bath off and turn the radiators on. A plumber didn't arrive, just another girl who was a waitress. After a lot of fiddling around we managed to turn the hot tap off. Then she couldn't get the radiators to work, and said she'd look at the boiler. A few minutes later she returned and said she'd turned it on. There's nothing like having a hotel where they don't bother to have any central heating even though it's October and cold. She ran the bath for me because the hot tap was too hard for me to switch off. The radiators in the bathroom came on but the one in my bedroom simply never did. I lay in the bath which wasn't as deep or as hot as I would have liked and then I went down to dinner.

The restaurant was off the reception area of the hotel and piped music prevailed. The printed menu was mostly fish. I ordered a Caesar salad. Some bits of tired ordinary lettuce (not Cos) arrived, although it did have bacon and some bits of anchovies, two large pieces of toasted bread (not croutons), and some parmesan. It had no dressing on it so it was taken away and returned with vinaigrette dressing. When I asked where the Caesar salad dressing was, some glutinous substance was brought in a small bowl. By then it was too late to start all over again. I ordered blackened swordfish but what appeared was a piece of tuna steak or it might have been swordfish that had been cooked in a lot of olive oil – forget the blackened idea. It was on a bed of allegedly roasted vegetables but which turned out to be a mushroom and a piece of pepper dripping with more olive oil. I had some new potatoes. After lots of Rioja I simply didn't feel the pain, but the idea of this place advertising itself as a fish restaurant was a joke. The food was obviously cooked by someone who had no idea of what they were doing, and as for roasted vegetables, I was just speechless. But what's the point in complaining? Because so many things had gone wrong (I'd received about eight visits from the staff) I was given some free drinks. I went to bed and fell into a deep sleep.

I was awakened at 6.30 am by the sound of people leaving their rooms – the hotel was built on the box principle where if someone even six rooms away from you coughs, sneezes or closes their door, you can hear it. I lay wide awake waiting for another travelling salesman to get up, brush their teeth and leave. Finally my breakfast was brought without the hot water and lemon that I'd ordered by a woman who couldn't speak a word of English, so I had to reorder in French.

When I presented *The Midnight Hour*, a political discussion series on BBC2, my boss was Charlie Courtauld, who now looks after *Question Time*. He called up and said he'd like to walk with me as I was near his home. He turned up in a rainbow-coloured sweater with a large hole in the front, black shoes and navy-blue linen trousers. It was pouring with rain and I don't know who looked the worse, him or me. He gave up after about an hour of empty lanes.

I walked through Newton Bromshold, taking a track off to the left which said 'Village only', went past some pretty cottages and headed south on a lane. The rain and grey sky were obviously part of Britain's continuing hurricane season. The lane soon degenerated into a wide muddy bridleway and it was extremely heavy going. I could hear continuous sounds of pheasant shooting from woods nearby. By Oakley Hunt Kennels two goats stared at me from a field, one a rather nice buttery cream colour. Then I came to a sign across the path, 'Private woodland, action will be taken against unauthorized entry to the Worley Wood Estate', and there was lots of barbed wire wrapped round the top of the padlocked gate to stop me climbing over it.

I crossed a ploughed field and had about ten pounds of mud on each foot that was extremely hard to dislodge. On the far side the farmer had ploughed right up to the edge so it was very tough going. I walked through miserable set-aside fields then along a very full ditch. I stopped by a sign with two skulls and crossbones on it that said, 'Danger, stop, do not proceed, shooting ranges ahead'.

I crossed over the main road to Riseley, then took another footpath heading south-east along the edge of a field. It stopped raining and the sun was weakly glimmering through the clouds. I had rather stupidly worn my light-weight boots which were completely worn out anyway, with a hole at the side of each foot where the stitching had split, and now both were full of water, little boats on each leg. I ate lunch and changed my socks which got wet the minute I put them on. I walked down the road towards Bedford, past a sign saying 'M Forster and Dad, North End Farm', which brought a smile to my face in the dreary weather. As I headed south on a B road to Bletsoe I could see on the horizon huge aircraft hangars. A beautiful old rectory had a sign 'Care for the residential in a homely environment'.

I turned left at the church in Bletsoe that had a square tower and an interesting weather-vane. On the parish field a massive bonfire lay ready for November 5th, dripping wet. Then I turned south along a busy road but realized I was too far off my line so when I got to Wigney Wood I turned east along a footpath, circling the Royal Aerospace Establishment site around a chainlink fence with triple barbed wire along the top. A lot of anonymous concrete buildings with small windows, an office block with a lot of glass and a water tower with a lot of aerials on the top were inside the fence. It looked like a set for sci-fi movies, with a large decompression chamber in the middle. It was now really pouring with rain.

I circled the perimeter of the top secret Aerospace Establishment, navigating a three-foot gap between a ten-foot chainlink fence and a wood. Underfoot was a sea of mud, and I was wet through. I entered Bedford by finding Grave Lane, where pots of honey were for sale by a little wooden hive in someone's front garden. What a sad and sorry sight they looked. Grave Lane eventually joined the road down the hill into Bedford, where I turned into the car park of the Mowsbury Park golf course. I was so wet and cold that I sat in the car with all the heaters on for 25 minutes to warm up.

Waiting to meet me in the clubhouse was the leisure director in a grey suit, who gave me lots of advice about how to cross a golf course, as if I haven't crossed 500 already on this walk. The rain had stopped and the course was filling up. Men in plaid sweaters, one wearing a Westminster Gym sweatshirt and a plaid flat hat chatted to me and wanted to know where I'd walked from. We crossed the golf course dodging the balls, shaking off a local photographer who had been phoned by the leisure director. I went through a copse on a bridleway and saw the best crop of sloes of the walk, and it was too bad I didn't have time to stop. I crossed a road and entered a housing estate.

I was on the eastern outskirts of Bedford as my line didn't go through the town centre. Near to the golf course the houses were detached and somewhat pretentious. I noted with delight that some people had added Doric columns in front of their double garages, while others had two-colour crazy paving, creating a kind of Arizona theme with the inevitable tufts of pampas. As I progressed further into the estate and the houses got smaller there were gardens that I really enjoyed. The last of the dahlias (my favourite flower) were looking gorgeously vulgar, yellow, maroon, spiky petals standing proudly to attention. The roses, a bit frowsy and past their best, were still blooming and had been pruned to within an inch of their lives. There were hydrangeas too, some faded and some a wonderful dusty pink. I enjoy looking at people's front gardens far more than crossing a ploughed field. You can tell so much about the British character from what they do in their bit of green. Some of the wheelie bins had been decorated and I passed one with a Mr Blobby face on it and another painted with a dog. One house had been painted white and had pink wooden shutters with little hearts cut out of them stuck around the windows to add a kind of Tyrolean chalet look. People were out mowing their lawns in military stripes. There were no dirty cars here as they all looked freshly washed, unlike my own car which was covered in bird shit and leaves, undriven and unloved.

I walked down Putnoe Lane and right on to Church Lane. I passed a modern housing estate with smaller gardens, just handkerchiefs of grass enclosed by the inevitable privet. I crossed Gulvington Green, and went past the children's playground where mums were chatting on the bench. The green had the inevitable war memorial and looked freshly mown. I walked down Barkers Lane with its Roman Catholic church on the corner, a rather unfortunate modern building with a barrel-vault roof that looked more like an aircraft hangar than a place of worship. I find that a lot of modern churches are the last place I'd want to pray. I went to Middlesbrough Cathedral a couple of years ago to a friend's mother's memorial mass and had trouble finding it because I actually mistook it for the giant superstore next door.

My favourite garden so far had a monkey puzzle tree in the centre of the lawn, and red salvias interspersed with white alyssum. Outside one semi-detached house a huge array of radio masts sprouted, owned by a ham radio enthusiast or perhaps a secret minicab company. There was a large area of allotments where men had rolled-up shirt sleeves and were digging their leeks furiously, soil was being tilled and turned, and there was even a woman helping out, a rare sight on allotments. I grew all my own vegetables for seven years until my back could take it no longer, and there are few things I like better than looking at other people's allotments and wishing that I had grown that spinach or those leeks. I skirted the industrial estate and headed for Bedford's Country Park.

A bridge took me across the fast-flowing River Great Ouse and into the Priory Country Park and Marina, the green artery of Bedford. To my right was the Travel Inn (£38 a night), a marina and a lake. In the marina the boats were all moored behind high steel gates with masses of barbed wire. Burglary was obviously a problem. All the small craft had the inevitable names: Foxy Lady, Laughing Water, etc. I walked around and then realized I couldn't get out, so I retraced my steps and was pointed in the right direction by a bird watcher wearing wellingtons, a flat hat and a large pair of binoculars. On the side of the lake the coarse fishermen were already in place.

By the water's edge, sitting on a bench was local publisher and John Bunyan expert, John Nicholson. He had a navy blue overcoat, a flowing grey beard and long silver hair, and a wide-brimmed trilby hat and sparkling eyes. A modern version of Bunyan, Bedford's most famous inhabitant.

Bunyan, author of *The Pilgrim's Progress*, was born in 1628 just south of the town. He was imprisoned in Bedford gaol for 12 years for refusing to accept the ban on his brand of plain Christianity, preached by the Independent Congregations. Bunyan had become a preacher in the mid 1650s but when Oliver Cromwell's protectorate ended and the monarchy was restored, his style of worship was banned. In prison he wrote *The Pilgrim's Progress*, the story of Christian's journey to the Celestial City, and it was published a year after his release. It has been translated into over 200 languages, and outsells Shakespeare in some places. According to John, although the popular view is that Bunyan was a devout, pious man who wrote a best-selling book about belief, in reality he was a rebel, voicing the true feelings of ordinary people who were sick of corruption and extravagance.

'The people who have erected statues and open museums in Bunyan's honour are doing him a disservice – he would have been horrified at such idolatry – it stood for everything he opposed,' said John. 'He wouldn't accept the monarchy, he wouldn't accept archbishops and the established church. Wars have been fought to get rid of bishops and this is the belief that had governed the country, and which Bunyan subscribed to. If he was alive today he'd be considered a real radical, even by the reformed Labour party.'

Didn't John think it was ironic that the church has claimed Bunyan as one of their own? John agreed: 'It's more than ironic, I think it's hilarious. They have actually had the Archbishop of Canterbury involved in delivering a sermon on John Bunyan.' I asked John what message I should take from *The Pilgrim's Progress* to help me complete my long walk. 'I think you should be inspired, because Bunyan changed the whole idea of a journey anyway,' said John. 'You are doing more than getting yourself fit.'

Then John read me a stirring passage from the book itself:

The Pilgrim's Progress from this world to that which is to come. Delivered under the similitude of a dream, wherein is discovered the manner of his setting out, his dangerous journey and safe arrival at the desired country. As I walk through the wilderness of this world, I lighted on a certain place. There was a den. And I laid me down in that place to sleep. And as I slept I dreamed a dream, I dreamed and behold I saw a man clothed with rags standing in a certain place. With his face from his own house, a book in his hand and a great burden upon his back. I looked and I saw him open the book, and read therein and as he read he wept and trembled and not being able longer to contain he'd creak out with a lamentable cry, saying what shall I do?

'The idea of any journey was transformed by Bunyan's book,' said John. 'Before that the idea of a pilgrimage meant crusades to the Holy Land. Bunyan said the Holy Land is here, in Bedford. *The Pilgrim's Progress* is more than just a literary classic, and it will be relevant to your journey through England because you're going through both the landscape which he knew, and you are also experiencing some of the inner learning, or the inner adventures which Christian experienced.'

Inspired by the exploits of Christian, and the idea of John Bunyan as a militant Leftie, I said goodbye and continued on my own journey to my celestial city, London.

The only other riveting fact I could come up with about Bedford was that during World War II the town was England's home of popular music. The BBC Symphony Orchestra and Music Department moved here from London. In July 1944 Glenn Miller gave his first live concert in Britain from the Corn Exchange in Bedford.

I entered the wildlife reserve on the south side of the lake, and got lost because none of the maps had 'You are here' signs on them. It was a pleasant spot with lots of bulrushes, ducks and the occasional heron. There was a whole series of weirs and waterways and eventually I rejoined the River Ouse and crossed it by a lock, and then crossed Cordington sluice-bridge over the River Great Ouse. Then I was in the Priory Business Park with its large bland new buildings.

I ended the day's walk by the A421 at Cordington Cross to the south-east of the town centre.

DAY 36

BEDFORD TO CHICKSANDS
Airships and military intelligence

I spent all last night throwing up after eating a bad oyster, so I felt a bit hollow to say the least. It was the rush hour. I passed the Autoglass factory and had to navigate a giant roundabout under Bedford's southern bypass. I walked past the A603 to Sandy and turned off to Cardington. Two hangars loomed enormously in front of me, dominating the horizon from the minute I first saw them. Every other building in Bedford seemed tiny and low in comparison. I entered the village of Cardington and passed a pair of old cottages with a big plaque on the front announcing that they had been refurbished by Bedford Borough Council in 1998. Unfortunately the pebble-dash exterior looked very 1950s council rather than 1760 and the detailing wasn't too great either. Next door was the cemetery, rows of stones and yew trees that could have done with a trim. A large tomb had a sad inscription: 'Here lie the bodies of 48 officers and men who perished in HM Airship R101 at Beauvais in France October 5th, 1930.' The airship, the R101, had taken off from the hangars behind. It made the magnificent bulk of the two buildings seem sombre and monumental in the bright sunlight.

Cardington church had a square tower, a turret to the side of it and a weather vane. The village green had a Victorian village hall, an old school and various brick cottages around it. At the end of the green were more pebble-dashed cottages all with identical dark-green doors. With hollyhocks spilling on to my path I turned right and headed for the giant hangars past a double-fronted Victorian mansion called The Little House. Parish Cottage was a fine Victorian building with pointed windows which had been leaded and an extension which had probably been the chapel.

Cardington was built around a large Victorian estate as there were plenty of similar cottages with leaded windows and elaborate porches, all painted dark green. I crossed a field at the back of the hangars that was newly planted and then walked over a bit of a bonfire and some rusting vehicles, and finally some pretty deep weeds to reach the back of the pair of two structures. According to my notes, they were the largest hangars in Britain, built over 80 years ago, and were originally owned by the Admiralty. One was being used by the Building Research Establishment to test different building constructions and the other was being used for storage. The northern ends of both buildings were held up by a complicated girder structure. They were built of corrugated metal and the oldest was a listed building. As I walked down the side, it seemed just like walking next to an airship or a boat; the pale green exactly matched the green of the grass around it and the flat windows seemed like port-holes in their sides. I sat and drank a coffee and just contemplated the sheer size of them, overawed by their bulk. I tried to imagine the scene when they housed luxury airships.

Inside I talked to one of the managing directors of the Building Research Establishment. He explained what tests were currently being carried out inside Hanger No. 2, now an enclosed laboratory dedicated to experimental fire research. It contained a six-storey timber house, a seven-storey concrete building, an eight-storey steel building, a house and part of a plane! The floor area was twice the size of the pitch at Wembley.

Very impressed, I rejoined the road out of Cardington, past detached Victorian cottages with high octagonal chimneys and the letters SW1894 on plaques above them. With fields at the front and back they were highly desirable residences.

I walked in a T-shirt, an unusual occurrence these days. The lane meandered south, straight for quite long sections, with no hedges on either side but large old plane trees still looking as if it had been part of an old estate even though the farmers had subsequently managed to plough up all the hedges. On the long straight sections new trees had been planted at regular intervals, and with a ditch on either side of the road with bulrushes and the absence of hedgerows, it seemed more like France than England. The trees had been recently pollarded, adding to their neat Continental appearance. The ruins of Manor Farm lay hidden behind a moat and a thicket of trees. I crossed the flat land to the south of the hangars and the road curved slightly and started to climb a hill. I passed a corrugated metal barn on my right, not unlike the hangars themselves, only this one was painted black. A large house on the other side of the road had 1881 on the plaque above the door.

A man and his wife went past me in the car, then turned round and came back crawling behind me. He leant out of the window and said, 'Excuse me, would you mind stopping and I'll pull over and we can have a chat. My wife and I are fans of yours.' I replied, 'I'm sorry I can't stop, I've got to meet my film crew.' 'Oh,' he said, 'so what are you doing?' and then he proceeded to interview me while driving along at 5 miles an hour. So I told him and said goodbye and hoped I hadn't appeared too rude. People can't really understand when you're walking why you don't want to stop on a busy main road. Also, if you stop for more than five minutes you lose your pace which is I guess about four miles an hour on a relatively flat road.

At the top of the hill I turned right and headed for Warden Little Wood, a footpath that was part of a new access agreement. Ahead of me partridges scuttled into the trees and I could see another Victorian cottage. The grey clouds were massing but it was still warm, and inside the trees I'd be away from the breeze. Now dozens of pheasants scurried out of the sweetcorn field on my left and headed for the safety of the plantation. The track was pretty well used and muddy but now was the middle of the pheasant-shooting season and away on my right I could see a trailer collecting logs. The pine gave way to poplars and beech, and the ground was relatively sandy underfoot. Between the two forests was a large expanse of corn. On the edge of it, before the trees started again, was about a ten-yard-wide expanse of grass and I could see a series of horse jumps, and next to me was a 'Caution, footpath' sign. Some of the jumps were made of logs, some gates and some twigs placed vertically, just like a mini Grand National.

Warden Great Wood was older and larger with fir trees planted relatively far apart, I guessed about 20 or 30 years old. A grey squirrel crossed my path holding a large nut in its mouth and in a clearing about 20 pheasants were busy tucking into something. Gradually the forest gave way to oak, plane trees and beech. I followed the edge of a field with an impressive ten-foot hawthorn hedge surrounding the forest, heading due south for Dead Man's Cross. I could see the traffic on the A600 streaking past ahead of me.

I had spoken to the knee expert in London on the phone about the scan I was to have on my knee. He'd agreed to order a scan of my lumbar area as well because I was concerned that the disc I'd slipped twice in the past was inflamed and causing the pain in my groin, my hip and in the front of my leg. I hoped it wasn't serious but I was in quite a lot of pain now.

Dead Man's Cross had a 40-mile speed limit written in red all over the road. The Red Lion pub had its own white courtesy bus which was a kind of minivan. I reached North Wood End Road, and turned into Rowney Warren Wood. It was full of horse chestnut trees. I walked on a broad path through it heading south. The first person I saw was a man on his hands and knees wearing thick yellow plastic gloves, the kind you use for cleaning drains or doing the gardening, and he had a Sainsbury's plastic carrier bag. I assumed he was collecting wild mushrooms but it turned out he was in fact collecting chestnuts. I thought he was getting in early for Christmas to either dry or cook them but he said instead that he owned woodland and he was going to plant them. He had the most enormous bag of conkers – and I thought he was bonkers!

Leaving conker man to his frenzied search, I set off down the path. In the undergrowth I saw a small deer move behind a tree. Squirrels scampered up and down the tree trunks. It was a thoroughly pleasant walk. People were out exercising their dogs, which all seemed to be overweight labradors. At the end of the wood I crossed over on to a narrow farm track, went past an enormous farm estate on the edge of which was a vegetable packing business. I walked up a road that was marked into lanes, one of which said 'Visitors', so I followed it to a barrier. This was DISC, the Defence Intelligence Security Centre. It trains all three armed forces in intelligence, security and psychological operations. They've got dozens of different courses and apparently it's one of the few places where all the armed services train together. From 1950 to 1995 the American Air Force were based here, so DISC is a relatively new operation.

There was a three-man team waiting to take me on my straight line, which ran right through the base: Commander Plommer from the Royal Navy, Lieutenant Colonel Morrison from the Army and Commander Kevin Telitt from the Royal Air Force. Commander Kevin seemed to assume control and off we marched down the road. I was fascinated to see that the men at the gates were in camouflage wear carrying guns, and yet there were families walking about and signs of normal life. Commander Kevin assured me that a quarter of the people on the base were women and people came here for courses as short as a week and as long as a year, but he was very vague about what they actually did. When I asked if it was decoding satellite pictures they all said, Yes, that kind of thing. There was a building I was very interested in called JSPI which turned out to be the Joint Services Photographic Intelligence Unit, where they learn to read satellite pictures and photographs of enemy installations and guerrilla camps taken from the air.

As we walked along I realized how smart my escorts were. I'd forgotten what a high level of grooming you have to achieve in the armed forces. Lieutenant Colonel Morrison had a trim moustache and very shiny red ox-blood shoes which he told me he polished with a special polish from Sweden (we walkers are fanatically interested in shoe polish). The Royal Navy and Royal Air Force chaps both had black shoes buffed to a fine hue. It turned out that their families lived off base because that was the easiest way to cope with all the changes and Commander Kevin was off to college in London for a year and he didn't know where he would be sent after that. At the end of the base we shook hands and I passed a sign that I photographed with some very peculiar writing on it: 'Black Tahiti bikini', and so on, apparently the various states of alertness in the armed forces.

I said goodbye to them and went on my way. They had been anxious to point out that the image that the armed forces get in the press is a bit negative at the moment because the daily papers were continually focusing on sexual harassment cases. I asked Lieutenant Morrison why, if the army is going all hi-tech, and people are using computers, and this kind of intelligence work demands that you know how to read a code, do recruits still have to square bash? He replied that a certain amount of regimental discipline was still required. So, in other words, although they want intelligent people who can use computers and read codes, they've still got to be able to run up and down a hill with a 30-pound rucksack. No wonder they have trouble recruiting. I suppose the truth of the matter is that the army in future will be made up of two ranks – cannon fodder and the technological elite.

Chicksands Priory was within the base, a few hundred yards away to the west. It was founded in 1140 and housed the English order of Gilbertines. They were all evicted 400 years later when one of Cromwell's commissioners paid a visit and found 'two nuns not barren'. There are local legends about the fallen nuns, and a ghost is said to appear from time to time. Sadly on this occasion she was elsewhere.

Feeling rather weak, I cut the day's walking short.

CHICKSANDS TO ST PAUL'S WALDEN
What price new homes?

I started on Ampthill Road outside the DISC base, and headed for the village of Campton. It was grey and very windy. I was walking over a bed of conker shells along a little lane, exhausted and pretty depressed, plus I had a heavy period, period pain and knee ache, so I'd really hit the jackpot regarding ailments. I decided to adopt a new-age approach and visualize all my various pains and shrink them in my mind, otherwise I would go nuts.

On the outskirts of the village I passed a long hedge of lavender still flowering and scented, which was very soothing in my current frame of mind. Then it was down Rectory Road and into the village that had late-Victorian and early-Edwardian houses with coloured brickwork making interesting patterns around the windows. There were wonderful brick houses in this area, probably because of the local brick factories. I'd seen bricks used with real wit and style, and the Victorian wooden gables and porches made the houses look charming. The village was on the edge of an estate with a large field on my left with old iron railings, a pedigree herd of cattle and fine parkland with large trees. I walked through the village, down Mill Lane, then along what looked like someone's driveway that became the footpath, skirting along by a river. There was no one in sight, and in fact I hadn't seen anyone all morning, just a cat scurrying across my path in this stormy weather.

I crossed the river on one slippery footbridge and then back again on another, following a greasy path, the rain of the last few days making this very slow going. Suddenly there was a house ahead and a lot of footpath modification signs in plastic nailed to posts flapping in the wind in the driveway. How are we supposed to understand these things? They are always placed at two feet off the ground and are almost certainly incomprehensible to the average walker. By the playing field on the outskirts of Meppershall a huge bonfire was under construction with table tops, bits of trees and rubbish all thrown in a big pile.

I walked up to a white Bedford van, parked by a house being renovated. I'd hoped and hoped to see one in Bedford – but no luck. To me this horrible vehicle sums up everything that's unpleasant about male drivers. White Bedford van drivers are the cowboys of the road, rampant egos and, no doubt, small dicks, always cutting up women drivers and hooting like mad when they can't overtake you. In their minds they're Damon Hill but in reality they're sad bastards driving a delivery vehicle. I'd been told that, incredibly, Bedford vans were now collector's items as production had stopped six years ago. The owner of this particular specimen was nowhere in sight. So Bedford's gift to the world was John Bunyan and vans, I mused as I meandered out of Meppershall.

At a T-junction I took a footpath past an exotic display of six-foot yellow daisies, gone to seed and growing wild, escapees from someone's garden. I picked one as a souvenir to carry with me, a little bit of sunlight to cheer up my day. I crossed a field with some horses in it, went over a stream, crossed a couple more fields, and in the final one to the road the footpath was non-existent, so it was a hard trudge into the wind with soil clinging to my boots. At the road into Upper Stondon I was pretty high up and could see for miles to the south across Bedford. A water tower on my right was festooned with aerials. A group of middle-aged men in running shorts came towards me in dribs and drabs saying hello, out on some fight-the-flab morning run. Luckily for them they had the wind behind them. It was so windy that patches of blue sky began to appear but by now in my journey I had learnt not to trust the weather. I was keeping my waterproofs in my backpack as no doubt they would be back on within an hour.

All Saints at Stondon was a magnificent arts-and-crafts-style church, each stone outlined in thick white mortar. Like a piece of two-dimensional graphic design it really was special, with a short squat tower, a pointed, tiled red roof and two tiers of windows. Sadly there was a notice on the wooden gate to the cemetery that said 'Regretfully silk flowers are not permitted in the churchyard'. On what grounds, I asked myself – taste, style, discrimination, or the fact that perhaps sheep were going to eat them and choke to death.

The road curved lazily down the hill and I had wonderful views to the south and east over Bedford, gradually descending into Lower Stondon which, as is often the case, wasn't nearly as stylish as its Upper counterpart. Now I was truly in the territory of garden nurseries and every other house seemed to be offering winter pansies for sale at ludicrous prices, whole boxes for £3. Lots of people had little plastic wind tunnels in their gardens where they were growing them.

On the main road in Lower Stondon, I entered a nursery to buy some pansies for my roof garden. It turned out to be a motor museum, probably Britain's only combined nursery and vintage car exhibition centre. From Daimlers to daisies! Maureen, the boss, had a peach tint to the front of her hair and was wearing a very trim trouser suit, and looked to be in her 50s. She told me they had over 300 cars on display. To reach the museum you went past the cash tills, through the garden centre and a small wrought-iron gate and then through a bewildering succession of sheds that John, the owner of all the cars, had built around his huge collection. It seemed that there were another 20 or 30 vehicles waiting to be brought there so they were going to have to put up yet another building. This ramshackle collection of sheds housed a superb display of tanks, motorbikes, bubble cars, American cars, plus all the usual gems that make Jeremy Clarkson drool. They were worth over £3 million and the casual passer-by on the road would have no idea of what lay behind the garden centre. A small sign simply said 'Garden Centre and Museum'. There were pre-war cars, a Rolls-Royce room, army vehicles, a hall of vans and trucks, there was the Bond car that you had to bounce to start with a motorbike engine, two beautiful Allards. It was fascinating and quirky in the extreme – one man's taste run riot. Sadly I wasn't as enthralled by all of this as my film crew. I have cured myself of car mania.

The story of me and cars starts with learning to drive in California. I was crap but my boyfriend at the time rented me a shocking pink Mustang convertible and that became my car for the next four months. I was very happy in that car and had dyed pinky red hair to match. Men used to shout 'Hey, red' at me as I drove it up and down Sunset Strip – they probably thought I was some kind of hooker.

Maureen and I didn't have too much in common because she obviously adored cars, and was very witty about them. This museum was clearly the product of a couple of eccentrics and Maureen said its fame was spreading. People were coming from all over Europe via the East Midlands airport on special trips to the museum. I could believe it. To me the sad thing was the way the cars were all jammed in, one hall after another, or one shed to another to be brutally honest, and when I asked her if she ever got them out and actually drove them, she looked at me as if I was barking mad. I have to admit though I did have a little day-dream about the E-type as I walked off out of the village heading for open fields through a caravan park.

I left Stondon behind me, a pretty featureless place, and walked on a path between two ploughed fields almost due south. Behind me a dog was barking incessantly. How do people live with such a noise? I heard a shout come from a house further along on the estate, 'For Christ's sake, shut up.'

I photographed a 'No footpath' sign that someone had sprayed over, while at the back of a disused barn two men were loitering around looking suspicious. They kept staring at me, perhaps considering doing something they shouldn't. Then I realized I'd made a mistake and had taken the wrong footpath out of Stondon, so I cut across to the west, circling around some fields, hoping I would arrive back at the path I should be on.

I took a pleasant green track with the grass freshly mowed under my feet, over a series of confusing drainage ditches which took all my wit and the compass to navigate. I could see the church tower at Holwell across a couple of fields to the east. I had a splitting headache, probably the result of not drinking coffee for two days on my new healthy-living phase.

Pirton and Stondon both sound exactly like villages out of a Ruth Rendell novel, somewhere Inspector Wexford would be uncovering a body. Pirton had a colour poster for a grand fireworks display they were to have on bonfire night, adults £2, children £1. I didn't approve of that as I thought bonfires were supposed to be free. I walked past the end of the High Street, a large field in front of the church with its short square tower and fine brick houses, some half-timbered. The field, according to the map, once held a motte and bailey, a fortified tower with a moat round it. At the junction of Walnut Tree Road and Hitchin Road I turned right, heading south-east for Stevenage.

Hitchin Road was straight and a total racetrack. Cars whizzed by. It was a long haul uphill with a huge and beautiful copper beech tree at the crest of the rise to focus on and keep my mind off the vehicles nearly slicing me in half. About 200 yards past the tree a white van came straight towards me and wouldn't move over. When I motioned that he could perhaps give me a foot more space he gave me the 'V' sign. Did he know his number plate was captured on film? Now the road was slightly more twisting, which increased the danger. I walked through somewhere called Offley Bottom that sounds more exciting than it was. I was heading for the village of Preston but first I had to cross the A505, a busy dual carriageway. In the spate of 100 yards I saw three dead weasels, one run over by a car and two lined up on the grass verge. A motorbike rider with shoulder-length black hair came out of a bridleway and recognized me, incredulous. The sky went grey and it could have been early evening instead of early afternoon. When it started to rain I upped my pace and soon I was boiling hot.

At the Carters Lane sign another phrase had been added – 'Known as Wibbly Wobbly Lane'. It was only just wide enough for a car so I hoped I wouldn't run into any traffic. But soon a new navy-blue Mercedes came belting up the road towards me, driven by a woman with long blonde hair and shiny earrings, and nearly hit me. Who are these people driving around in these expensive cars in the middle of the day? I was now in Hertfordshire, the stockbroker belt, commuter belt, green belt, whatever. I'd skirted around Hitchin, which lay to the east.

This was fine rolling countryside, in spite of being so close to London, not quite ironed out into gruesome suburbia. There were plenty of fields with horses grazing and on my left I saw a hawk hovering motionless near a hedge. The large farms had well-manicured farmhouses and gardens around them, and I doubted if any of these were the farmers who would be going bust this year.

I crossed the A505 at Offley Cross and took a bridleway, Hoars Lane, straight ahead. It was a beautiful old drovers' road, sadly made unattractive by piles of rubbish. I'd been making a list of the garbage that I most frequently saw on my journey; it's the kind of thing that walkers get obsessed with. Top of the list comes an empty can of Diet Coke, second is a can of Coca-Cola, the third and fourth on the list the boxes that they have come in, closely followed by Castrol Oil bottles, and so on. Hoars Lane at one point was very narrow. Then I walked through mulberry bushes and sloe bushes, a thoroughly enjoyable stretch through a couple of miles of undulating rich farmland.

I joined a road that was to lead into the village of Preston and on my right was wonderful parkland and a couple of houses that were interesting architecturally. There was a large farm with wooden barns stained dark brown with corrugated metal roofs and stables, a very expensive place. The barns and all the farm buildings were empty. A British Telecom van was drawn up outside the door in front of the house by a lovely hedge of lavender. On the map it's listed as Offley Holes Farm but when I walked past there was no name and two expensive-looking horses were grazing in the hilly paddocks behind. It was probably a pop star retreat.

I climbed up a hill through high hedges and walked along a muddy lane towards Preston, with a series of relatively small fields on either side, the sky dark grey and the wind whipping up a storm. In Preston the first house I saw was a garish half-timbered cottage with brickwork panels, the plaster panels painted bright sky-blue, the timbers black. I turned right at the junction of Chequers Lane and Butchers Lane. Overhead huge jets were preparing to land at nearby Luton Airport. A perfectly ordinary brick double-fronted house had what looked like a rocket nose cone under a tarpaulin in its driveway – how mysterious. I was in commuter land with empty houses and nothing much happening during the day. I'd only seen two people all day, both elderly. Now there was a flurry of activity, with mothers on the school run. Apart from that the only people I saw were builders, workmen and gardeners. Preston village green had a weird contraption under a tiled roof, like a kind of series of spinning wheels. Perhaps it was a form of public punishment like stocks, for householders whose gardens didn't come up to scratch.

I went down past the Princess Helena College and down School Lane, a large building with a lot of white paint, fake Georgian. This was a very posh bit of the green belt. I turned south into Hitch Wood with lofty beech trees, orange in the autumn, and lots of leaves underfoot. I startled a fox that ran away in front of me. The tracks were all overgrown and the blue footpath arrows didn't make any sense, so I headed south-east and saw a hare speeding away. It was an idyllic place.

On the lane into St Paul's Walden the Hertfordshire Way crossed my path, a green sign with a stag's head on it. St Paul's Walden was a small hamlet with a neat brick pub and a flint church set well back from the road. A farmer went past with a black labrador in the back of his truck leaning out the side. I walked down a deserted lane through East Farm Hall with the Walden herd on the notice-board. It was very grand parkland around here.

On Bullocks Hill I took a right-hand fork and met Annie Palmer, who was wearing a blue jacket and had long hair, and was in her 40s, I guessed. Annie, a school dinner-lady, was an active member of CASE, the Campaign Against Stevenage Expansion. We had a lively discussion overlooking the proposed site for 10,000 new houses west of Stevenage, a couple of fields to the north. According to Annie, on the edge of these fields were sites of special scientific interest. As far as I could see Stevenage was a pretty horrible place before this expansion, and the only reason I would argue against building any more new homes around it is that perhaps some money should be spent to make Stevenage a nicer place to be. The site was divided from Stevenage by the A1(M) and it meant that only one road would take all the people from the new development into Stevenage, again a hopeless bit of planning. I knew the Government wanted to build 10,000 new homes in the area but it did seem odd to build them in two and a half square miles of green belt.

Green belts were devised as a way to protect the countryside, by creating zones which surrounded major cities where development was strictly limited. The plan was to stop cities expanding so much they joined up. Here, I had walked between Hitchin and Luton. If Stevenage's proposed expansion went ahead on these pleasant rolling fields, I could see that the landscape I had just walked through would be altered for ever.

According to Annie, the problems stemmed from the fact that figures for housing needed were based on the number of households, which was all wrong. Nowadays people left home earlier, they wanted to live alone. More marriages broke down and there were more single parents. The old idea of a family unit had gone for ever, and so more homes were needed. Annie claimed it would be better to develop city sites where the people needing homes already lived, keeping families close together, and to refurbish existing communities, rather than build all of a county's housing requirements on one site. It seemed that Hertfordshire county council was against the development, but Stevenage council was in favour. The final decision on whether to go ahead wouldn't be taken until 2001, but meanwhile the number of protesters was growing and demonstrations were planned. A government task force chaired by the architect Lord Rogers was advising councils on how to maximize inner-city brown-field sites, and not before time.

Stevenage has the highest unemployment rate in the county, and hopes the scheme would provide jobs. But they also hope to attract hi-tech investment to the area, so wouldn't the development end up being for the middle-classes, not low-cost social housing at all? I have yet to be persuaded that John Prescott ever gets out of his executive gas-guzzling Daimler and walks in the countryside, so I wasn't hopeful for Annie and her army of protesters. And surely the revitalization of Stevenage wouldn't be achieved by concreting over a field outside it. The town itself should be declared an Enterprise Zone, like Margaret Thatcher's triumph with the Isle of Dogs, and placed in the hands of a planner or an architect with vision.

ST PAUL'S WALDEN TO WELWYN GARDEN CITY

A city for healthy living

As I was so close to London, I could go home and sleep in my own bed. The next morning I got the underground and then the train to Welwyn Garden City. The crew were supposed to be there half an hour ahead of me but as I left the station I saw their car in front, they had obviously gone for breakfast which slightly annoyed me as we were supposed to be ready to start at 10 am. I made the fatal mistake of saying this to the director who started shouting at me, whereupon I nearly burst into tears. What a happy little band we were. Everybody was finding something to moan about now; we're all tired of the weather and the walking. It'd all taken so much more out of everybody than I could have ever have predicted. It was miles harder than the previous year's walk climbing mountains in Wales. Here we were in the green belt, absolutely shattered.

I started at the spot where I did the interview with Annie, and to the north you could clearly see Stevenage across the ploughed fields. By Rustling End Cottage, a pretty brick house, I turned south and skirted the wood on a muddy track, then some ploughed fields, one with turnips in it, and emerged at the north end of Codicote.

It was a main road and cars whizzed past me. I walked past shops, pubs, and then a stretch with trees and larger houses. Then pretty Old Welwyn with its duck pond and on the wall just up the street was a blue and white enamel sign saying 'Royal Society for the Prevention of Cruelty to Animals, please slacken hame or bearing rein when going uphill, complaints of cruelty to be forwarded to the Secretary at Headquarters'. The village atmosphere was sadly ruined by the traffic rushing down the High Street. I carried on down the London Road past a Victorian school that had been converted into houses. It was a grey blustery day and it had already rained once and looked as if it would do so again. It was unsettled, a bit like everybody's mood.

Then I took an even busier road parallel with the noisy A1(M). The sun came out fitfully and ahead of me in a lay-by a man stuck a home-made yellow card in the back window of a battered Bedford van saying 'For sale, £1,500 or near offer', got out a bucket and a sponge and started cleaning this rather sad vehicle. I entered the leafy suburbs of Welwyn Garden City. My directions led me to a cul-de-sac where a lot of workmen were busy at work on a large detached house. There was an unmistakable air of cosiness and warmth and I felt nothing horrible was going to happen in Welwyn Garden City. I noticed a development of new houses called Scholars Mews but it had none of the charm of the original dwellings.

Throughout my long walk from Edinburgh I had tramped through miles of suburban development and passed hundreds of new houses being built around villages and towns the entire way down my route. Now I was in Welwyn Garden City, the Utopian dream city that set the benchmark for rural living when it was built in the 1920s. To my mind, all the suburban sprawl, all the new brick boxes I'd sneered at, seemed pale, cheap, feeble imitations of the original concept so brilliantly realized at Welwyn. It was the concept of Sir Ebenezer Howard, whose first project was at nearby Letchworth, and was founded in 1911. Howard was a philosopher, social reformer and town planner. His ideal Garden City was to be limited to 6,000 acres, of which the city only occupied 1,000 acres, the rest being given over to industry and architecture. Industry would be surrounded by farmland, there were to be six residential areas, and everything was to be built to a master plan. He thought that the town would have its own food supply, jobs and be self-sufficient. People of all classes would live there.

Howard managed to buy the land for Welwyn in 1919. He planned a city of 40-50,000, and chose a French-Canadian architect, Louis de Soissons. De Soissons chose a neo-Georgian style and built in red brick made from local clay.

I sat on the steps of the library as pensioners went past me with their books. I felt absolutely drained, and started to cry, for no reason, just exhaustion, and day after day of poor weather and being filmed. No one took any notice. I went and sat inside in the hall, and snivelled a bit more. I was cold and tired, and sick of looking smiley for the benefit of the cameras. After five minutes, I pulled myself together and went back out to the crew.

I walked round the old part of Welwyn with David Irving who trained as an architect in Edinburgh and I would guess to be one of my contemporaries. He was wildly enthusiastic about the place and when I told him I thought it all seemed rather cosy he completely agreed. He pointed out Ebenezer Howard's own house and then that of the chairman of the corporation, somebody who obviously had a larger than life personality as his house was at an angle to the road and in a completely different architectural style to everyone else's. The cul-de-sacs were designed with larger houses at one end and then terraced houses for workmen at the other. It all made for a harmonious environment, with homes for people of all income brackets living side by side.

Today even the workmen's cottages are highly desirable residences, way beyond the price bracket of any workmen. What made Welwyn such a desirable place to live was the large amount of gardens and green spaces, something that planners have skimped on ever since. Ebenezer Howard called it a town for healthy living, where urban slums were banished and people's health would improve in the clean air.

The centre of Welwyn was designed to be not more than 15 minutes walk from anybody's home (as was their place of work) and so we soon came to the town centre, a glorious avenue of poplars, almost a mile long, very French but not surprising as Louis de Soissons trained in Paris. In the centre of the avenue was the shopping area, with a rather dreary modern addition, the Howard Centre housing shops, cafés and the station. Sadly the advent of the railway killed Howard's dream of a self-sufficient city, as the commuter was born. I said goodbye to David Irving, crossed over the railway bridge and then a black metal bridge, down some steps, past the Shredded Wheat factory and then turned south heading out of town, past a series of glorious 1920s and 1930s factory buildings, some in need of occupants and some restored behind high wire fences. Here was the home of Cresta Silks and Murphy Radio. The Polycell building with its arched roof was part of the 1932 British Instructional Films Studio, Hollywood in Herts.

I was plagued by a group of three local teenagers, one attractive black girl, one black boy on a bike and a sad white youth who was trying to be black, mouthing off at me in a kind of rap-speak. Is there anything more pathetic than teenagers who wish they were a different colour? I told them what we were doing and then walked down the other side of the road as their desperate attempts to be on camera became more and more irritating.

At a traffic roundabout I took the turning towards Hatfield and Hertford along a road heading out through town where I passed a brick sculpture in high walls, protecting a new estate. David Irving had told me that unlike Stevenage, Welwyn only had to provide 1,000 new homes to meet its Government target and that didn't involve any over-development, but more filling in, although he did admit that there wasn't much land to fill in. Welwyn still remains a harmonious and desirable place to live, with detached houses fetching over £180,000 and even the workers' cottages highly sought after. The architecture has been much parodied but of all the new developments I have walked through since Edinburgh not one has spent the money on the landscaping that Welwyn has. And you can't build homes without shops and places to work nearby – another lesson no one seems eager to learn.

Without the help of a Welwyn street map I made a bit of a detour on my way out of town but I did notice that the newer council estates on the southern edge of Welwyn seemed rather bereft of the Ebenezer Howard spirit. Gardens had been shrunk down and although the houses were in red brick it all seemed a bit threadbare. Since World War II housing standards have declined and the standards that now apply seem rather low compared to Ebenezer Howard's. Howard was passionate about the total environment, and if they build the 10,000 houses outside Stevenage it will be like just another estate with no heart unless there's landscaping and a whole variety of homes.

My final stretch outside of Welwyn was down Gypsy Lane to the Mill Green Golf Club, heading south towards the A414. Ahead of me two golfers wheeled their caddies and ahead of them cars flashed past on the road.

I finished for the day, determined to stop being a misery and pull myself together. At least Welwyn was an extremely pleasant environment. Was I doing a Ffyona Campbell and becoming a nightmare bitch? I hoped not.

PART SEVEN

South of Welwyn Garden City

to Greenwich

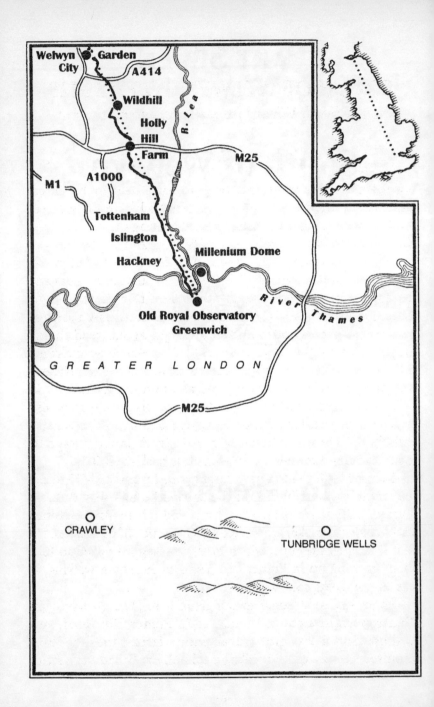

DAY 39

SOUTH OF WELWYN TO THE M25
The Pinball Wizard from Pinner interviews me

I woke up with a migraine, tried to eat a healthy breakfast although my digestive system was still a bit trashed from the recent food poisoning. I got the underground to King's Cross and then the train to Welwyn, and finally a lift to the A414 by the golf course. It was sunny with a few clouds, but a fine autumn day and warm, thank goodness. There had been hurricanes, gales and torrential rain and flooding all weekend with over ten people killed. I crossed the A414, went down a little road, past a sawmill and over a river, swollen and with bright green weeds being dragged sideways by the current. A load of people were already fishing, men with their sons because today was half-term holiday. I was going to walk with Elton John, an old friend I first met in 1978. I even attended his short-lived wedding in Sydney and remember singing 'Love Divine, all Loves Excelling' in a tiny chapel with about 30 people in blistering heat. Barry Humphries was next to me and sang a completely different tune to all the Brits!

I waited for Elton to arrive. He'd phoned from the M25 to say the traffic was terrible. When he arrived he was very suitably dressed, in new trainers, a tracksuit and a Jean-Paul Gaultier khaki-coloured parka. We walked down a series of back lanes. He kept farting all the time, which made me laugh. I talked to him about growing up in Pinner and he asked me about walking. It was an easy-going conversation.

Elton was no stranger to the green belt. He'd grown up in Pinner, born in a council house at 55 Pinner Hill Road, and in those days it was quite rural, with a farm opposite. Elton admitted he was 'quite nice' as a schoolboy; 'I had very strict parents. I wouldn't say boo to a goose basically.' At Pinner Grammar School he had to endure rugby. 'Because I was fat and I wore glasses they put me in the scrum,' he said. 'Which I hated. Boys didn't play tennis, girls played tennis. And girls played hockey. I'd loved to have played hockey.'

From 11 he went to the Royal Academy of Music on Saturdays. 'Except when I played truant. When I hadn't done any practice I used to get the 183 bus down to Pinner, then the Metropolitan line up to Baker Street, go round on the Circle line for three hours. And then come back home. I did that quite a few times actually.'

At 16 Elton started playing in hotels in Willesden and Harlesden to get money to pay for his equipment. My parents had moved to Perivale and I remembered seeing him play in a hotel lounge around that time. I remembered too seeing him in his yellow boiler-suit phase. It came from Mr Freedom, owned by Tommy Roberts. Keith, at Smile, was doing my hair and he did Elton's too. I went with everyone from the hairdresser's to see Elton at a club called Bumpers in the 1970s.

Elton didn't leave home till he was 21 – and then moved to Northwood Hills, about a mile from Pinner! 'When I started to make it I moved to London. To the Water Gardens off Edgware Road. And I went very grand immediately. My manager John Reed said you can't drive a Ford Escort so you should get another car. So I got an Aston Martin. I've never looked back. It was purple!'

Elton and I nearly met in the 1950s. His cousin Roy Dwight played football for Fulham, and Elton would go and watch from the players' bench. I too was at Craven Cottage, in those golden years when Fulham were in the first division, watching Johnny Haynes from the terraces with my dad, a life-long supporter. Elton's real club was always Watford though, and he'd stand on the terraces cheering them on. Now of course he's the chairman.

By now Elton, with his famously low attention span, was getting bored with the rather bland Herts countryside – weren't we going to pass anything historical? Sadly not. Was he a keen walker, I asked, changing the subject. 'I like to walk down Regent Street, Oxford Street, Bond Street ... in the direction of a shop!' he giggled, 'I used to go camping as a kid with my parents. I loathed it.'

We climbed over a stile and continued up a quiet lane. Elton mightn't be a walker, but rather touchingly he had bought the book of my last giant walk across England and Wales and read it in one sitting. Now he turned the tables on me – why did I like walking so much? I replied that I did it for the isolation and solitude, but the paradox was that when you were being filmed, you always had people with you. But the bits of the walk which weren't filmed (about one third) were far more enjoyable. I explained I wasn't really into macho walking like climbing mountains. Large areas of open moorland were my favourite terrain. Elton wondered what I thought about – was it sex? I laughed. To be honest I just experience the light, the colours and the landscape, I said. The idea was to empty your mind of as much as possible.

Elton, if not keen on walking, was passionate about gardens and had wonderful ones at his houses in Windsor and Nice; 'When you create a garden you want it to last another 100 years, so you're always improving it. Which is difficult for me, I always want everything instantly. So you have to be very patient but I often go out and say why hasn't this or that grown. And the gardeners say well, it's a tree, it takes a little longer, you know. But I do love my gardens. When the weather's bad and the trees lose a couple of branches I get mortified. I hate losing plants and trees.'

I told Elton that being alone was something I'd got better at as I got older. Maybe walking helped. Up to when I was 50 I couldn't be by myself for a minute. What about him? 'I quite like being by myself sometimes. Just to zone out at home and be by myself. I never used to be any good at it at all, I always had to have people around. I agree, the older you get, the more tolerance you get for being on your own. Don't you like getting older?' I replied that it was OK, but I didn't like my body dropping one bit. Perhaps that's another reason I did so much walking, to try and arrest all that. And spent hours in the mirror wondering about my eyelids. Were they too droopy? Did Elton think old can look sexy? 'Yeah, absolutely.' I wished I could believe him. 'Well, Honor Blackman is an incredibly sexy woman,' said Elton. 'And so's Helen Mirren.' He wasn't entirely reassuring me. 'As you get older I think you get a different perspective on life. Something changes and you get much more opinionated – if that's even possible for you,' he said, laughing. It was true, I was definitely getting more like Victor Meldrew as the years passed. But Elton, in my opinion, was basically a much nicer person than me. 'Well, I've had to listen to so much crap and mediocrity, and you can say it when you're 50,' he added. I really hadn't mellowed. And I thought it was because I hadn't had children. I'd never had to be a family. I'd never been any good at any of that either, and I'd been completely self-centred. 'I can't imagine anybody wanting to have children actually,' said Elton. 'That's a horrible thing to say, but what a responsibility. I can't think of any bigger responsibility than that. And I know it involves an enormous sacrifice, I think, for your life, to bring up your children well.'

But with the constant travelling Elton did, how could he have any responsibilities? Didn't it drive him mad? 'I love playing, I hate the in-between bits like travelling, although we travel in great style. I'm a musician so I like to play, but it does wear you out after a while, and you have to change. In 1999 I'm going to do some solo concerts without the band, which means I can play completely different numbers, and be much more vulnerable on stage than I am with the band. I'll finish this tour and I probably won't tour for another three or four years. Then I'm going to do some different things.'

I wasn't sure he was going to like going over a couple of stiles, but he was fine about it. As we were walking along the road a couple of ramblers came in the opposite direction. When I said hello they more or less ignored us, so Elton said, 'Suit yourself.' The crew said that after we had passed them, the woman said to her husband, 'I do believe that's Janet Street-Porter.' There was no mention of Elton, which he found very entertaining.

Eventually we arrived at a pub and Elton told me he had been desperate to go to the loo the entire time. In the end he went behind a hedge and I went into the pub, only to find all the doors to the loos locked.

I left Elton, who was going to town to buy records in his Bentley. ('Guess who has the more glamorous lifestyle,' he chortled to the camera.) I walked south through leafy lanes towards a hamlet called West End, towards Wildhill. The sun was shining through the few leaves that remained on the beech trees and cobwebs were stretched across the road catching the sunlight like fine silvery silk washing-lines. I went past the tradesmen's entrance and then the grand entrance to Camfield Place which had an urn on top of each of its pillars and a sign saying, 'Warning, dogs running loose' in pale-blue paint. The village cottages looked as if it was all once part of a Victorian estate.

I took the B158, still seeing cobwebs stretched across the road. No other walkers had broken them. A large Southfork-type house was under construction with no less than four garages and a swimming pool. What contrasts I had walked past in the Green Belt – charming architecture, then 200 yards down the road a sweet pair of Victorian cottages and then the absolute lack of style that this home exemplified, no visual taste whatsoever. I passed another posh residence, Warrenwood Park, with a sign that said 'Guard dogs' and an entry intercom. I was now firmly in luxury commuter land, with high burglary potential and the resultant maximum security.

Then I took a long straight lane, along a pavement covered with twigs and debris from the wind of the last two days. The road was a racetrack and I nearly got knocked down by a man coming out of a side road who, even though I was halfway across it, drove straight at me. I shouted at him but what difference did it make? None really. Quite a few cars hooted at me and I guessed I must have looked a bit deranged. I passed a house called San Antonio and in front of me two chickens were pecking about on the pavement. They soon squawked back into their luxury grounds on my approach. A large sign said 'These grounds are protected by concealed video cameras'. Now the houses were definitely getting very *nouveau-riche*, with gables, well-manicured gardens and high steel gates, mock-Georgian cottages of baronial hall proportions. If I had a million pounds I wouldn't be living on this noisy road in Hertfordshire's answer to Beverly Hills. These homes were so big they had to be called 'house'. I passed Hertford House, Kentish House and so on. I heard a radio playing Mike and the Mechanics, it seemed appropriate as this was the neighbourhood of Marty Wilde and record producer, Mickey Most. I almost expected Cliff Richard to come down someone's driveway.

The A1000 was teeming with traffic, heading towards Potters Bar. I turned left on the B157 and as I ate my sandwiches by the side of the road, cars thundered past and a Great Dane barked ferociously and tried to clamber over a six-foot wooden fence opposite; thankfully it held. Now the rain was tipping down. A huge black cloud hung overhead.

On Coopers Lane Road heading towards the M25 the rain was pelting down but the sun eventually came out. I passed a sign for deer and another one for horses; could it really be that rural this close to the M25? In a meadow on my right horses were grazing and it seemed a tranquil rural environment. When I put my waterproof hood down as the rain had stopped I could easily hear the sound of the M25. It was a background curtain of noise, constant and never rising above a steady drone. On top of that was the dripping of the rain from the trees, the intermittent popping sound of someone pheasant shooting in a wood nearby, and of course the sound of cars hurtling along this lane in the rain well over the speed limit. I went past Fir Wood with its footpaths and 'No horses' sign. The trees on my walk today had been magnificent, huge 150-year-old specimens, remnants of another era when the green belt was simply part of wealthy people's estates.

The verges of the road were clogged with leaves and yet through them were poking the most astonishing variety of mushrooms, probably because the trees were so mature and of so many varieties. I turned down by a footpath sign opposite where an old school was being demolished and new homes built – another intrusion into the green belt – but I suppose it was justified on the grounds that it was using an existing site. My path was pretty brambly and overgrown and the roar of the motorway grew ever closer. I went over a stile and a concrete road on a bridge took me over the M25. I felt like screaming, 'Don't ever build another road like this one.' What justification could there be? The visual and aural pollution was devastating. How could John Prescott *not* get people out of their cars?

DAY 40

M25 TO HACKNEY
I meet Waynetta Slob and sit for a portrait

I had the most God awful hangover and was an hour late to start walking this morning, and I had to drink a whole bottle of Orangina to get my system kick-started. I crossed the M25 and picked up a footpath skirting Hollybush Farm, then crossed a road and followed a pleasant track due south between some trees and a field marked 'The Round London Trail'. Having gone down a hillside I headed west along a series of footpaths that were completely waterlogged. The water went right over my boots, and soon both feet were saturated. Apparently there had been torrential rain in the early hours of the morning. Two walkers came towards me. 'This part's a bit wet,' I said. 'Wait until you see it further down,' they said gleefully, as only ramblers can. By the time I got to the next road I had mud splattered up both trouser legs and I was soaking right up to my knees.

I entered Enfield Chase and had a pleasant walk down through the woods. I was immediately accosted by a man wearing an Enfield Forest Ranger's jacket. 'Have you got a permit to film here?' he said. I said, 'We've come all the way from Edinburgh to London without ever requiring a permit to walk on a public footpath through a public park.' He replied, 'You need one in Enfield but as it's you, just get on with it', followed by a nod and a wink. I asked him what all the people were doing who were sitting around having a cup of tea and he said they were volunteers restoring some fences and that there was an old moat in the grounds. I'd walked past an obelisk earlier but it seemed it had been moved here in the 1930s and there was nothing very special about it, although it made a fine landmark and standing by it you could see right down across London to Canary Wharf tower and my final destination in Greenwich.

Having crossed Trent Park and skirted round Pets' Corner we found ourselves at the back of the Southgate Hockey Club, which had a fine all-weather pitch, but sadly no players or spectators in evidence. I crossed Enfield Road and went south-east via a series of suburban streets full of detached 1930s to 1950s houses, some with Doric columns, some with two Jaguars in the driveway, and all looking pretty well cared for. This was Oakwood Park, very near to where my granddad lived when I was little. He was a train driver on the Piccadilly line. He and my granny (my father's parents) had a very long garden and at the end of it there was a pond with ducks and chickens. Granddad had dug most of the garden up to grow his own vegetables. In the upstairs bedroom he had made a laboratory. He was really interested in science and gardening, and I suppose that in another era he would have had further education and been an engineer like my father.

Then I went up Wades Hill and down it, noticing that there were plenty of personalized number-plates in evidence. I passed Winchmore Hill station and the green, a pretty collection of older houses and shops, down Station Road, then over Green Lanes and down Farm Road. I walked past large playing fields and open spaces approaching the North Circular. Once again, like the M25, the noise was deafening. I took the underpass below the North Circular, and a graffiti slogan said 'I was blind to see how much you mean to me'. The last couple of houses before the road had extraordinary coloured stones in the front garden and giant plaster lions, real suburban follies. I hadn't seen anyone walking all morning, it was as if suburbia was a place where you just had a car to go everywhere. There hadn't been anyone popping down to the corner shop for a paper because the corner shops were few and far between.

On the south side of the North Circular I was in Tottenham and the houses were smaller, large council estates probably sold to their owner/occupiers, and I could see the first of London's tower blocks ahead. I walked past a primary school, but as it was half-term the grounds were locked. There was a large sign saying it was protected by a security company. A boy ran across the street in front of me and shinned over the seven-foot railings. I could only admire his agility. Then he was in the school grounds and he ran around in an aimless fashion not really knowing what to do as he had no one to play with.

The post-war council blocks had been recently repainted and refurbished with the balconies enclosed to give a more Mediterranean feel if that's possible in the London Borough of Haringey. I went down through more pebble-dashed houses on to White Hart Lane where I turned left and entered Tottenham Cemetery, a magical place, where my path took me on a narrow paved path between iron railings with tombstones on either side. I emerged on Church Road by All Hallows Church and Bruce Castle, a Grade 1 listed building built in 1514 by a member of Henry VIII's court. Once the manor house for Tottenham, the castle has been altered and rebuilt over the centuries – it was a school and has been a museum since 1906. It had a magnificent clock tower, from which Lady Constantia, the first wife of Lord Coleraine (whose family lived here in the 17th and 18th centuries) jumped to her death. Her ghost was supposed to haunt the building. In the 16th century rich Londoners built country retreats in Tottenham, but the area really got developed when the railway arrived in 1872. I wondered how much of old Tottenham remained outside this special conservation area. Meanwhile, the weather was foul. There were some children playing in the park and as I walked past they shouted out, 'Oh, it's you, can we be on the telly too?' This area still felt like it had some community spirit left; after all, London is still a collection of villages like this one.

I went past a neat row of almshouses, built in 1859 by the Draper's Company as homes for retired sailmakers and the 'deserving' poor from the parishes of Bow, Bromley and

Stepney. Their neat appearance behind a stretch of green lawn was in total contrast to the jumble of newsagents, video shops, grocers and discount stores further down the street. Immigrants from other parts of Britain and overseas moved into Tottenham from after the French Revolution. Catholics were joined by the Irish in the 19th century, and there was a large Quaker community. The rise of the working-class population coincided with the railway, and today Tottenham is still an interesting ethnic mix, with large Greek and West Indian communities.

I stopped at a tailor's shop and met Alex Vasiliou, who had come to Britain from Cyprus 25 years ago and never returned. He made suits for the President of Cyprus and British MPs. Alex even employed a Turkish Cypriot and on the wall of the shop was a poster – 'Come to Cyprus for your holidays', with a large map of the island. Friends and relatives from the neighbourhood dropped in all day for coffee and a gossip. The shop was a jumble of half-finished suits with people sewing away. A woman was finishing one suit off while a man was tacking another. Alex told me that he'd moved out of the area to Cockfosters. I got the impression that he found it too rough now. He said that young people didn't want to go into the business. His son was a car engineer and his daughter was at college so when he eventually retired the business would close. When Alex started there were half a dozen tailors in that particular stretch of Tottenham and now he was the only one left. He was a charming man, who confided that Michael Portillo was one of his close friends. I asked if he'd met Steven Twigg, the new MP, and he gave a weak smile and said no.

Each suit was entirely made by hand and took a week to make. It would cost between £450 and £500, a third of Savile Row prices. I felt rather sad that all Alex's craft was going to die out with him and this shop would probably end up as one more late-night supermarket selling rubbishy food and sliced bread. Before I left Alex couldn't resist giving me a kiss on both cheeks.

I went along Bruce Grove that joined the A10 and turned left on Monument Way. A man was silently executing a series of

Kung Fu moves in slow motion on an asphalted playing area. I walked through a series of streets to a particularly ghastly series of factories where I met Kathy Burke. By then it was starting to drizzle again and we walked along the edge of the River Lea which actually would have been pretty if the weather hadn't been so bad. Kathy was wearing a brown comfy cardigan, cotton trousers and trainers. What I loved about her was that she was completely unpretentious; she's just the way she is. A highly intelligent woman, she didn't do well at convent school but finally got into Anna Scher's acting classes at 16 after being on the waiting list for three years.

We walked across a recreation ground and then followed the towpath along the curve of the River Lea. To the north-east lay a whole series of reservoirs, on the site of Bronze and Iron Age Tottenham men and women. In 894 the Danes sailed right up the River Lea followed by King Alfred, who diverted the river to strand them. During the Saxon period the Manor of Tottenham actually passed into Scottish hands for nearly 200 years!

Kathy Burke was born and bred in Islington, where she still lives, but this was the nearest my line would go to her 'manor'. Since *Scum* Kathy has had a glittering career with parts ranging from drama series like *Mr Wroe's Virgins* for BBC2, to Waynetta Slob in Harry Enfield's comedy shows and the beaten and abused wife in Gary Oldman's award-winning film *Nil by Mouth*. She recently starred in the outrageous TV sit-com *Gimme Gimme Gimme* by Jonathan Harvey, complete with orange wig and huge white specs. She's nothing if not versatile!

Kathy had a bit of a cold and was dying for a fag. Did she do much walking? 'I go for a waddle up Upper Street,' she said. 'I get a bit hot, then I get out of breath because I smoke too much!' I apologized for the appalling weather, but Kathy didn't seem too fazed by it. She said she preferred the winter, 'getting snug and making soup at home' was really enjoyable. How had she started acting? 'When finally I got into acting classes I can still remember the first time I went there because I didn't get up and do anything.

Or even say anything other than my name and what school I was at. But I remember coming home exhausted because I think I was so excited by it all. I just loved it. I would be deeply upset if I was ill and had to miss a lesson and I went for about three or four years. Then when I started acting professionally I got moved to the Friday group, which was where all the professional actors were.' What was the very first thing she got paid for? 'The film, *Scrubbers*. The director, Mai Zetterling, went to Anna Scher's and spotted me. I couldn't believe it when they phoned up and said you've got an audition for a film! My dad was terrified and he wasn't happy about it at all until he found out it was with Mai, who used to be his pin-up!'

As Kathy's success had grown, had she thought of moving from Islington? 'I'm going to move but I'm not going to move out of Islington. I'm going to get a bigger place but I'm going to stay in the area.' But aren't there two Islingtons – the Tony Blair Islington of sun-dried tomatoes, polenta and swanky restaurants, and then Kathy's working-class Islington? Kathy agreed: 'Yes – I'm Essex Road, Islington, which has always been the poor end of it. But there has always been the posh end of it too. I used to clean in a house up in Alwyne Villas when I was a kid. And I remember the poshness seeping in more, when a flash off-licence opened in Upper Street that also did little snacks. When I was nine years old I remember leaving the school at lunchtime and ordering an egg mayonnaise [she put on a snooty voice] and I'd never eaten mayonnaise before that. About once a week I'd save up my little bits of dinner money and bunk out of school and go and get myself a posh egg mayonnaise! I went to primary school just off Duncan Terrace in Islington and I'd walk through Camden Passage with all its antique shops. I used to walk into these antique shops and say, "I don't think I'll buy this today, I might come back tomorrow," imagining that the shop owner would be convinced that I was from the posh bit of Islington.'

Did Kathy think things were changing for women like herself? Ten years ago it would have been hard for a woman to act, write and direct. She seemed to have really worked hard on not just being pigeon-holed as a character actress. 'When I was growing up the people that I admired were people like Victoria Wood,' Kathy said. 'She seemed to be doing everything from the start. I just thought she was amazing and so I never felt like I shouldn't be writing and directing – I went ahead and did it anyway.'

Would she like to do Lady Macbeth? What about the classical theatre? 'It doesn't really appeal to me, all that sort of stuff. It's not that accessible. But I don't know, I'll see what happens. I might come to it later. I like to perform anywhere really. Just as long as the play is decent enough – I'll do it in a barn if it's a brilliantly written piece. Now I've said that, I'll probably get all these people that own barns, do you know what I mean, sending me plays!'

Now it was really pelting down and I didn't want Kathy's cold to get any worse. We'd been walking for about an hour, stopping every now and then for her to have a cigarette and a cough! I asked her about the excitement when she won the Best Actress Award at Cannes for *Nil by Mouth*. Had she been surprised? She hadn't even been in Cannes. 'I couldn't go out because I was in the middle of doing *Tom Jones* for the BBC. But it was lucky because on the day of the awards I had the weekend off. Gary Oldman phoned me up in the morning and told me that I had won Best Actress. Then it really was action stations, a bit like a movie happening to me! They organized an aeroplane and helicopters and luckily only a couple of weeks before it had been Harry Enfield's wedding. So I had a very nice Mark Powell suit and just grabbed that. Then I got changed on the aeroplane and did my make-up on it! Really exciting!'

I thought that Kathy's award was well deserved, and also marked a departure from the glamorous leading lady to one that reflected real life. 'I was very proud of *Nil by Mouth* when I first saw it. I was just amazed by it,' said Kathy.

We'd reached Springfield Park and climbed up the hill where I said goodbye to Kathy, one of my inspirations. We gave each other a hug and she went home for a cup of tea, while I slogged slowly on in the rain.

I didn't fancy having lunch in the pretty basic park café so I got a lift to one just down the road which had only been open a couple of weeks. It was run by a girl who seemed a bit inexperienced but nice all the same. I had some lasagne and a cup of tea, the first hot lunch I'd had for weeks. While I was sitting there, two black guys came in. One was covered with gold jewellery. They spoke to the girl as if she was a piece of dirt. I found it so totally offensive I had to stop myself turning round and saying something. Anyway, my lunch was very cheap at £3. Then I was dropped back at Springfield Road to carry on walking through the dreary back streets of Tottenham, up Mount Pleasant, a misnomer although it did have fine views all the way to the M25 to the north and the green belt. I walked past the Lennox Lewis college and there wasn't much going on there; apparently it was having a funding crisis. Every now and then black or white young men would appear and just hang about. I don't know if they were buying or selling drugs but this section of my walk was a strange combination of well-cared-for terraced houses and some pretty run-down council estates where a sense of slight menace pervaded the air.

I crossed a large green open space and then a main road. At the far side I started walking towards Chatsworth Road. A black guy and his girlfriend came towards me. He was all attitude and looked pretty surly. I was going to say hello but then I didn't. It's funny how when you leave the green belt behind and you are walking city streets you stop saying hello to other walkers. He'd just gone past me, maybe 25 yards, and then he turned round and he said, 'Hi, it's you isn't it,' and started waving furiously so I waved back and suddenly we were friends. Then it was a long slog down Chatsworth Road, one of the best and most cosmopolitan mixtures of shops and ethnic groups on my whole walk. Every single nationality that lives in north London was represented here: Kosher butchers, hallal butchers, regular butchers, Afro beauty salons, Italian restaurants, African shops,

Muslim bookshops, and a pub that had been converted into a Thai food restaurant. What a fantastic mixture! As I passed the Afro beauty salon a girl came out and said hello. She looked immaculate but then she probably worked there. In the window of the shop next door (which was closed) was a large pile of dried fish stacked up against the glass – nothing else – and a phone number to ring if you wanted to buy any of these particularly unappealing specimens. According to the girl from the beauty shop, it was African.

A couple of people recognized me and waved, and finally at the end of Chatsworth Road I turned right into Barnabas Terrace to meet people from the Core Charity. But first I sat in the crew's car and dried my hair with an old towel. I tried to dry my legs a bit by putting the heater on, then I went into the Core premises and met everyone and did what I had promised, which was sitting for my portrait to be painted.

Core Arts was set up six years ago by Paul Monks as a charity. All the people who go there have, at one time, received treatment for mental illnesses. Most of them had never tried to paint or make music before. I perched on a stool in a kind of Alice-in-Wonderland-style set they had built and about 15 people had their easels arranged very tightly together all around me. It was intimidating at first and then very entertaining. I asked them to keep me amused and one woman read me a poem she had written about comparing a bonsai tree to being a lesbian. Well, that was a first. Another guy told me lots of jokes. They were almost all chatty to various degrees, and some very bound up in their work. There were some older people in their late 60s, and the youngest, a black girl whose hair stood straight up on her head, interviewed me as if she was Trevor MacDonald or Anna Ford. I really enjoyed the experience and I hadn't thought that I would. At the end of it I looked at what they had done. One man who hadn't said a word had all his hair slicked back and on his canvas he had simply painted a red square and a white circle. I didn't know what to say.

I had tea with the portrait painters, eating an iced bun with a cherry on it. That was the end of my day's walking. It had started to pelt with rain again. That night I went to the opening for the Turner Prize. I didn't drink much at the Tate Gallery. Elton John came and I walked round with him and David Furnish. Sam Taylor-Wood's film was particularly good. Later Sam, Jay Jopling, Gary Kemp and I went out drinking. The less said about the rest of the night the better.

DAY 41

HOMERTON TO GREENWICH
I visit the Dome and mark the birthplace of Time

I walked down Barnabas Road in Homerton, around Well Street Common and into the wonderful Victoria Park. There was a kind of divine symmetry about my line taking me through this leafy open space. Not only had this route taken me through the valley in Yorkshire that has been my second home for 20 years, but it was also now taking me within a mile of where I'd lived in Limehouse for ten years. Twenty years ago I lived in Narrow Street with my third husband, the film-maker Frank Cvitanovich.

He had loved Victoria Park so much that he made a brilliant TV documentary about it, a text-book example of fly-on-the-wall artistry. In one sequence two men sat on a park bench on a blazing hot day, watching a bowls match and waffling on about nothing in particular. Mesmeric stuff. I learnt so much from Frank, now sadly dead, and I remembered his film vividly as I walked through the park, past the bowling green, the lakes, the tennis courts (where I used to play on Saturdays) and the bandstand. There were few other strollers on this particular morning, unlike the scene on Sunday mornings when intense rivalries are acted out on the football pitches.

I took the Three Colt Bridge over the Grand Union Canal and down St Stephen's Road to the Tredegar Square Conservation Area. Captain Cook had lived in a terraced house round the corner from here on the Mile End Road, and now the whole area around here of Georgian and Victorian houses is undergoing massive gentrification. This part of London was traditionally the first stopping-off point for immigrants over the centuries, from Jews to Huguenots, from Greeks to Bengalis.

Nowadays the workers' cottages around Coborn Road are highly sought after by city workers, and the council has spent a lot of money on Victorian street lamps, cast-iron bollards and plenty of barriers to deter through-traffic. You can tell an area's on the way up when you've got a delicatessen next to a Chinese take-away.

I crossed Bow Road and walked past more Georgian and Victorian buildings to another secret delight (in the same league as Victoria Park), the Tower Hamlets Cemetery. The Industrial Revolution brought an increase in deaths as well as in wealth and in the middle of the 19th century there was an explosion in cemetery building and new burial grounds sprang up all around London. The Tower Hamlets Cemetery was built in 1841 and now it's been designated a nature reserve. It's 27 acres and an overgrown wilderness of neglect, with graves falling down in brambly splendour. One just inside the entrance bore a large name 'FRED', and was toppling at 45 degrees. The inscription read 'Life's race well run, life's work well done'. I wondered what job good old Fred had spent his life on. I passed the family crypt of Charles (Charlie) Brown, owner of the Railway Pub in Limehouse and a local hero. Over 10,000 people attended his funeral in 1904. I crossed through an open green space, sad to leave this last piece of nature running riot.

Then it was back to ugly 1960s council estates around Bow Common, where children in an adventure playground rushed up to a chainlink fence and wanted to know when they'd be on TV. I wished some of these city kids, whose only play areas are pathetic squares of asphalt, could have tramped over some of the wild moors that I had on this journey. Like everywhere else on my route, any open space owned by the council involved a large notice-board with a lot of rules, starting with the word 'No'.

I couldn't imagine how many golf courses I had walked over and moaned about en route from Edinburgh, so imagine my joy when I passed a sign saying 'No Golf' on a particularly depressing stretch of green in Poplar.

I crossed the busy East India Dock Road and made my way down to Poplar High Street. Bombing during World War II had devastated this area, and then Maggie Thatcher's Enterprise Zone had meant a second wave of post-war building. The giant tower at Canary Wharf was a constant reminder of all the changes, never being out of my sight. The original development in the 1980s had ground to a halt by the early 1990s, but now the first developers (the Reichmann family) had reclaimed it and further building had started again on the next phase of the grandiose scheme. Britain's highest building had been my workplace for a year, when I set up Live TV. From my office on the corner of the 23rd floor I had one of the best views of London, right down past the Thames Barrier. It almost made up for some of the most unpleasant bosses I've ever worked for.

Now the group of buildings around it housed banks, investment houses, half a dozen newspapers and publishers. All where, before, dockers had lived and worked. Canary Wharf had gone from being a hard-to-let white elephant to a desirable location, full of shops, cafés and restaurants. The surrounding areas were full of flats and warehouse conversions accessible via the Docklands Light Railway and soon-to-be-completed (hopefully) Jubilee line extension. I love this glittering skyscraper skyline and the curved glass arch where the railway enters the building. It's so exhilarating.

I crossed over Aspen Way in a plastic tube, skirted the warehouses of West India Quay (now being restored – they were where I'd made the TV series *Network 7* for Channel 4 in 1986) and crossed over the water on a floating pontoon bridge made of steel.

I climbed up the steps to Cabot Square and walked around the fountain, where workers were sitting and having their lunch. Then it was down Cubitt Steps and over the even more exciting Limekiln Dock Bridge to South Quay and a dreary slog along Marsh Wall and Manchester Road, past endless little modern brick boxes and monumental 1960s tower blocks. This part of the Isle of Dogs has no personality whatsoever.

I reached the park by the southern tip of the Isle of Dogs. But before I took the foot tunnel under the Thames to my final destination, I decided to make a short detour to the Millennium Dome, less than a mile downstream and, courtesy of the Port of London Authority, I boarded a bright-red rubber dinghy with a powerful outboard motor outside the Poplar and Blackwall District Club. The river looked grey and choppy and there was a still breeze blowing. Unfortunately my captain, a jolly Nigel type (who made me wear a red life-vest over my waterproof and rucksack) turned the boat so quickly as we left the jetty, that a giant wave crashed over the boat and soaked both my legs to thigh level. I wasn't very happy, especially when we got to midstream and the freezing wind kicked in. Luckily, the journey past Greenwich to where the dome sits next to the Blackwall Tunnel was uneventful.

I lived for ten years from 1973 on the banks of the Thames at Limehouse and had seen a dramatic decline in the commercial use of the river. In fact the ground floor of my house had been a barge repair workshop and about 15 barges had been moored outside when I moved in. Over the years the number shrank drastically and the remaining vessels just seemed like relics from a previous era. River traffic dwindled to tourist boats with irritatingly inaccurate commentaries and disco boats which drove me bonkers at 3 am, endlessly circling about while playing clapped-out Rolling Stones records.

There had been much talk that the declaration of an Enterprise Zone on the Isle of Dogs and the opening of the City Airport would lead to a growth in river transport, but it had never happened. One hydrofoil company after another had given up. And for all the trendy flats being built on the Thames below Tower Bridge, there didn't seem a rush of occupants commuting to work by water. And will the Dome itself revitalize the river? From this short journey I could see that outside the Enterprise Zone it was the same old story – disused wharves and dereliction, interspersed with the odd factory or printing works. Maybe the new tube line, rather than the Dome, was the key, but construction had been stricken by problems and it was behind schedule. Another problem for river traffic was the enormous rise and fall of the tide – 20 feet. But the two new piers being built at the Dome had been designed to cope with that and to handle seven boats at a time each carrying up to 300 or 400 passengers. There were plans for a new water-taxi service as well as pleasure boats.

We arrived by the Dome, which to my mind looked a bit grubby and grey, and not quite the pristine white spacecraft-style structure of the architects' drawing. On the edge of the river was a sign announcing that this was to be the site of the Eco Garden. At the moment it was a muddy bank held together by netting. I stepped gingerly out of the dinghy, handed back my life-jacket and clambered up the bank. I was outside a chainlink fence surrounding the construction site and a long way from where I had arranged to meet Zaha Hadid, the architect responsible for the Mind Zone.

I walked around a short distance and climbed over some rocks to find myself on the perimeter road around the Dome. Security seemed lax to say the least. It was a sea of mud and even I, someone not short of a vivid imagination, couldn't imagine how this cheerless windy grey smelly industrial zone of South East London could be landscaped and turned into the eighth wonder of the Western world in the time available. The inside of the Dome could work on the level of Las Vegas or a giant fairground attraction, I would allow that, but given the appallingly inconsistent British weather and the raw unprettified environment, I wasn't optimistic about first impressions. As far as I'm concerned, just plonking down a Dome doesn't create an experience; it should be integrated into the river and the landscape.

A mud-spattered Land Rover drew up and I was offered a lift around to the site offices. Now I was wet, cold and covered in mud. Zaha emerged in a stylish bright-orange nylon Yohji Yamamoto quilted puffy coat, like a cocoon around a long black dress and high-heeled black shoes. One of our most high-profile and effervescent architects, she seems to have trouble getting buildings built in the UK, whereas abroad she was acclaimed. By coincidence Zaha and I attended the same college, the Architectural Association in London, world renowned for its encouragement of radical free-thinkers. I'd left after two years (seduced in 1967 by a career in journalism). Zaha arrived in 1972, and is without doubt the most distinguished female graduate in decades. She is regarded as a fine teacher, and really rose to prominence when she beat Sir Norman Foster in an international competition to design the Cardiff Opera House in 1995, although the commission never went ahead owing to local opposition. She had recently designed a fashion exhibition at the Hayward Gallery which was well reviewed, but was building more important work abroad – an Arts Centre in Cincinnati, and a housing project in Vienna. Why had she been relegated to temporary installations like the Mind Zone in Britain? Born in Baghdad, she's lived here since college days. With her large frame, mass of hair, exotic clothes and throaty voice, she's not short of an opinion or three. Maybe she's too charismatic for most dreary British developers and town councils, but surely architecture needn't be dominated by men as we approached the Millennium? It must have changed, surely, since my student days in the 1960s, when I was one of just five girls in a year of 95 boys? Why weren't there more successful female architects? Apart from Zaha there were few women architects in this country really making a mark. 'Or anywhere else actually,' she added, smiling ruefully. 'People ask me this question all the time. And I really don't have an answer. My best students have always been female students, whether here or in Columbia or at Harvard or the Architectural Association. It doesn't make any sense to me. The best students of my contemporaries were the women and my students have always been very good. I don't know what it is. I think they are intimidated in the workspace.'

Did women architects have to be very thick-skinned? After all, the way her work had been presented in the press and the philistine things that people said about it, must be hard to take. 'I think you have to have incredible confidence and determination. I'm damned if I'm going to let them get the better of me. But about the issue of women, it doesn't make sense to me because they can succeed in other professions. Whether it's law or medicine, for example, which are equally tough. Or in the arts or in the theatre. But for some reason architecture is so blocked to women. The fundamental problem is that it isn't just a male-run profession but also that the clients are a brotherhood. And that's really the bottom line. You can't really go drinking with them and so on. I see from my female friends who have kids that something else becomes more important than socializing, and architecture is so time-consuming. And it's tough, but there's no need for it to be so tough.'

It was depressing news if architecture was as masculine and closed to original women as it was in my day, 30 years ago. I left Zaha arguing about whether she had to wear steel-capped wellingtons for a site meeting, and rejoined my boat for a much drier ride back to the Poplar and District Rowing Club.

In Island Gardens I braved the freezing wind and sat outside the café drinking tea and eating a slice of cake. Now it was time to enter another dome – the pretty glass one topping the entrance to the Greenwich foot tunnel, my route under the Thames. I shunned the lift and ran down the metal spiral staircase to get warm. Built in 1902, the tunnel is open 24 hours a day, and is just under a quarter of a mile long. Faced with 200,000 white tiles, it's been filmed and photographed thousands of times. I prefer it to a boat trip any day. It was packed with tourists and had the inevitable sad busker plunking on his guitar. I talked to Mr Williams, who operated the lift at the other end. A charming West Indian, he had a radio playing to enliven his somewhat monotonous existence. His working environment underground was light years away from my office in the sky at Live TV. What did I have to moan about? He'd been working 12-hour shifts for eight years – the busiest day of the year for him was the London Marathon. He got continually asked why the *Cutty Sark* was on dry land, but couldn't really come up with a satisfactory answer.

I emerged into a grey afternoon in Greenwich. It looked like I was going to end my walk in the rain, but that wouldn't be surprising. I walked past the *Cutty Sark* (dreading that any of the dozens of tourists would ask me why it was on dry land!), up King William Walk and into Greenwich Park. My goal, the Old Royal Observatory, sat proudly on top of the hill, a throng of visitors heading to and from it. Designed by Sir Christopher Wren and founded by King Charles II in 1675, the Observatory has now become a mere tourist attraction. No scientific work has been done here for years, although it houses a splendid museum. It's just become another facet of theme-park Britain, a sad end for a proud and noble institution that for one brief moment truly was the birthplace of time. The money saved by closing the Observatory (about £2 million a year) was less than half of one per cent of the cost of the Dome. The telescopes had moved ages ago, but the Observatory had offered research and technical support for astronomers at its base in Cambridge, now to be axed. I walked into the courtyard as rain began to fall and stepped on to the line in the ground marking 'Longitude 0°', the place where east meets west, the Greenwich Meridian.

So I'd made it to the home of time, and the place, where for me at least, the third Millennium will officially begin. Like all the rest of my walk, my final day had been a mixture of blatant optimism (the Dome) and sadness (Victoria Park and now the Observatory), but as I headed off to the pub to celebrate I thought it would be a long time before I'd forget the extraordinary people and events my straight-line route had thrown up.

I'd walked over 450 miles, often in appalling weather, and I'd seen a unique slice of Britain on my difficult journey. Now I just hoped I could regain my sense of humour!